Indicator

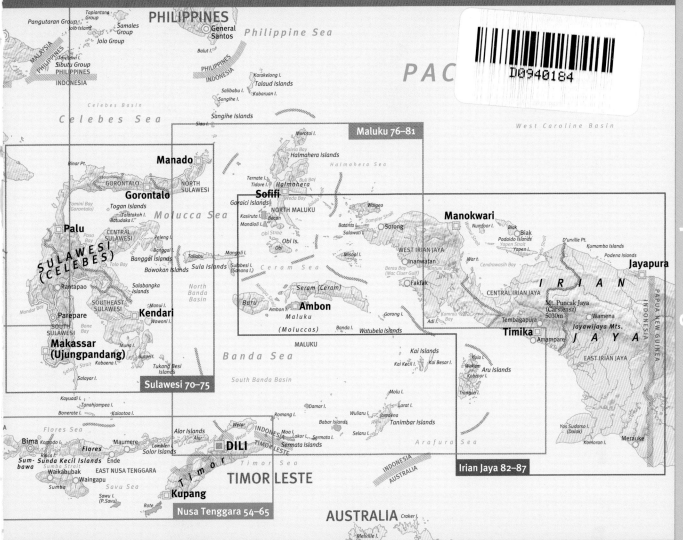

Scale 1 : 14 500 000

LEGEND

TRANSPORT FEATURES

AIR

✈ Airport
✛ Airfield

ROAD

CITY PLANS

Tollway/Highway
Ramp
Tollway/Highway (u/c)
Major Street
Secondary Street
Large Minor Street
Small Minor Street
Track
Footpath

AREA MAPS

Tollway/Highway
Tollway/Highway (u/c)
Major Street/ Provincial Road
Secondary Road
Secondary Road
Minor Road
Track
Footpath
Trek with Guide
Trek without Guide

GENERAL TRANSPORT FEATURES

🚐 Minibus (Angkot) Terminal
🚌 Bus Terminal
Ⓟ Car Park
▭ Gate
→ One-way Arrow
🅖 Petrol Station

WATER

4 hours — Ferry Route and Travel Time
⛴ Ferry Terminal
⚓ Harbour

RECREATIONAL FEATURES

DINING & ACCOMMODATION

🅗 Hotel
Ⓡ Restaurant
🅕 Food Centre

ENVIRONMENTAL AMENITIES

Forest
Nature Reserve
Park/Open Space

RECREATIONAL AMENITIES

🏖 Beach
🗼 Monument
🏛 Museum
★ Place of Interest
❶ Tourist Information
🎥 Cinema
✈ Travel Agent/Airline Office

SHOPPING

Ⓜ Market
Ⓢ Shop/ Shopping

SPORTS AMENITIES

🤿 Diving
⛳ Golf Corse
⛵ Sea Sport Centre
🏟 Stadium
🏄 Surfing

BUILDINGS

Building with Known Shape
▲ General Building

PHYSICAL FEATURES

+ Elevation Point
▭ Lake/Sea
Sand
Swamp
— River

GENERAL FEATURES

BOUNDARIES

INDONESIA / MALAYSIA — International Border
State / Province Border

DIPLOMATIC MISSIONS

📬 Embassy/Consulate

EDUCATION

🏫 School
■ Higher Education

PLACES OF WORSHIP

卐 Hindu Temple
✝ Church
☪ Mosque

PUBLIC AMENITIES

🅑 Bank
✛ Hospital
✳ Police
✉ Post Office

STRUCTURES

— Dam
🗼 Lighthouse/ Tower

URBAN AREA ZONE

Built-up Area
Park/ Garden
Other Area

LOCALITIES

CITY PLANS

KUTA Municipality
SANUR Village Administration
40141 (POSTCODE)
Sanglah Village

AREA MAPS

◼ Large City
◻ City
◉ Large Town
◎ Medium Town
○ Small Town
○ Village
○ Small Village

GLOSSARY

INDONESIA	ENGLISH	DEUTSCH	FRANÇAIS	NEDERLANDS
Bukit	Hill	Hügel	Colline	Heuvel
Candi	Temple	Tempel	Temple	Tempel
Danau, Tasik	Lake	See	Lac	Meer
Gunung	Mountain	Berg	Montagne	Berg
Jalan	Street	Straße	Rue	Weg/Straat
Kebun	Garden	Garten	Jardin	Park/Tuinen
Muara	Estuary	Flußmündung	Embouchure	Riviermond
Pantai	Beach	Badestrand	Plage	Strand
Pasar	Market	Markt	Marché	Markt
Pelabuhan	Harbour	Seehafen	Port	Haven
Pulau	Island	Insel	Île	Eiland
Rumah Sakit	Hospital	Krankenhaus	Hôpital	Ziekenhuis
Selat	Strait	Meerenge	Détroit	Zeestraat
Sungai	River	Fluß	Rivière	Rivier
Taman	Park	Parkanlage	Jardins	Tuinen
Cagar Alam	Reserve	Reservat	Réserve	Reservaat
Tanjung	Cape, Point	Kap	Cap	Kaap
Teluk	Bay	Bucht	Bai	Baai
Toserba	Dep't Store	Kaufhaus	Grand magasin	Warenhuis

Indonesia
Travel Atlas

© Periplus Editions (HK) Ltd.
All Rights Reserved
Second Edition
Printed in Singapore
ISBN-13: 978-0-7946-0105-8
ISBN-10: 0-7946-0105-7

Distributors:
Indonesia
PT Java Books Indonesia
Jl. Rawa Gelam IV No. 9
Kawasan Industri Pulogadung
Jakarta Timur 13930
Tel: (021) 4682 1088
Fax: (021) 461 0207
e-mail: cs@javabooks.co.id

Japan
Tuttle Publishing
Yaekari Bldg. 3rd Floor 5-4-12 Osaki
Shinagawa-Ku Tokyo 141 0032
Tel: (03) 5437 0171
Fax: (03) 5437 0755
e-mail: tuttle-sales@gol.com

North America/Latin America/Europe
Tuttle Publishing
364 Innovation Drive
North Clarendon, VT 05759-9436, USA
Tel: (802) 773 8930
Fax: (802) 773 6993
e-mail: info@tuttlepublishing.com

Asia Pacific
Berkeley Books Pte Ltd
130 Joo Seng Road, #06-01
Singapore 368357
Tel: (65) 280 1330
Fax: (65) 280 6290
e-mail : inquiries@periplus.com.sg

HOW TO USE THIS TRAVEL ATLAS

The Indonesian Travel Atlas is grouped into eight chapters, each covering a major geographical region of Indonesia. Some of the chapters cover thousands of islands while other chapters only cover one island and perhaps a few small small offshore islands considered to be part of the main island geographically and culturally.

Each chapter begins with a map of the entire region covered, with boxes showing the areas detailed on the pages following and a page number to allow the user to go directly go to the desired page.

Pages two and three show a map of the entire Indonesian Archipelago, in addition to the nearby countries of Malaysia, Brunei Darussalam, Singapore and Timor Leste. This map is keyed with colour-coded boxes that indicate the basic coverage of each chapter. Each chapter contains maps of large areas of general interest, more detailed maps of smaller regions and maps of key cities and towns of particular interest to visitors and travellers. The largest city maps include an index of points of interest with hotels and restaurants also listed where space permits. The maps, wherever possible, are arranged so that towns are shown adjacent to the regional maps allowing the user to look for nearby points of interest and find out how to travel from one town to another.

The Index at the end of the Atlas contains lists of cities, towns and villages that appear on the various maps. These are only keyed to the page number where they are located to help the user find the general area where the place is located. There are separate index lists for places of interest and national parks and nature reserves.

PERIPLUS

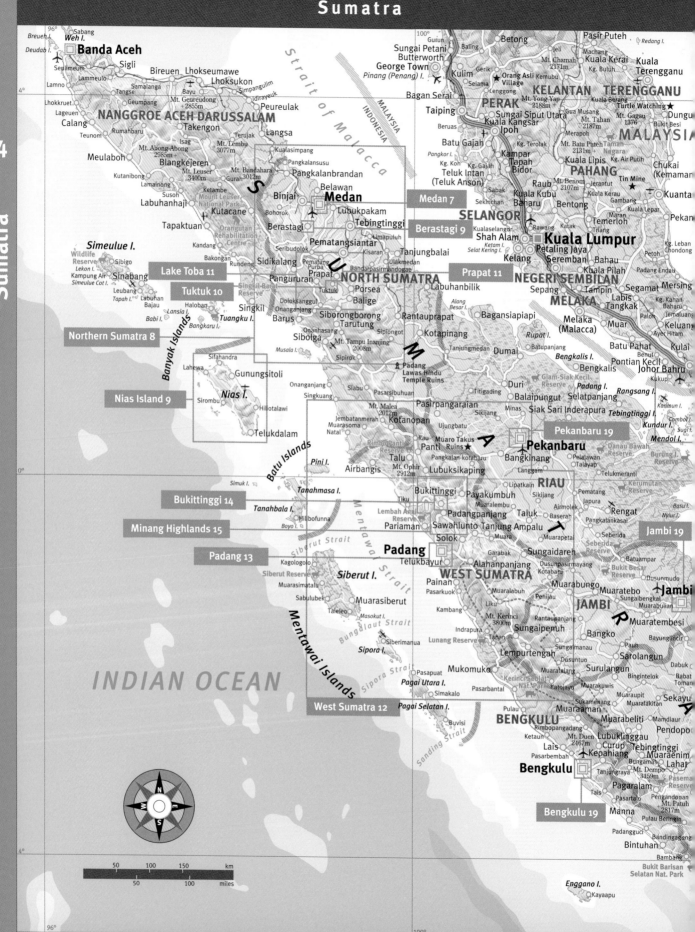

Sumatra

4

Scale 1 : 5 500 000

Map Labels

Laut Cina Selatan
(South China Sea)

4°

Laut I.

Teluk Butun
Salor I.
Natuna Besar I.
Binjai
Panarik

Lagong I.

Anambas Islands

Mubur I. Matak I.
Siantan I. Bajau I.
Jemaja I. Airabu I.

Mida I.

MALAYSIA
INDONESIA

Natuna Sea

Kg. Tekok Selang
Tioman I.
Pemanggil I.
Aur I.

Sibu I.
Tinggi I.

OHOR
Mawai
Kota Tinggi

SINGAPORE
■ **Singapore**

Batam I.
Bintan I. Mapur I.
Rempang I.
Poto I.
Numbing I.
Tanjungpinang Gin Besar I.

Riau Islands

Mesanak I.
Termiang I.
Buaya I. Limas
Bakong I. **Lingga I.**
Kelume Sambau
Penuba Selayar I. Tengkis
Maroktua Lanjut
Labu
Singkep I.

Lingga Islands

Tambelan Besar I.
Benua I.

Karimata Strait

0°

Berhala Strait

┌──────────────────────────┐
│ Riau Island Group 16   │
└──────────────────────────┘
┌──────────────────────────┐
│ Batam & Bintan Is. 16   │
└──────────────────────────┘

┌──────────────────────────┐
│ Palembang 18   │
└──────────────────────────┘

Bangka Island
Belinyu

Kelapa
Mentok Sungailiat
Pudingbesar
Sungaiselan ✈ **Pangkalpinang**
BANGKA BELITUNG

angkalangresik Koba
Talang Selengku **Belitung Island**
Payung Tanjungpandan
SOUTH SUMATRA Liat I. Manggar
Lubuklancang Mendanau I. ┼ Badau
Palembang Lepar I. Gantung
Talang □ Sungai Gerung Toboali
betutu ✈ Plaju Membalong Dendang
elumbang Tulungselapan
Prabumulih Kayuagung
elimbing Muarakuang
Pagergunung
Pagerdewa Sungaibelidah
Peninjauan Betung
Umbulan Gayohpecoh
Baturaja Talangbatu
Martapura Pakuanratu Lebaktebang
Gedongratu Dintiteladas
Muaradua Menggala
Bukitkemuning Surabaya
LAMPUNG Way Kambas
Gunungsugih National Park
Simpangsender Kotabumi Kotagajah
Liwa Mt. Tangkitebak
2115m Metro Sukadana
Tanjungkarang □ Labuhanmeringgai
Krui Pringsewu
Kotaagung ■ **Bandarlampung**
Ngaras Panjang
Tabuan I. Telukbetung
Baradaragung Legundi I. Bakahuni
Balimbing ● Merak

┌──────────────────────────┐
│ Bandarlampung 19   │
└──────────────────────────┘

104° 4°

SUMATRA

Sumatra indeed has something for everyone — lush rainforests, exotic flora and fauna, cascading rivers, sparkling crater lakes, shimmering white sand beaches, and an incredibly diverse array of traditional ethnic groups who inhabit some of the most spectacular volcanic landscapes in the world. It is neither the largest landmass in the Indonesian archipelago (Irian Jaya and Kalimantan are larger), nor the most populous (Java has three times as many people), but by most accounts it is the most varied and interesting island to visit.

Sumatra straddles vital waterways at the western end of an immense island chain. It is truly continental in scope; vast lowland rainforests and coastal wetlands are cut by a network of broad, silt-laden rivers that snake across the island for up to 800 km before emptying into the South China Sea. Unlike all the other islands of a similar scale, however, Sumatra is also volcanic — its lofty range of western peaks forming a longitudinal "spine" dotted with lakes and fertile upland valleys.

Sumatra is the fourth largest island in the world after Greenland, New Guinea and Borneo, with a land area of some 473,481 sq km — roughly the size of Spain.

Well over a dozen major ethnic groups live on the island, speaking more than 25 different languages and hundreds of dialects. Sumatra today supports 40 million people — over 20 percent of Indonesia's population — with a land area and population density similar to that of California, though far less urbanized.

Found here are some of Indonesia's most dynamic peoples. The Acehnese of the north are fervent Muslims renowned for their fierce resistance to Dutch rule. The Minangkabau of West Sumatra have migrated throughout Indonesia and today form the economic and intellectual elite in many areas. Sumatra's largest group, the Malays, were the great seafaring traders of Asia in pre-modern times, and their tongue forms the basis for the national languages of Indonesia and Malaysia. Last but not least, the Batak of the northern highlands around Lake Toba are one of the nation's most resourceful and flamboyant groups.

VOLCANOES AND CRATER LAKES. The geography of Sumatra is best considered as a series of parallel longitudinal slices running northwest to southeast along the main axis of the island. In the extreme west is a sparsely inhabited chain of islands — from **Simeulue** in the north to **Enggano** in the south — that is separated from Sumatra by a submarine trench which plunges to depths of 2,000 m.

The western fringe of Sumatra itself is a narrow but complex coastal strip, alternating between fertile alluvial soils where rice is grown and inhospitable swamps that are gradually being drained for agriculture. Rugged foothills rise steeply from this coastal fringe to the mighty **Barisan Mountains**. The highest non-volcanic peaks (about 3,400 m) lie within the **Gunung Leuser National Park** in the northern part of the island. Sumatra's highest volcano is **Mt. Kerinci** — at 3,800 m, the highest Indonesian mountain outside of Irian Jaya.

Also found along this central axis is dramatic **Lake Tujuh** — a crater lake, 5 sq km in area, perched at an altitude of 2,000 m atop **Mt. Tujuh**. It is best seen from the southern slopes of adjacent **Mt. Kerinci**, but can also be reached directly from the town of **Sungaipenuh**. Impressive mountains are also found in the limestone areas around **Bukittinggi** and **Payakumbuh** in West Sumatra, as well as in the **Lhoknga** area of Aceh in North Sumatra.

Huge **Lake Toba** in North Sumatra is Southeast Asia's largest lake, covering 1,146 sq km. It occupies the caldera of a massive volcano which exploded some 100,000 years ago in the most powerful volcanic eruption ever known. The island of **Samosir**, which stands in the centre of the lake, and the lake's eastern shore are all that remain of the shattered cone.

NATURAL RESOURCES. The island is extremely rich in natural resources. Its coal, tin, bauxite, oil, gold, natural gas, timber, rubber, tea, palm oil, cacao, and coffee together account for over half of Indonesia's export income, while its long coastline is dotted with harbours providing access to seas teeming with tropical marine life.

Oil is found mainly in the east, between **Riau** and **South Sumatra**, both on land and off-shore. The enormous Arun gas field, which ranks as one of the world's most productive fields, is in southeast Aceh. In South Sumatra, at **Muaraenim**, is a very large open-cast coal mine. Small amounts of gold are mined, though the important metals are aluminum (bauxite) and tin.

WILDLIFE. Sumatra's wildlife is the stuff of adventure books. Huge elephants, large skulking cats and elusive rhinos inhabit dense tropical forests amidst a tangle of enormous trees, twisting lianas, and weird, wonderful flowers. The island's remarkable biological wealth is partly due to it's great size and diversity of habitats, and partly to its periodic connections with the Southeast Asian mainland during the past few hundred thousand years. The island has no fewer than 196 different species of mammals, 20 of which are found nowhere else.

MEDAN

Medan, the provincial capital of North Sumatra, is a cosmopolitan city of over 2 million inhabitants and a booming commercial centre for the region's huge oil and agri-businesses. As a result of major international investments in plantation agriculture from the 1870s onward, it grew from a tiny village to a prosperous colonial city by 1943. Today it is by far the largest city on Sumatra, and the fourth largest in the nation — after Jakarta, Surabaya, and Bandung.

The colonial-period main street, Jalan Ahmad Yani, with its many European-style buildings, is still known locally as Kesawan, the road to the sawah, or rice fields. Behind an iron grill fence alongside numerous Chinese shops, stands the mansion of a former millionaire, Tjong A Fie — who made and lost a fortune in the booming plantation world of the 1920s and '30s. Opposite his house is the **Cafe Tip Top**, once a favourite haunt of Medan's colonial society and still in almost original condition — where one can sit along the sidewalk sipping iced Vienna coffee, eat some of their Dutch-style koekjes and watch the world go by.

At the northern end of Jl. Ahmad Yani are the offices of London-based **Harrisons and Crosfield Ltd.**, built of Aberdeen granite imported as ballast during the 1920s, and now occupied by P.T. London Sumatra, the British Consulate and the British Council Library.

Around the town square (Lapangan Merdeka) to the north of Jl. Ahmad Yani are several colonial buildings, notably the old Town Hall, the Bank of Indonesia building (formerly the exclusive **Witte Societeit Club**, built in 1879), and the Hotel Dharma Deli. On the corner of Jl. Balaikota, the colonial era Post Office stands virtually unchanged, with the Nienhuys fountain just outside.

Maimoon Palace, the ceremonial palace of the sultans of Deli, with its yellow trim (yellow stand for Malay royalty) and typical east coast Malay architecture, stands majestically on Jl. Brigjen Katamso. Designed by an Italian architect and completed in 1888, it has patterned tiles and elegant moorish archways supported by large pillars covered with floral patterns. Performances of Malay dance and music are held here to accompany weddings and other festivities.

One block to the east across the single track railway, on Jl. Sisingamangaraja, is the **Mesjid Raya**, or Grand Mosque, with its imposing tiled archway and royal burial ground.

At the corner of Jl. Imam Bonjol and Jl. Palang Merah, in the courtyard of the **Danau Toba Hotel**, with its traditional Batak-style entrance, is the former Dutch Assistant Resident's house, now part of the modern hotel complex. Next door on Jl. Imam Bonjol is the Buddhist **Vihara Borobudur temple**. To the north along Jl. Imam Bonjol is another square dominated by the modern Batak-style **Provincial Assembly** building, the Benteng Restaurant and Convention Hall built on the site of the original military barracks, and the Dirga Surya Hotel.

Further west on Jl. Diponegoro is the Provincial Governor's office, a single-storey, shuttered colonial structure with neo-classical pillars, originally the Deli Tabaksproefstation. Immediately behind this, the Medan Club, with its fine timber pillars and open design, was built by Allied prisoners-of-war as a Shinto temple for use by officers during the Japanese occupation.

To the south, overlooking the **Babura River**, is the **Vihara Gunung Timur**, the largest Chinese temple in Medan, perhaps in all of Indonesia. Nearby is the **Immanuel Protestant Church** — a fine example of art-deco colonial architecture.

Nearby **Kampung Keling** (Jl. Zainul Arifin), a busy commercial centre, is the original centre of Medan's Indian community. Its high-walled **Shri Mariamman** temple devoted to the goddess Kali was built in 1884; the entrance is topped by a small ornamental pyramidal gateway.

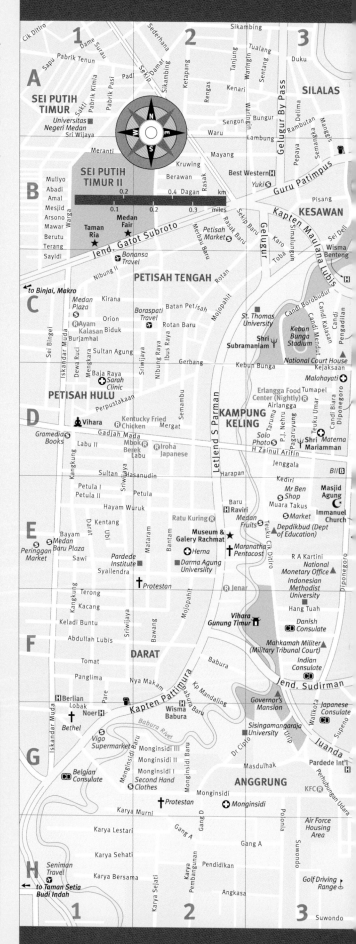

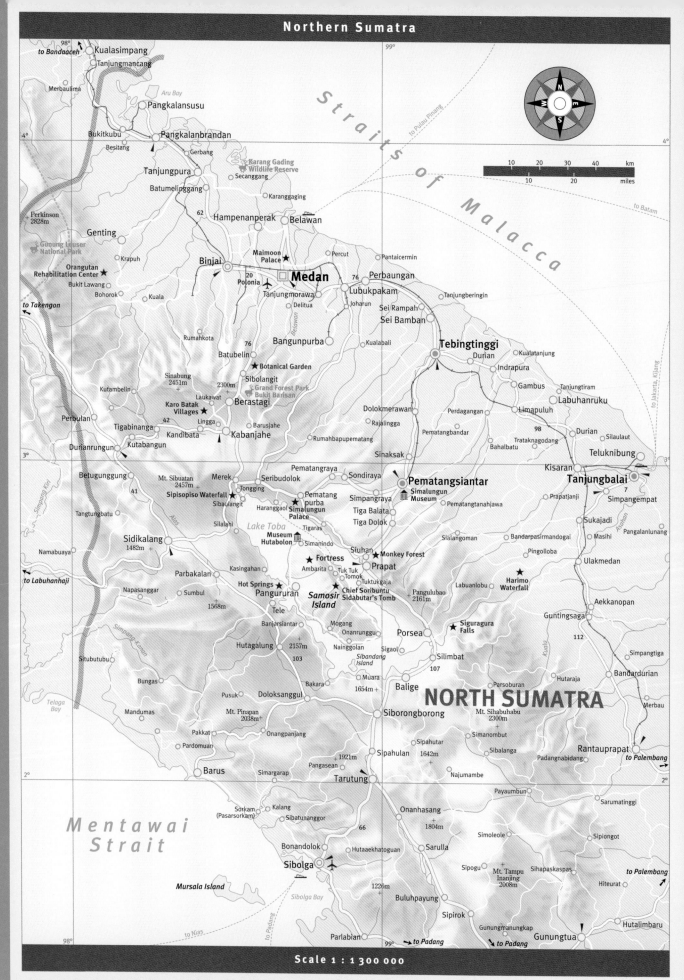

NORTH SUMATRA

North Sumatra, with its colourful and mixed population, is Indonesia's most populous province outside of Java. Dynamic Bataks, Malays, Javanese, Indians, and Chinese have created a fascinating kaleidoscope of modern and traditional Indonesian culture. The economy, long established on the basis of plantation agriculture, now supplemented by the huge Asahan aluminum project and various service industries, is one of the strongest in the nation.

There are two major ecological zones — a fertile, swamp-fringed eastern plain and a central volcanic core formed 70 million years ago by tectonic movements. A narrow coastal plain lies to the west and a chain of sparsely-inhabited islands are located 125 km off the western coast, of which Nias is the best known.

Pematang Siantar, North Sumatra's second largest city, is the administrative and commercial hub of the Simalungun plantation area, founded by the Dutch early in this century. Colonial houses stand amidst the urban clutter at 400 m above sea level, it is notably cooler than the coast. The Simalungun Museum has an interesting collection of *pustaka laklak* — bark books written in Batak script used by datuk magicians to record their sacred formulae.

The **Sibolangit Botanical Garden**, a patch of undisturbed rainforest with giant ferns and moss-covered trees, lies on an escarpment overlooking Sembahe and the lowlands on the road between Medan and Berastagi. Twenty-four km south of Kabanjahe, the road between Berastagi and Prapat touches the northern rim of the Toba basin at Merek, and a sideroad from there winds down to the lakeshore past a spectacular waterfall, known as Sipisopiso ("Like a Knife"), which shoots out of a cave at the edge of the plateau and plunges 120 m straight down to a small, gushing stream below.

Lake Toba in Northern Sumatra, was formed by one of the most violent volcanic eruptions ever known — a cataclysm which created volcanic deposits over 600m thick and hurled ash as far as the Bay of Bengal. A second series of eruptions some 30,000 years ago built up a new volcano inside the older one.

The explosion also resulted in the formation of a zoogeographical boundary in the Toba area. Species such as the orangutan, the white-handed gibbon, Thomas' leaf monkey and 17 types of birds are found only to the north of this region — while the tapir, tarsier, Sumatran rabbit, banded leaf monkey and 10 species of birds are found only to the south of it. Apparently, the eruption created a vast, desolate region that many wildlife species were unable to cross.

The west coast of North Sumatra, with its narrow plain, steep hills and deepwater bays, is one of the most scenic parts of Sumatra. The 66 km road down to **Sibolga** from Tarutung follows the sinuous **Silindung Valley** through deep ravines and dense forests across steep fern-covered slopes — rounding 1,200 hairpin bends that afford magnificent views of **Tapanuli Bay** as you approach the coast.

The town of **Sibolga** is the administrative centre for Central Tapanuli and a major port for steamers and ferries bound for Nias. The town is noted for its seafood, and the bay is dotted with islands — the largest of which is Pulau Mursala, known for its clear waters and bountiful marine life.

BERASTAGI

The delightfully cool and picturesque town of Berastagi nestles at the northern edge of the **Karo Plateau**, 68 km south of Medan. At 1,330 m elevation, the climate is deliciously mild during the day and bracing at night. This is the perfect base for an exploration into the thick pine forests, soothing hot springs and traditional villages of the volcanic Karo highlands.

NIAS

Nias is a small island, 130 km long and 45 km wide (slightly smaller than Bali), lying just 125 km off Sumatra's west coast — close enough that the latter's volcanic peaks can be seen on a clear day. Like the other western islands off Sumatra, however, Nias stands apart — the island's rugged terrain, malarial climate and warlike population served to isolate it from mainstream Sumatran culture for many centuries. The main point of entry to Nias is Gunungsitoli, the district capital. Aside from a few local architectural embellishments in the town square, it resembles many other Indonesian port towns.

Central Nias is extremely inaccessible, yet has some of the island's greatest art treasures. Villages along the Gomo and Tae rivers are particularly important; Orahili Idanö Gomo, Lahusa Idanö Tae and Tundrumbaho are known for their striking plazas with vertical and horizontal megaliths. The village of Holi has a unique old "big house" with pyramidal tombs in the square commemorating the great ancestral chiefs.

The island's most spectacular area, however, is the South — reached by boat from Sibolga or Gunungsitoli. The most important village here is **Bawömatalowo**, with a massive flight of stairs at the main entrance.

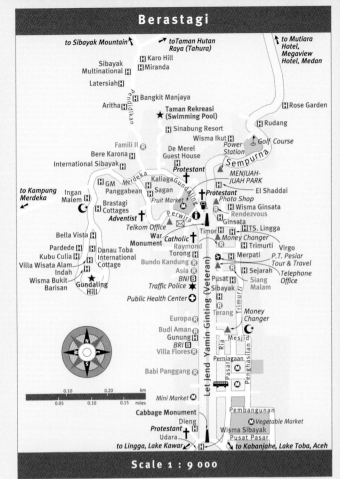

Berastagi

Scale 1 : 9 000

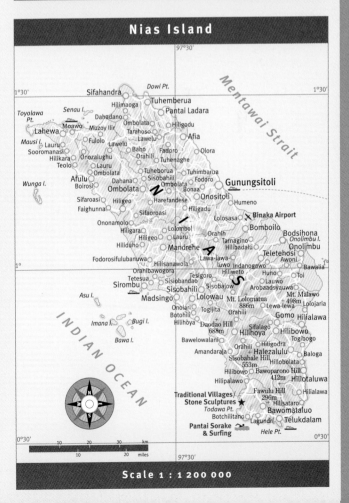

Nias Island

Scale 1 : 1 200 000

LAKE TOBA

With the mystical island of Samosir at its centre, Lake Toba — a huge volcanic depression set high in the treeless mountains of northern Sumatra — forms the very heart of the beautiful but often harsh **Toba Batakland**. This is the largest lake in Southeast Asia — measuring 100 km long, north to south, and 31 km across — with a surface area of about 1,145 sq km. The island of **Samosir** alone, inside the lake, is 530 sq km — about the size of Singapore. This is also the world's deepest lake, over 450 m deep, though accurate surveys of the lake floor have yet to be made. The lake's surface lies 906 m above sea level, but may once have been 150 m higher. The water level has begun to subside again in recent years and no adequate explanation for this has yet been given.

SAMOSIR ISLAND, the huge, arid "Island of the Dead" in the middle of Lake Toba, is a stark remnant of a second powerful explosion that rocked this volcanic cauldron some 30,000 years ago. At that time, a subsidiary peak formed which then subsequently split and slumped back into the earlier crater. The eastern part now forms the Prapat peninsula and the Uluan shore down to Porsea; the western edge forms Samosir.

The island, which measures 45 km by 20 km, was in fact originally a peninsula. It became an island after the Dutch dug a canal through the narrow, 200 metre isthmus connecting it to the mainland at Panguruuran in 1906. This action, it is said, caused considerable consternation among the local inhabitants, as they feared the island would slip into the lake and disappear.

The eastern side of the island rises very steeply up from a narrow strip along the lake shore to a central plateau towering some 780 m above it. The plateau slopes gently back to the southern and western shores of the island and is dotted with tiny villages that cling precariously to clifftops pierced by deep ravines.

The Samosir plateau is largely barren — with scattered forests, marshes and a small lake.

A bridge connects Samosir to the mainland at **Pangururan**, the sub-district administrative centre. Just past the bridge on the mainland, a small road to the right leads up to a popular hot spring on the slopes of **Mt. Pusuk Buhit** (1,981 m), sacred mountain of origin for all Batak peoples. This is where the first ruler — Si Raja Batak — is said to have descended from the heavens.

Samosir is accessible by regular ferry from the resort of **Prapat**, but also by less frequent ferries from **Haranggaol** and **Tigaras** on the **Simalungun** shore to the north. The two main landing points on Samosir are **Tomok** — a traditional village with beautiful stone tombs and houses — and **Tuktuk**, where the island's many hotels and restaurants are concentrated.

During the northeast monsoon (September — January) a strong wind known as alogo bolong, the "great wind," often springs up at midday from the heights, creating waves of over a metre in height, making it dangerous for boats.

TUKTUK

Just to the north of **Tomok** is the small peninsula of Tuktuk Ni Asu ("Dog Peninsula") with its sandy beaches and scores of hotels offering budget accommodations.

Some 19 km further north is **Simanindo**, where the elaborately decorated house of Raja Sidauruk is now a museum. Here visitors can witness a traditional *torton* dance and *sigalegale* puppet performance. The *sigalegale* traditionally served as a receptacle for the soul of the deceased in Batak funerary rites, though the custom may have originated only about 100 years ago in the **Balige** area.

PRAPAT

Prapat occupies a small, rocky peninsula jutting into the lake, and has recently expanded southward over a ridge into the adjacent village of **Ajibata**. A resort since before World War II, the town has boomed in recent years with the opening of many new hotels.

The area around **Porsea** is where the 60 m wide **Asahan River** drains Toba to the east. The alluvial plain formed by the river and its tributaries is extremely fertile and dotted with prosperous villages. The road descends steeply into the **Asahan Valley**, where the river enters a narrow ravine with vertical walls 250 m high cut from the soft volcanic tuff. This is the site of the Inalum hydroelectric plant, the largest such plant in Indonesia.

The ravine narrows at **Siguragura** to a mere cleft in the rocks and the river plunges over a spectacular 220 m waterfall into another cleft further down known as **Sampuran Harimo** ("Tiger Falls"), from whence it plunges once again into the vale of **Tangga**, through yet another falls.

Balige is an important market town at the southern end of the lake, 65 km from **Prapat**. The large town market is built in the traditional Tapanuli style, and is known for its textile production. At the southwestern corner of the lake, is **Bakkara** — the former seat of the mystical Batak priest-kings, the Sisingamangaraja.

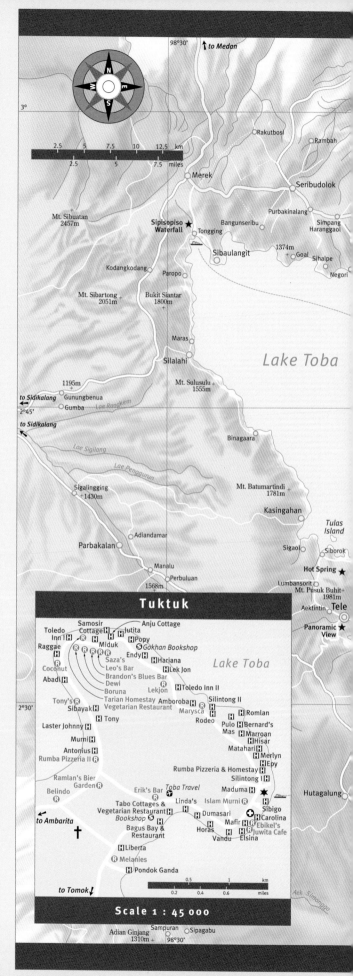

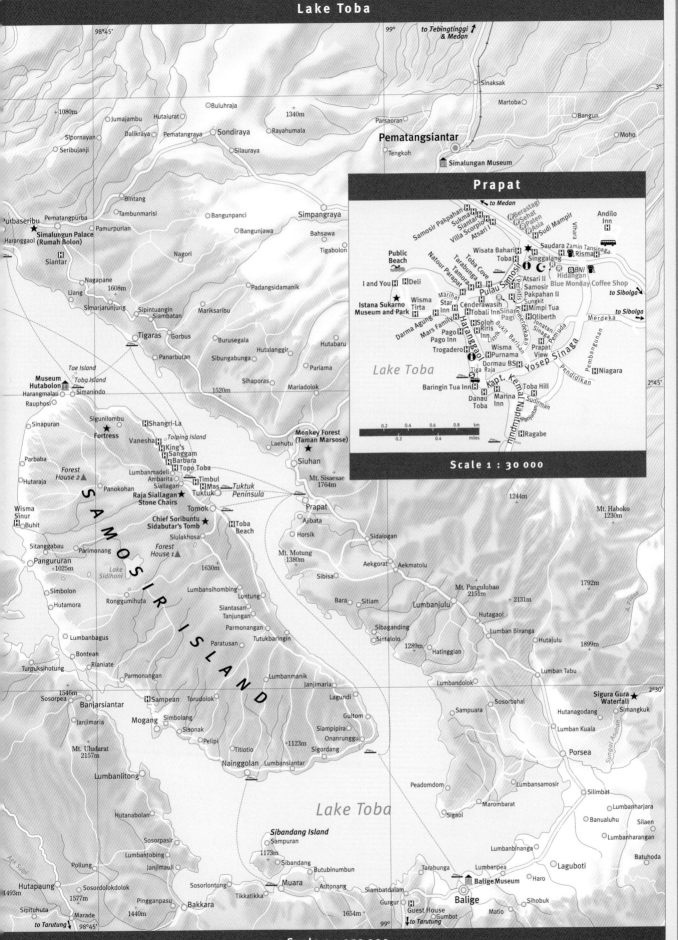

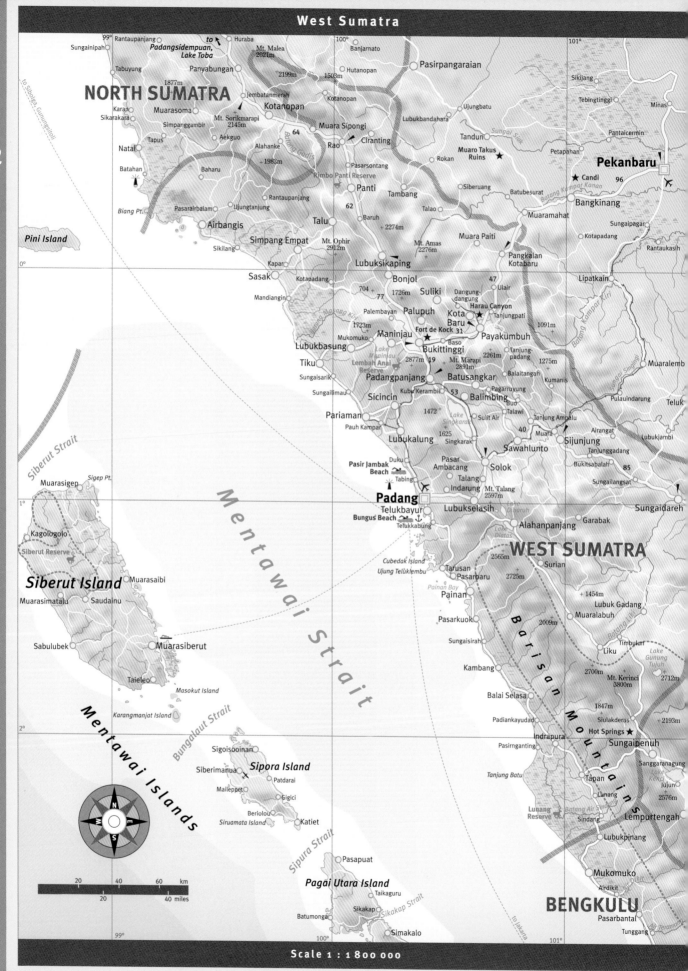

Sumatra

12

NORTH SUMATRA

WEST SUMATRA

BENGKULU

Pini Island

Siberut Island

Mentawai Islands

Mentawai Strait

Siberut Strait

Sipora Island

Pagai Utara Island

Siberut Reserve

Bungalaut Strait

Sipura Strait

Barisan Mountains

Rantaupanjang
Sungainipah
Tabuyung
Huraba
Banjarnato
Mt. Malea 2021m
Pasirpangaraian
Sikijang
Tebingtinggi
Minas
to Padangsidempuan, Lake Toba
Panyabungan
Hutanopan
Ujungbatu
1877m
Karan
Muarasoma
Jembatanmerah
Kotanopan
Lubukbandahara
Tandun
Pantaicermin
Sikarakara
Simpanggambir
Mt. Sorikmarapi 2145m
Muara Sipongi
Muaro Takus Ruins
Pekanbaru
Natal
Tapus
Aekguo
Rao
Ciranting
Rokan
Batubesurat
Petahan
Candi
96
Batahan
Baharu
Alahanke
Pasarsontang
Siberuang
Bangkinang
Pasarairbalam
Ujungtanjung
Panti
Tambang
Talao
Muaramahat
Sungaipagar
Rimbo Panti Reserve
Rantaupanjang
Kotapadang
Rantaukasih
Airbangis
Talu
Baruh
Muara Paiti
Lipatkain
Simpang Empat
Mt. Ophir 2912m
Pangkalan Kotabaru
Sasak
Kotapadang
Lubuksikaping
Kapar
Mandiangin
Bonjol
Suliki
Ulair
704
1726m
Dangung-dangung
Harau Canyon
Palembayan
Palupuh
Kota Baru
Tanjungpati
Maninjau
Fort de Kock
Payakumbuh
Lubukbasung
Komukomo
Bukittinggi
Baso
Tanjung-padang
Tiku
Mt. Marapi 2891m
Balaitangah
Muaralemb
Sungaisarik
Padangpanjang
Batusangkar
Pagarruyung
Kumanis
Sungailimau
Kubu Kerambil
Balimbing
Pulauindarung
Teluk
Sicincin
Buo
Tanjung Ampalu
Pariaman
Talawi
Sijunjung
Lubukjambi
Pauh Kampar
Sulit Air
Airangat
Lubukalung
Singkarak
Muara
Sawahlunto
Tanjunggadang
Bukitsabalah
Pasir Jambak Beach
Duku
Pasar Ambacang
Solok
Sungailangsat
Tabing
Talang
Indarung
Sungaidareh
Padang
Mt. Talang 2597m
Telukbayur
Lubukselasih
Alahanpanjang
Garabak
Bungus Beach
Telukkabung
WEST SUMATRA
Cubedak Island
Ujung Telúklembu
Tarusan
Surian
Pasarbaru
Painan
Pasarkuok
Muaralabuh
Muarasigep
Lubuk Gadang
Sigep Pt.
Sungaisirah
Liku
Kagologolo
Kambang
Mt. Kerinci 3800m
Muarasaibi
Balai Selasa
Muarasimatalu
Saudainu
Padiankayudad
Siulakderas
Hot Springs
Muarasiberut
Indrapura
Sungaipenuh
Sabulubek
Pasirnganting
Sanggaranagung
Taieleo
Tanjung Batu
Tapan
Masokut Island
Lunang
Jujun
Karangmanjat Island
Lempurtengah
Sigoisooinan
Sindang
Siberimanua
Sipora Island
Lubukpinang
Maileppet
Patdarai
Beriolou
Gigici
Mukomuko
Siruamata Island
Katiet
Airdikit
Pasapuat
BENGKULU
Taikaguru
Pasarbantal
Sikakap
Batumonga
Simakalo
Tunggang

Scale 1 : 1 800 000

20   40   60   km
20
40 miles

WEST SUMATRA

After Lake Toba, the fertile valleys and scenic lakes of the West Sumatran highlands are undoubtedly the most memorable — and also the most often visited — sights on the island.

West Sumatra is actually composed of three distinct regions — a volcanic highland, a long coastal plain, and a string of jungle-clad islands lying about 100 km offshore. The province is dominated by the **Barisan Mountains** — two parallel ranges of mountain peaks interspersed with broad valleys and several highland lakes. Many mountains are covered in pristine montane forest.

The highest peak in West Sumatra is **Mt. Kerinci**, a dormant volcano standing 3,800 m high. A number of others rise above 2,000 m, notably the smouldering **Mt. Marapi** (2,831 m) to the southeast of Bukittinggi. The central and northern highlands of the province contain several valleys which form the ancient cultural heartland of the region. Three of these are the homeland of the Minangkabau who have spread throughout the entire archipelago.

The mountainous southeastern portion of the province is still wild; much of it is included in the huge **Kerinci Seblat National Park**, which encompasses several stunning crater lakes.

The **Mentawai Islands** consist of four large inhabited islands — Siberut, Sipura, North and South Pagai — and numerous smaller ones. Most are still covered in tropical rainforest and fringed by unspoilt coral reefs teeming with marine life.

PADANG

Padang is the provincial capital of West Sumatra and the principal gateway to the Minang highlands. The port, which is 6 km south of the city, is the largest on Sumatra's west coast. The **Provincial Museum** on Diponegoro stands in a park and is built in the traditional Minang style known as "Gajah Maharam."

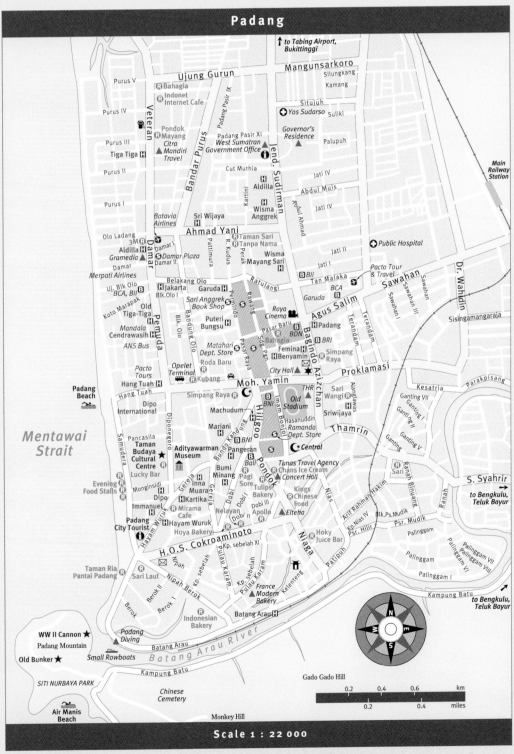

Padang

Scale 1 : 22 000

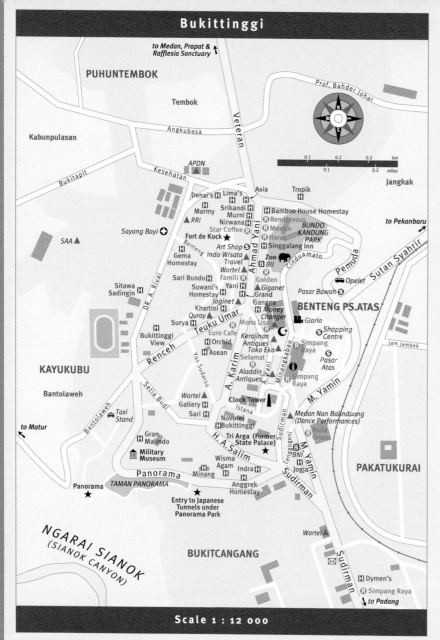

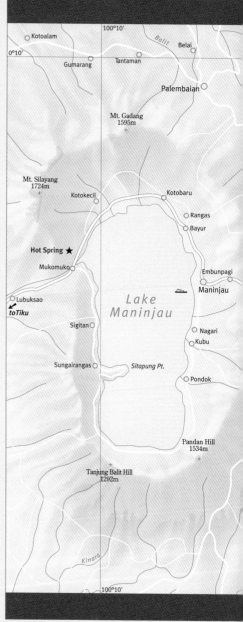

BUKITTINGGI

The town of Bukittinggi (literally "high hill") lies at the centre of the Agam valley. While Padang is the modern commercial, educational and administrative centre of the province, Bukittinggi is the cultural capital of the Minang realm. The largest city in the highlands, it grew up around a Dutch post, **Fort de Kock**, built in 1825. Although less than a degree south of the equator, the city is cool due to its elevation — 900 m above sea level.

Bukittinggi's principal landmark is the **Clock Tower** (Jam Gadang), which has a miniature Minang house perched on top overlooking the main square. Jalan Ahmad Yani is lined with antique and souvenir shops, restaurants and offices. Unique stair-streets lined with more souvenir shops lead down from here to Jl. Cinduamato.

Bundo Kanduang Park at the top of Jl. Cinduamato offers a good view of the town and surrounding area. The name of the park refers to the legendary "Great Mother" symbolic of the matrilineal Minang. The museum in the park is housed in a traditional Minang rumah gadang, complete with thatched roof and flanking granaries. A small fortune in fine gold jewelry is on display; for several centuries this area was the archipelago's leading producer of the precious metal.

MINANG HIGHLANDS

The ancient homeland of the Minangkabau — the *luak nan tigo* or "three valleys" of western central Sumatra — is an incredibly beautiful highland region of lush rice fields, towering volcanoes and spectacular crater lakes. These three valleys roughly define the corners of a triangle centering around sacred **Mt. Merapi** (2,891 m), the highest and most active volcano in the area and the spot where, according to local legend, the first Minang ancestors are thought to have settled.

To the south and east of the volcano is the valley known as **Tanah Datar** ("Level Land"), with its focus around the small town of Batusangkar. This is where the royal Minang court was located from the 14th to the 19th centuries. Ancient tombs, inscriptions, palace sites, megalithic stones, and other remains dot the area. Tanah Datar was renowned for its gold and iron mines in former times.

The **Agam valley** lies to the north and west of Merapi and is centred around the town of Bukittinggi. This area developed rapidly during the last two centuries as a result of contacts with Europeans on the west coast. The third and most fertile of the valleys is known as **Limapuluh Kota**. It lies to the east around the large town of **Payakumbuh**. Megalithic remains abound here and it is thought that this may have been the earliest of the valleys to have been settled.

Framing these valleys is a tightly-packed cluster of volcanic peaks and two enormous crater lakes, **Maninjau** and **Singkarak**. As in the Toba area, these volcanoes have contributed to the fertility of the soils, and as a result the Minang highlands have been relatively densely populated for many centuries.

West Sumatra's most famous sight is, undoubtedly, **Lake Maninjau** (literally "to look out across") — a lake 17 km long and 8 km wide set inside an ancient crater that is surrounded on all sides by steep, 600 m jungle-clad walls. Lake Singkarak is similar in size and scenic beauty to **Maninjau**.

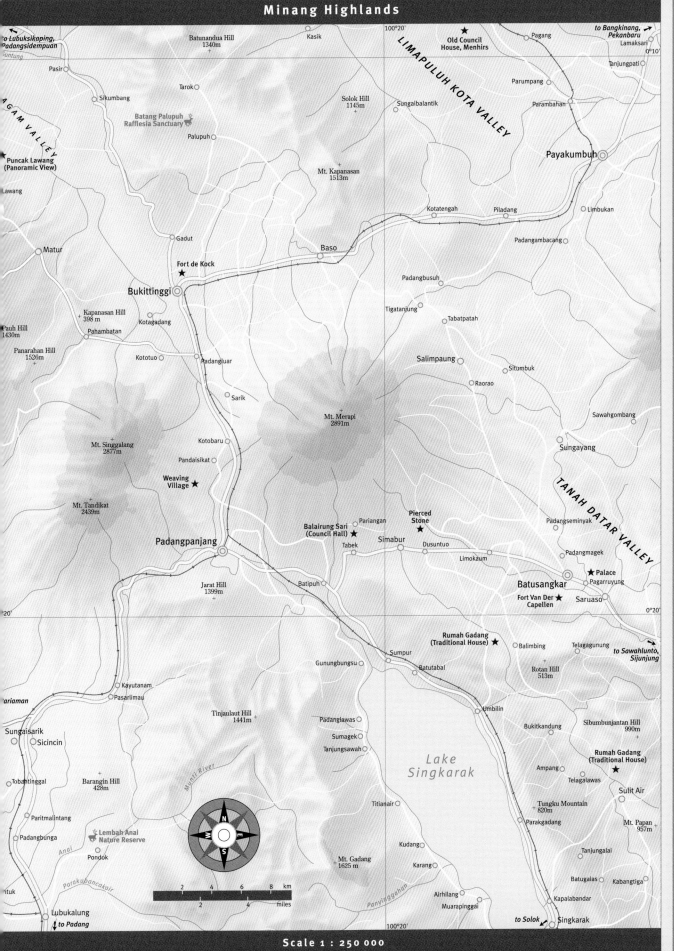

to Lubuksikaping,
Padangsidempuan

to Bangkinang,
Pekanbaru

100°20'

★ Old Council
House, Menhirs

Pagang
Lamaksari
0°10'

Tanjungpati

Batunandua Hill
1340m

Kasik

LIMAPULUH KOTA VALLEY

Parumpang

Pasir

Sikumbang

Tarok

Solok Hill
1145m

Sungaibalantik

Parambahan

Payakumbuh

Batang Palupuh
Rafflesia Sanctuary

Palupuh

Puncak Lawang
(Panoramic View)

Mt. Kapanasan
1513m

Kotatengah

Piladang

Limbukan

Lawang

Padangambacang

Matur

Gadut

Baso

Padangbusuh

Fort de Kock ★

Tigatanjung

Tabatpatah

Bukittinggi

Kapanasan Hill
398 m

Kotagadang

Salimpaung

Situmbuk

Pauh Hill
1430m

Pahambatan

Raorao

Panarahan Hill
1526m

Kototuo

Padangluar

Sawahgombang

Sarik

Mt. Singgalang
2877m

Kotobaru

Mt. Merapi
2891m

Sungayang

Pandaisikat

TANAH DATAR VALLEY

Weaving
Village ★

Mt. Tandikat
2439m

Pierced
Stone ★

Padangseminyak

Balairung Sari
(Council Hall) ★

Pariangan

Padangmagek

Padangpanjang

Tabek

Simabur

Dusuntuo

Limokaum

Palace ★

Jarat Hill
1399m

Batipuh

Batusangkar

Pagarruyung

20'

Fort Van Der ★
Capellen

Saruaso

0°20'

Rumah Gadang
(Traditional House) ★

Balimbing

Telagagunung

to Sawahlunto,
Sijunjung

Sumpur

Gunungbungsu

Batutabal

Rotan Hill
513m

ariaman

Kayutanam

Pasarlimau

Umbilin

Bukitkandung

Sibumbunjantan Hill
990m

Sungaisarik

Sicincin

Tinjaulaut Hill
1441m

Padanglawas

Sumagek

Tanjungsawah

Lake
Singkarak

Rumah Gadang
(Traditional House) ★

Ampang

Sulit Air

Tobahtinggal

Barangin Hill
428m

Muntir River

Telagalawas

Paritmalintang

Titianair

Tungku Mountain
820m

Mt. Papan
957m

Padangbunga

Anai

Lembah Anai
Nature Reserve

Parakgadang

Pondok

Kudang

Tanjungalai

Parakubancakair

Mt. Gadang
1625 m

Karang

Batugaias

Kabangtiga

htuk

2   4   6   8   km

2   4   miles

Airhilang

Muarapinggai

Kapalabandar

Lubukalung

to Padang

Panyinggahan

to Solok

Singkarak

100°20'

16

Sumatra

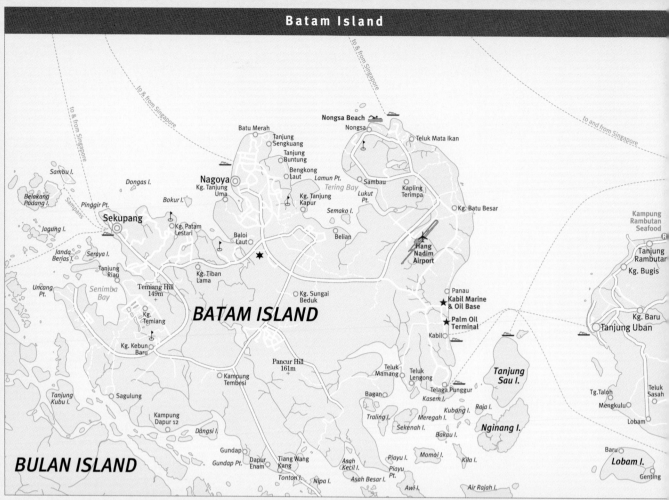

Batu Merah · Tanjung Sengkuang · Tanjung Buntung · Bengkong Laut · Nongsa Beach · Nongsa · Teluk Mata Ikan · Sambau · Kapling Terimpa · Kg. Batu Besar

Nagoya · Kg. Tanjung Uma · Kg. Tanjung Kapur · Lamun Pt. · Tering Bay · Lukut Pt. · Semako I.

Sekupang · Kg. Patam Lestari · Baloi Laut · Belian · ★ Hang Nadim Airport

Belakang Padang I. · Sambu I. · Dongas I. · Bokur I. · Jagung I. · Janda Berias I. · Seraya I. · Pinggir Pt. · Sampans · Tanjung Riau · Uncang Pt. · Senimba Bay · Temiang Hill 149m · Kg. Tiban Lama

BATAM ISLAND

Kg. Sungai Beduk · Kg. Temiang · Kg. Kebun Baru

Panau · ★ Kabil Marine & Oil Base · ★ Palm Oil Terminal · Kabil

Kampung Rambutan Seafood · Tanjung Rambutar · Kg. Bugis · Kg. Baru · Tanjung Uban

Pancur Hill 161m · Kampung Tembesi · Teluk Mamang · Teluk Lengong · Telaga Punggur · Bagan · Kasem I. · Kubong I. · Raja I. · **Tanjung Sau I.** · Tg.Taloh · Mengkulu · Teluk Sasah · Lobam

Tanjung Kubu I. · Sagulung · Traling · Meregah I. · Sekenah I. · Bakau I. · **Nginang I.**

BULAN ISLAND · Kampung Dapur 12 · Dangsi I. · Gundap · Gundap Pt. · Dapur Enam · Tiang Wang Kang · Tonton I. · Nipa I. · Asah Kecil I. · Asah Besar I. · Piayu I. · Piayu Pt. · Momoi I. · Kita I. · Air Rajah I. · Awi I. · **Lobam I.** · Baru · Genting

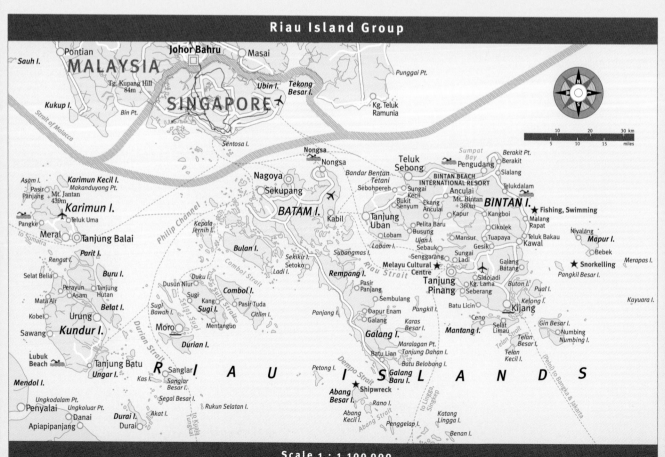

Sauh I. · Pontian · **Johor Bahru** · Masai · Punggai Pt.

MALAYSIA · Tg. Kupang Hill 84m · Ubin I. · Tekong Besar I.

Kukup I. · Bin Pt. · **SINGAPORE** · Kg. Teluk Ramunia

Strait of Malacca · Sentosa I.

Nongsa · Nongsa · Sumpat Bay · Berakit Pt. · Berakit · Sialang

Asam I. · Pasir Panjang · **Karimun Kecil I.** · Makanduyong Pt. · Nagoya · Sekupang · Bandar Bentan Tetani · Sebohpereh · Teluk Sebong · Pengudang · BINTAN BEACH INTERNATIONAL RESORT · Telukdalam

Karimun I. · + Mt. Jantan 439m · Teluk Uma · **BATAM I.** · Kabil · Sungai Kecil · Sungai Senyum · Anculai · Mt. Bintan +360m · **BINTAN I.** · ★ Fishing, Swimming

Pangke · Meral · Tanjung Balai · to Sumatra · Philip Channel · **Bulan I.** · Kepala Jernih I. · Tanjung Uban · Ekang Anculai · Pelita Baru · Busung · Kapur · Kangboi · Cikolek · Teluk Bakau · Kawal · Niyalang · **Mapur I.**

Parit I. · Sekikir I. · Setoko I. · Ladi I. · Subangmas I. · Lobam I. · Mansur · Gesik · Tuapaya · Kawal · Bebek

Buru I. · Rengat I. · Dusun Niur · Duku I. · Pasir Tuda · Ujan I. · Sebauk · Sungai Ladi · Senggarang · ★ Snorkelling · Merapas I.

Selat Belia · Perayun · Tanjung Hutan · Sugi · Kang · Citlim I. · Pasir Panjang · Melayu Cultural Centre ★ · Sidojadi · Galang Batang · Pangkil Besar I.

Mata Air · Perayun Asam · Combol I. · Sugi Bawah I. · Mentangun · Panjang I. · Pasir Panjang · Sembulang · **Tanjung Pinang** · Kg. Lama · Seberang · Buton I. · Pual I. · Kayuara I.

Kobel · **Urung** · **Belat I.** · Moro · **Durian I.** · **Sugi I.** · Dapur Enam · Galang · Karas Besar I. · Batu Licin · Ceno · Selat Limau · Gin Besar I. · Numbing I. · Numbing I.

Sawang · **Kundur I.** · Lubuk Beach · Tanjung Batu · Sanglar · **Galang I.** · Batu Lian · Maralagan Pt. · Tanjung Dahan I. · Batu Belobang I. · Kelong I. · **Kijang** · Telan Besar I. · Telan Kecil I.

Mendol I. · Ungar I. · Kas I. · Sanglar Besar I. · Segal Besar I. · Petong I. · Batu Baru I. · Abang Besar I. · ★ Shipwreck · Rano I. · (Pelan) to Bangka & Jakarta

R I A U Penyalai · Ungkodalam Pt. · Ungkoluar Pt. · Akat I. · Rukun Selatan I. · Abang Kecil I. · Penggelap I. · Katang Lingga I. · to Lingga-Singkep · Benan I. · **I S L A N D S**

Danai · **Durai I.** · Durai · Apiapipanjang

10 · 20 · 30 km · 5 · 10 · 15 miles

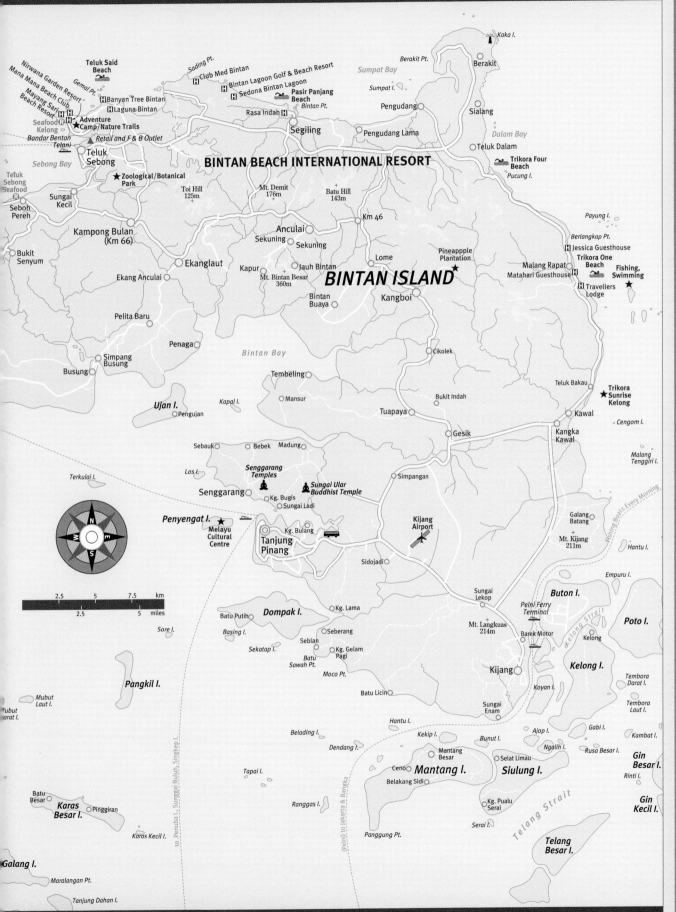

Teluk Said Beach

Nirwana Garden Resort
Mana Mana Beach Club
Mayang Sari Beach Resort
Banyan Tree Bintan
Laguna Bintan
Adventure Camp/Nature Trails
Seafood Kelong
Bandar Bentan Telani
Retail and F & B Outlet

Club Med Bintan
Bintan Lagoon Golf & Beach Resort
Sedona Bintan Lagoon
Pasir Panjang Beach
Rasa Indah
Segiling

Sading Pt.
Bintan Pt.

Sumpat Bay
Sumpat I.

Berakit Pt.

Kaka I.

Berakit

Pengudang
Sialang

Pengudang Lama
Dalam Bay

Teluk Dalam

BINTAN BEACH INTERNATIONAL RESORT

Trikora Four Beach
Pucung I.

Gemal Pt.

Teluk Sebong
Sebong Bay

Teluk Sebong Seafood
Seboh Pereh

Zoological/Botanical Park

Toi Hill 125m

Mt. Demit 176m

Batu Hill 143m

Km 46

Payung I.
Berlangkap Pt.

Jessica Guesthouse
Trikora One Beach
Malang Rapat
Matahari Guesthouse
Fishing, Swimming
Travellers Lodge

Sungai Kecil

Kampong Bulan (Km 66)

Bukit Senyum

Anculai
Sekuning
Sekuning

Ekanglaut
Ekang Anculai

Kapur
Mt. Bintan Besar 360m
Jauh Bintan

Lome

Pineappple Plantation

BINTAN ISLAND

Bintan Buaya

Kangboi

Pelita Baru

Penaga

Bintan Bay

Cikolek

Teluk Bakau

Trikora Sunrise Kelong

Simpang Busung
Busung

Tembeling

Mansur

Bukit Indah

Tuapaya

Gesik

Kawal

Kangka Kawal

Cengom I.

Malang Tenggiri I.

Ujan I.

Kapal I.

Pengujan

Sebauk

Bebek

Madung

Simpangan

Terkulai I.

Los I.

Senggarang Temples

Sungai Ular Buddhist Temple
Kg. Bugis
Sungai Ladi

Kijang Airport

Galang Batang
Mt. Kijang 211m

Hantu I.

Senggarang

Penyengat I.
Melayu Cultural Centre

Kg. Bulang
Tanjung Pinang

Sidojadi

Sungai Lekop

Empuru I.

Buton I.

Pelni Ferry Terminal

Poto I.

Batu Putih

Dompak I.

Kg. Lama

Seberang

Basing I.

Sekatap I.

Seblan

Kg. Gelam Pagi

Batu Sawah Pt.

Moco Pt.

Mt. Langkuas 214m

Barek Motor

Kelong

Kelong I.

Tembora Darat I.

Tembora Laut I.

Pangkil I.

Sore I.

Batu Licin

Koyan I.

Mubut Laut I.
Mubut Darat I.

Batu Besar

Karas Besar I.
Pinggiran

Karas Kecil I.

Kijang

Sungai Enam

Gabi I.

Ajop I.
Ngalih I.

Kambat I.

Rusa Besar I.

Gin Besar I.

Hantu I.

Belading I.

Dendang I.

Tapai I.

Ranggas I.

Kekip I.

Ceno
Belakang Sidi

Mantang Besar

Mantang I.

Bunut I.

Selat Limau

Siulung I.

Rinti I.

Gin Kecil I.

Kg. Pualu Serai

Serai I.

Telang Besar I.

Telang Strait

Galang I.

Maralangan Pt.

Tanjung Dahan I.

Panggung Pt.

to Penuba I., Sungai Buluh, Singkep I.

(Pelni) to Jakarta & Bangka

Fishing Boats Every Morning

Kelong Strait

2.5 5 7.5 km
2.5 5 miles

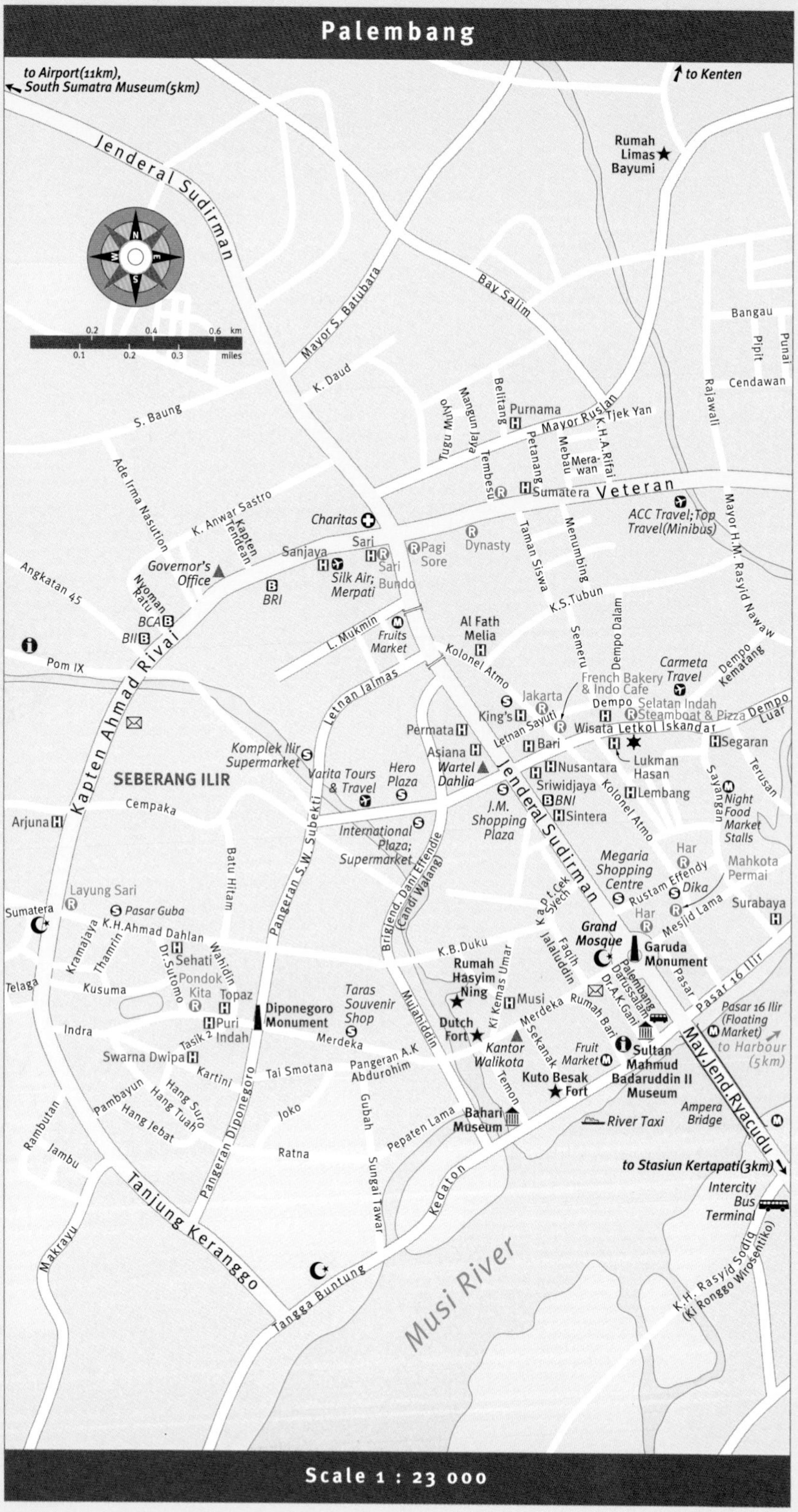

Map of Palembang (Scale 1 : 23 000)

Map labels include:
to Airport(11km), South Tsumatra Museum(5km); to Kenten; Jenderal Sudirman; Rumah Limas Bayumi ★; Mayor S. Batubara; Bay Salim; Bangau; Pipit; Punai; Cendawan; Rajawali; S. Baung; K. Daud; Tjek Yan; Purnama; Belitang; Mangun Jaya; Tembesi; Peranap; Mebal; Mahkmin; Mera-wan; Sumatera; Veteran; Mayor H.M. Rasyid Nawal; Mayor H.M. Rasyid Nawal; Mayor Ruslan; ACC Travel; Top Travel(Minibus); Ade Irma Nasution; K. Anwar Sastro; Kapten Tendean; Charitas +; Sanjaya; Sari; Silk Air; Merpati; Pagi Sore; Dynasty; Taman Siswa; Menumbing; K.S.Tubun; Governor's Office; Nyoman Rati; BCA; BII; BRI; Sari Bundo; Al Fath Melia; Semeru; Dempo Dalam; Carmeta Travel; Dempo Kematang; Dempo Luar; Angkatan 45; Kolonel Atmo; French Bakery & Indo Cafe; Dempo Selatan Indah; Pom IX; Fruits Market; L. Mikmin; Jakarta; King's; Steamboat & Pizza Dempo; Wisata Letkol Iskandar; Segaran; Letnan Jalmas; Permata; Asiana; Wartel; Dahlia; Letnan Sayuti; Bari; Nusantara; Lukman Hasan; Terusan; Komplek Ilir Supermarket; Hero Plaza; Varita Tours & Travel; Candi Walang; Sriwidjaya; BNI; Lembang; Sayangan; Kaptea Ahmad Rivai; SEBERANG ILIR; Cempaka; J.M. Shopping Plaza; Sintera; Night Food Market Stalls; Mahkota Permai; Arjuna; International Plaza; Supermarket; Megaria Shopping Centre; Har; Surabaya; Layung Sari; Batu Hitam; Rustam Effendy; Dika; Sumatera; Pasar Guba; Kramalaya; K.H.Ahmad Dahlan; Wahidin; K.B.Duku; Fatih Jalaludin; Har; Mesjid Lama; Telaga; Sehati; Pondok Kita; Topaz; D.Sutomo; Rumah Hasyim Ning; Grand Mosque; Garuda Monument; Pasar; Kusuma; Puri; Indah; Tasik 2; Diponegoro Monument; Taras Souvenir Shop; Mauland; Musi; Merdeka; Rumah Bari; Pasar 16 Ilir; Pasar 16 Ilir (Floating Market); Indra; Swarna Dwipa; Kartini; Pangeran A.K. Abdurohim; Tai Smotana; Kantor Walikota; Temon; Kuto Besak Fort; Fruit Market; Sultan Mahmud Badaruddin II Museum; Dutch Fort; Sekanak; to Harbour (5km); Rambutan; Jambu; Makrayu; Hang Suro; Hang Tuah; Hang Jebat; Pambayun; Joko; Ratna; Pepaten Lama; Gubah; Bahari Museum; River Taxi; Ampera Bridge; Maul Jend Ryacudu; Pangeran Diponegoro; Tanjung Keranggo; Kedaron; Sungai Tawar; to Stasiun Kertapati(3km); Intercity Bus Terminal; Tangga Buntung; Musi River; K.H. Rasyid Sodiq (Ki Ronggo Wirosentiko)

Scale 1 : 23 000

The Riau Islands, on the other hand, are one of Indonesia's best kept travel secrets. Easy to reach from Singapore on fast and comfortable hydrofoils, the islands of Batam and Bintan have good facilities and beaches. The realm of former pirates and traders, these islands are currently the scene of a multi-billion-dollar investment fever.

BATAM is the Indonesian island just opposite Singapore. It is only slightly smaller than Singapore, and would in fact seem to share many of the latter's geographical features — yet this sleepy, half-forgotten island was until recently considered to be of little or no value.

The key to Batam's success is careful planning. The entire east coast is being developed into a modern container facility known as Asia Port that will accommodate ships of up to 150,000 tons. Next to it, Hang Nadim International Airport is being expanded to handle jumbo jets. The main town, **Nagoya** — formerly known as Lubuk Baja ("Pirates' Waterhole") — has become a busy trading centre.

Tanjung Uncang peninsula, at the western tip of the island, will serve as a complex for the processing of timber, rubber, palm oil, tin, bauxite, petroleum, and other Sumatran resources. Reservoirs and water treatment plants are in place, and excellent roads crisscross the island.

Perhaps the jewel in the crown, however, is the "New Town" at Batam Centre — an entire city with office blocks, markets, shopping centres, and suburban residential neighbourhoods on the beautiful bay of Teluk Tering, facing Singapore. This will be the island's administrative hub with a polytechnic institute and training centre.

The largest town and main point of entry on BINTAN is **Tanjung Pinang** ("Areca Palm Cape") — a picturesque trading community that borders a sheltered bay on the island's southwestern shore.

PEKANBARU

Pekanbaru, capital of Riau, is a booming oil town and one of the main gateways into Sumatra. There's a well-worn route from Singapore to Pekanbaru, so it is a pleasant base for exploring Riau's sights.

PALEMBANG

Palembang is a sweltering, bustling industrial and communications centre. With over a million inhabitants, it is Sumatra's second largest city (after Medan) and the sixth largest in Indonesia (after Semarang). Its booming economy is based on coal mining, plantation agriculture, oil refining, and fertilizer production.

Palembang straddles the 600-m wide **Musi River** at a strategic point just below the confluence of major tributaries providing access to the vast Sumatran hinterland. Despite its newly-found oil wealth, Palembang is a city with a 1,300 year history, beginning as the site of the ancient Buddhist Srivijayan empire.

The city's main landmark is **Ampera Bridge** — built by the Japanese as a war reparation. At the time, it was Southeast Asia's longest bridge. Running north from the bridge is Jl. Sudirman, Palembang's main street, joining with Jl. Merdeka at a large roundabout in front of the Grand Mosque, built by Sultan Machmud Badaruddin I in 1740, and recently restored to its former splendour. The **Sultan Machmud Badaruddin II Museum** faces the Musi River west of the northern end of the bridge. The museum building, a blend of colonial and traditional Malay architecture, was constructed by the Dutch in 1823 on the site of the former sultan's palace.

JAMBI

The modern provincial capital of Jambi combines the old seat of the former Jambi sultanate with a new administrative centre at Telanipura just to the west. This is a major tidal river port with a booming economy (palm oil,

RIAU

As a province Riau is composed of many disparate parts. Its land mass is huge (94,561 sq km) and it comprises not only 3,214 islands and four of Sumatra's largest rivers, but the greatest expanse of tropical rainforest on the island, hundreds of vital sea lanes and thousands of kilometres of sparsely-inhabited coastline. Riau also contains the most productive oil fields in Indonesia — pumping half the nation's crude, some 650,000 barrels a day.

The Riau mainland is a densely-jungled lowland formed by alluvial deposits brought by the Rokan, Siak, Kampar and Inderagiri rivers — all of which begin high in the western Barisan Mountain range and meander some 300 to 550 km eastward to the coast. The lowlands are not suitable for agriculture.

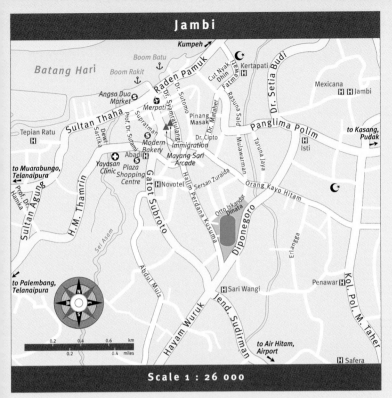

Jambi

Scale 1 : 26 000

Pekanbaru

Scale 1 : 20 000

timber, plywood, rubber). A floating population lives on rafts over the Batang Hari at Solok Sipin, just west of the city.

BENGKULU

Bengkulu is the smallest and least populated of Sumatra's provinces, yet its historical and natural charms abound. The province encompasses a 550 km long stretch of unspoiled sandy coastline which ascends rapidly to the lofty peaks of the **Barisan Mountains**. Tigers, elephants and rhinos still roam its pristine jungles, where the exotic rafflesia and wild orchids bloom.

Bengkulu was founded by the British in 1685 and occupied by them until 1825, when the Dutch took over. **Fort Marlborough** was built by the British East India Company between 1713 and 1719, and was carefully restored between 1977 and 1984. The former British Residency faces the fort. Just behind this is the old

Chinese quarter, where rows of two-storeyed wooden shop houses with ornately-carved balconies line both sides of the street.

BANDAR LAMPUNG

Lampung is one of the most interesting, and yet least known provinces of Indonesia. It occupies the southernmost tip of Sumatra — separated from Java by the shallow **Sunda Straits**, that are less than 30 km wide at their narrowest point. Lampung has been the area of Sumatra most influenced, socially and economically, by its densely populated and politically powerful neighbour.

The provincial capital and university town of Bandar Lampung overlooks a scenic bay. The city was formed by uniting Tanjung Karang, the former colonial administrative centre which lies on a hillside overlooking the bay, and the adjacent port of Teluk Betung, terminus of the southern Sumatra railway system.

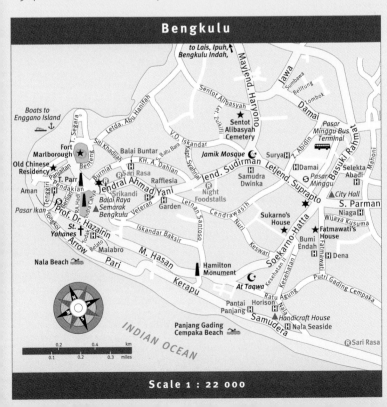

Bengkulu

Scale 1 : 22 000

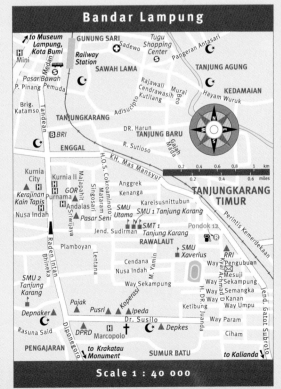

Bandar Lampung

Scale 1 : 40 000

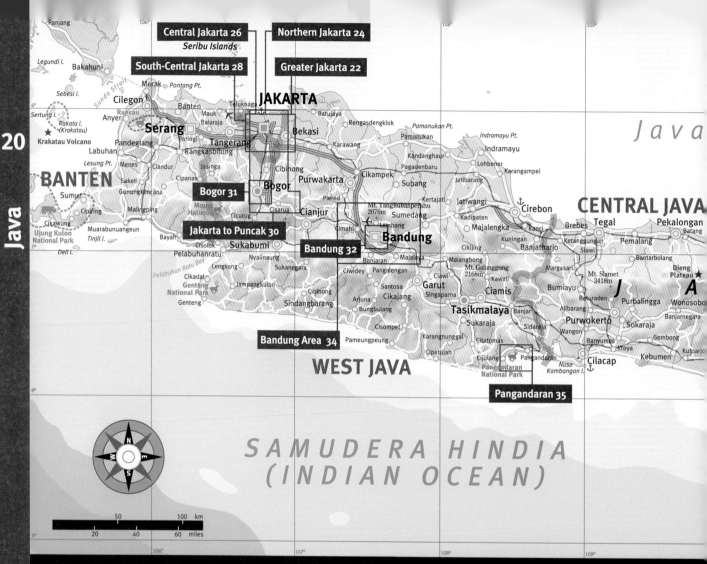

Scale 1 : 2 800 000

JAVA

Java has one of the longest records of human habitation of any place on Earth. It was here that million-year-old remains of one of man's earliest ancestors — "Java Man" (Homo erectus) — were discovered over a century ago.

For eons, the island was blanketed in a luxuriant mantle of tropical forest hosting an exotic assortment of wildlife. Violent volcanic eruptions periodically spread nutrient-rich deposits across the land, while the volcanic slopes provided ideal terrain which could be terraced for irrigated cultivation. Heavy monsoon rains, bubbling mountain springs and months of uninterrupted sunshine produced a bounty of grains, fruits and forest products.

Today, from the air, Java resembles a patchwork quilt of verdant rice fields interspersed by village settlements, palm groves and stands of rubber, teak, and sugar cane. The bright green vegetation contrasts vividly with rich, red-brown soils, and the landscapes are dominated by soaring, blue-grey volcanoes with balding tops, forested slopes and covered with rice terraces below.

This is the most fertile, the most productive, and also the most densely populated island in the world. With over 115 million people living in an area the size of England or New York State, the average population density is an amazing 850 persons per square kilometre. Although there are four cities with over a million inhabitants, and many more with over 100,000, the island is still predominantly rural. Java, constituting just 7 percent of Indonesia's total land mass, supports over 60 percent of the nation's huge population. It is the political, commercial and administrative centre of Indonesia.

However, many areas in the mountains and along the isolated southern shore are in fact still rather sparsely populated. Several of the island's densely packed agricultural zones, on the other hand, support more than twice the island average. In the fertile crescent around Yogyakarta in Central Java, for example, rural densities soar to an unbelievable 2,000 persons per square kilometre, with the majority still making a living from traditional wet-rice cultivation, practiced under the most labour-intensive conditions found anywhere.

VOLCANOES. Volcanoes are the very essence of Java. They have moulded the landscape and provided the basis for the island's rich soils. Frequent outpourings of nutrient-rich lava and ash are washed down by heavy rains across the foothills and plains, providing continuous renewal of the land.

The volcanoes form an irregular line running the entire length of the island — one of the most active segments in the circum-Pacific "Ring of Fire" that marks the boundaries of drifting continental plates. Java lies at the southern extremity of one of these plates, which during the Ice Ages formed a huge sub-continent encompassing all of Java, Bali, Borneo, Sumatra, the Malay peninsula, and the intervening area that now lies submerged beneath the shallow Java Sea.

While many peaks date back to the Tertiary era and have long since weathered and lost recognizable form, others are very young. Java and Bali together have 37 volcanoes officially listed, of which 13 have erupted in the last 25 years. The highest peak is **Mt. Semeru** at 3,676 m, which sends forth intermittent puffs of smoke. The most famous volcano is **Krakatau** in the Sunda Strait, separating Java from Sumatra, whose cataclysmic eruption in 1883 set up tidal waves that reportedly killed 36,000 people. **Mt. Merapi** (literally "Fire Mountain") to the north of Yogyakarta erupts most frequently.

Karimunjawa Islands

Sea

Bawean I.

Masalembu Besar I.

Semarang 40

Surabaya 42

Madura

Solo 41

EAST JAVA

Surabaya

Madura Strait

Malang 44

Yogyakarta – Solo Area 36

Mt. Bromo 45

Yogyakarta 38

Scale 1 : 2 800 000

With their potential for devastation, volcanoes are a mixed blessing, yet as the dust settles after each eruption, land-hungry farmers move back into the area to redevelop the fertile soils. In some areas the dangers are more subtle — as, for example, the clouds of odorless poisonous gas that sometimes waft across the **Dieng Plateau**. Yet the Javanese often seek a livelihood in the very jaws of volcanic death, as in the quarries of fresh sulphur formed by hissing fumaroles in the crater of Mt. Ijen, Java's easternmost peak.

The mountains are never far from the sea, and as a result, few of the rivers on Java achieve significant size. The two largest rivers on the island — the **Solo** and the **Brantas** — both originate near the south coast of Java, but wind around and between several peaks, finally emptying into the Java Sea near Surabaya. Similarly, the **Citarum River** in West Java flows out of the former lakebed around Bandung through a series of gorges and the **Jatiluhur Reservoir** before emptying into the sea at **Cape Karawang**, east of Jakarta.

The Java Sea to the north of the island is extremely shallow — less than 200 m at its deepest point. The Java Trench to the south, on the other hand, drops precipitously to 7,000 m. This trench marks a zone of violent subduction where the Indo-Australian plate is sliding northward beneath the Sunda plate.

AGRICULTURE. An astounding 63 percent of all land on Java is cultivated, compared to only 10 to 20 percent on other Indonesian islands. A third of this is irrigated farmland worked by small-holders who may or may not own their own plots — while another 7 percent is under cultivation by large estates growing tea, rubber, oil palm, cacao, and teak. At least 55 percent of the population of Java are farmers, and by far the most important crop is rice. Other crops of importance, such as maize,

soybeans, peanuts, cassava, and potatoes, are grown on dry fields, but rice is the staple food and beautifully engineered rice terraces and irrigation systems are a characteristic feature of the landscape.

NATURE RESERVES. Less than 150 km from the centre of Jakarta, on Java's westernmost tip at **Ujung Kulon National Park**, is the island's last refuge for the crocodile. More importantly, it is also the sole remaining haunt of the Javan Rhino — one of the rarest mammals on earth. **Gunung Halimun Reserve**, south west of Jakarta, still has some primary forest, and despite being surrounded by tea and clove plantations contains a wide variety of primates — some rare, like the Javan Gibbon, the Javan Leaf Monkey and the Silvered Leaf Monkey.

Around the eastern tip of Java are a number of reserves: **Mt. Ijen** is a steaming crater where sulphur is mined; Meru Betiri is where the last sightings of the Java Tiger were made several years ago and where giant sea turtles lay their eggs on the beach at night; the **Blambangan Nature Reserve** is a surfer's paradise; and Baluran is where the climate and landscape are almost East African.

POPULATION. In contrast to other areas of Indonesia and despite its huge population, the island of Java is relatively homogeneous in its ethnic composition. Only two ethnic groups are actually native to the island: the Javanese (primarily in Central and East Java) and the Sundanese (in West Java). A third group, the Madurese, inhabit the neighbouring island of Madura and have migrated to East Java in large numbers since the 18th century. The Javanese are by far the dominant group, accounting for about two-thirds of the island's total population, while the Sundanese and Madurese comprise another 20 and 10 percent respectively.

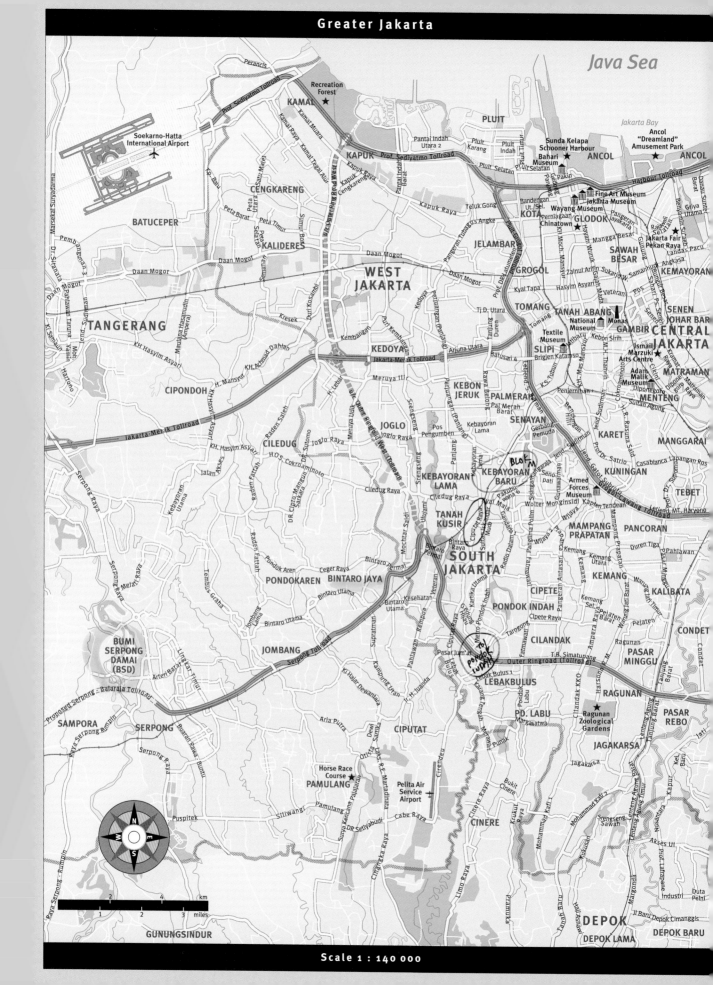

GREATER JAKARTA

Founded on the site of the ancient pepper trading port of Sunda Kelapa more than four-and-a-half centuries ago, the city of Jakarta is a vibrant commercial centre drawing together peoples from all over the vast Indonesian archipelago. It is the sprawling and rapidly growing capital of the world's fourth largest nation — a crowded metropolis of more than 10 million inhabitants, with a dynamic economy and a fast-paced lifestyle.

In the 15th century, **Sunda Kelapa** was an important coastal outpost for the inland kingdom of **Pajajaran**, competing for a share of the regional spice trade with a host of other riverine ports lining the strategic Malacca and Sunda straits. In 1527, the port was conquered by the joint Islamic forces of Banten and Demak and re-named Jayakarta — "City of Victory."

It was to this town that Portuguese spice merchants came and began a trading association. At the end of the 16th century, the Portuguese were followed by the Dutch, who with faster ships and better organisation soon took the lead in the spice trade. The Dutch moved their regional base from nearby Banten to Jayakarta. Under the leadership of an aggressive and determined envoy of the Dutch East Indies Company (VOC), Jan Pieterszoon Coen, the Dutch enlarged their fortress, which had been dubbed "Batavia" in honor of early Germanic tribes which settled in Holland. It was by this name that the city was to be known throughout almost 350 years of Dutch rule.

Batavia became the administrative and military hub of a vast and powerful trading empire that extended from the Cape of Africa across the Indian Ocean to the Indonesian archipelago, Formosa (Taiwan) and Japan. During the next two centuries, the fortunes of Batavia first waxed and then waned along with those of the VOC. Throughout the 17th century, a lucrative monopoly in eastern spices buoyed the city's economy. However, in the 18th century, the Company's trading activities increasingly suffered from drastic fluctuations in prices, while the high cost of maintaining a military presence in faraway corners of the eastern archipelago was compounded by rampant corruption within the VOC ranks.

Declining economic fortunes were mirrored by deteriorating physical conditions in the city. The fine canals Coen had designed to make Batavia an eastern version of Amsterdam were unsuited to the tropics. Sluggish and dirty, they soon silted up and became a breeding ground for mosquitoes and vermin. The solid but poorly ventilated Dutch buildings became infested with rats and epidemics of cholera, typhoid, dysentery, and malaria decimated the town's population.

Under Governor-General Daendels (1808-1810), the old fortress and town around the harbour were demolished. A new city centre was begun in the more salubrious southern districts, where broad, tree-lined boulevards and handsome civic buildings in neo-classical style laid the foundation for modern Jakarta.

Batavia prospered once again in 1830 after the institution of the "Cultivation System" of forced labor that generated millions of guilders in profits for the Dutch. Canals and roads were rebuilt, civic buildings increased in number and leafy residential suburbs appeared in Menteng, Cikini, and the surrounding areas. Batavia became known as the "Pearl of the Orient."

The city thus entered the 20th century as a small, but prosperous colonial capital with only about 300,000 residents. It underwent a process of rapid modernisation in the 1930s with the introduction of gas lighting, tramways and automobiles, and became the focus for a new class of young, Dutch-educated Indonesians who began to sow the seeds of nationalism and independence. In 1942, the Japanese invaded and Batavia was renamed Jakarta.

The post-war Soekarno era left an indelible stamp on the face of modern Jakarta. While struggling to rule a nation torn by factionalism and bereft of the colonial administration that had held it together since the days of the VOC, Soekarno dreamed of a capital that would embody the surging spirit of Merdeka ("freedom"). He commissioned grand parks, broad ceremonial boulevards, dramatic sculptures and monuments, thus creating a new "theatre state."

Under the "New Order" government (1966-1998), the city entered a dynamic period of development. Office towers and construction cranes dominated the skyline. Jakarta's suburbs expanded outward in all directions. **Kebayoran Baru**, one of the oldest of Jakarta's satellite suburbs, which centres around the bustling Blok M shopping complex, lies south of the end of Jl. Sudirman. Further suburban development now stretches south through Pondok Indah, an enclave of lavish villas, and on to Cilandak and Ciputat.

The **Ragunan Zoological Gardens** lie 15 km south of the city centre, just beyond Pasar Minggu. The ultimate visitors' experience awaits at **Taman Mini Indonesia Indah**, just off the Jagorawi toll road in south Jakarta. This 160 ha park provides a vicarious tour of the architecture and cultures of the vast Indonesian archipelago. The park also features several museums, an orchid garden, a bird park with walk-in aviaries, and cultural performances.

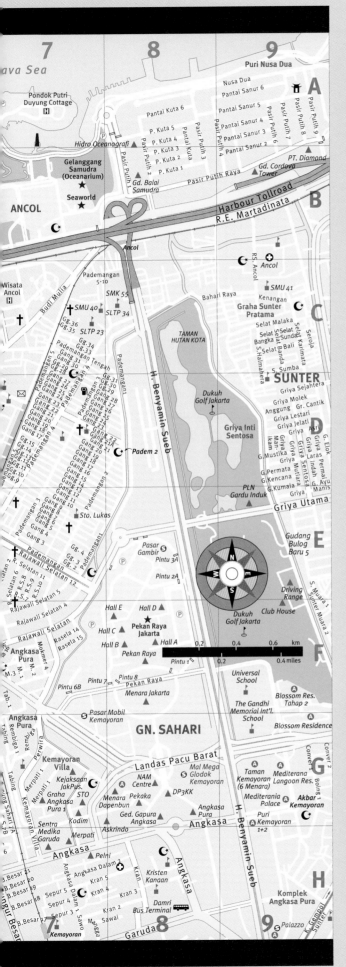

NORTHERN JAKARTA

Jakarta developed from north to south. The Dutch colonial city of Batavia grew up around the ancient spice trading harbour, **Sunda Kelapa**, located where the **Ciliwung River** meets the sea. The Dutch East Indies Company (VOC) erected a trading outpost here on the east bank of the Ciliwung, fortifying it with thick masonry walls and 15 large bastions. The **Uitkijk Lookout Tower** on Jalan Pakin provides an overview of the entire area. The tower was erected in 1839 and served as the customs house. To the north and across the river from the tower lies **Sunda Kelapa** port, in continuous use since at least the 12th century.

On the west side of the river, just north of the lookout, stands the **Museum Bahari**, a maritime museum located in an old warehouse that was built by the VOC in 1652. It once housed a vast hoard of trading goods — pepper, cloves, nutmeg, coffee, tea, copper, tin, and bales of Indian cloth. Behind the museum is the Fish Market. The market is hard on the nose, but surrounding it is a veritable rabbit warren of tiny shops crammed with seashells, ships chandlery, kitchenwares, fishing nets, stuffed turtles, model ships, shoes, and sealing wax.

The area immediately to the south and east of the harbour was the centre of the walled city known as **Kota** and still contains several relics of the VOC days. Between Kali Besar and Jl. Kakap stand the old VOC shipyards. South and west of the bridge on Jl. Kali Besar Barat, stands the home of Governor-General van Imhoff, dating from around 1730. Known as "Red House," it has fine Chinese woodwork characteristic of 18th-century Batavian houses.

The administrative centre of Batavia was situated some distance away from the noise and bustle of the port, around a square now known as **Taman Fatahillah**. The city founders built a splendid city hall from where the vast Asian trading empire was controlled. The square and its surrounding buildings were restored during the mid-1970s and the colonial administrative buildings were then converted into museums.

The city hall on the south side of the square has become the **Jakarta History Museum** — 37 rooms filled with old maps, antiques and memorabilia. Opulently appointed rooms now recreate the atmosphere of the VOC period. The hall was actually rebuilt three times; the current structure dates from 1710. It had a long and checkered career as a law court, administrative centre and even a prison.

A huge collection of wayang puppets from throughout Indonesia is on display in the **Wayang Museum** on the western side of Taman Fatahillah. A church once stood on this site and the tombstones of early Dutch notables are still preserved at the back. On the eastern side of Taman Fatahillah, in the neo-classical **Hall of Justice** dating from 1870, is the **Fine Arts Museum**. It houses a superb collection of rare porcelain and modern paintings.

The **Sion Portuguese Church**, east of the Kota train station, was built in 1695 for the mardijkers — a community of Portuguese-Indian mestizos brought to Batavia as slaves in the 17th century and later freed. It is the oldest church in Jakarta and still has the original pews, copper chandeliers, and a fine pulpit.

The Chinese have always played an important role in Jakarta's economy. In 1740, they were relocated just south of the fortress walls to an area now known as **Glodok**. A maze of narrow streets behind **Glodok Plaza**, which is filled with hawkers, foodstalls, and small shops. The **Dharma Jaya** temple was one of the earliest centres of worship for the Batavian Chinese. Founded in 1650, it is dedicated to Kuan Yin, the Buddhist goddess of mercy.

Modern Jakarta has expanded its playground along the northern coast and today, east of Sunda Kelapa, is the 200-ha Ancol Dreamland. The grounds include an 18-hole golf course, Fantasy World Park, SeaWorld Marina, and an art market.

INDEX

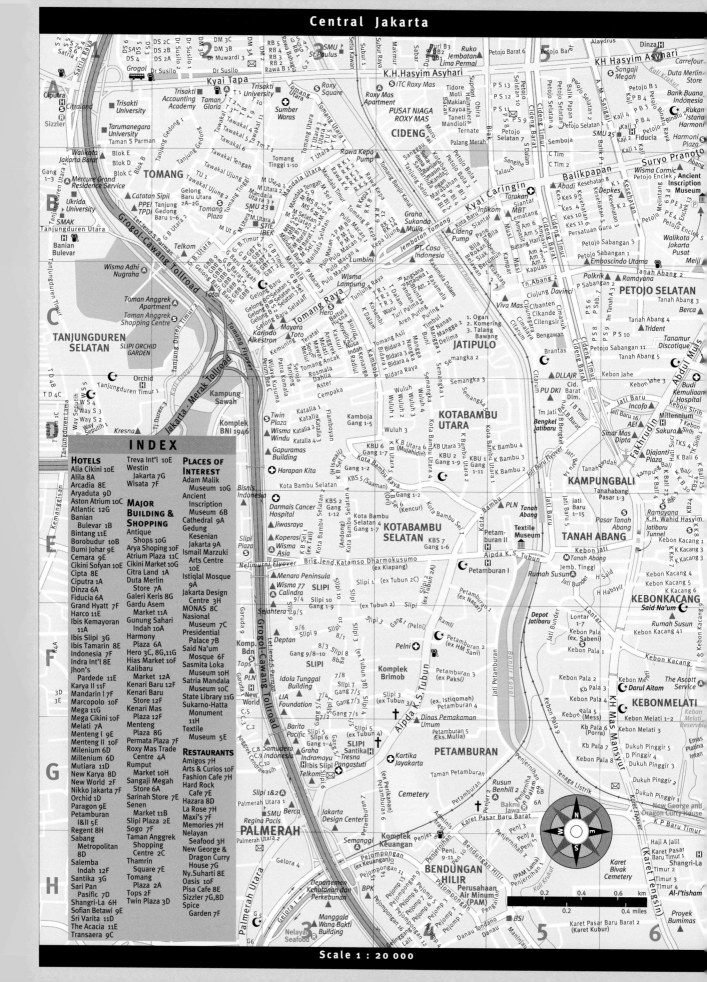

Java

28

KARET TENGSIN

GELORA

GROGOL UTARA

Komplek Polri

Komplek TVRI

Komplek Pln Senayan

Permata Senayan

Simprug Indah

GELORA

Gedung DPR/MPR (Parliament Bldg)

Youth Recreation Park/Taman Ria Senayan

National TV (TVRI)

Athletic Stadium

Main Stadium

Swimming Pool

Gelora Bung Karno

Istora Senayan (Sport Palace)

Tennis Courts

Senayan Golf Course

Senayan Golf Driving Range

Atlet Century Park

Jakarta Hilton international

Hilton Residence 1&2

Executive Club

Polda Metro Jaya

SENAYAN

KARET SEMANGI

Plaza Semanggi

Crowne Plaza

Komplek Menteri

Api Monument

Jakarta Int'l School

SENAYAN

SELONG

Al Azhar

Museum TNI-AD "Satria Mandala"

RAWA BARAT

GUNUNG

Kyai Maja

Pertamina (RSPP)

Mabak POLRI

ASEAN

MELAWAI

Blok M

PELA MAMPANG

PETOGOGAN

Kapten Tendean

Wolter Monginsidi

Pasar Burung

Melawai Raya

Singapore Int'l School

Permata Gandaria

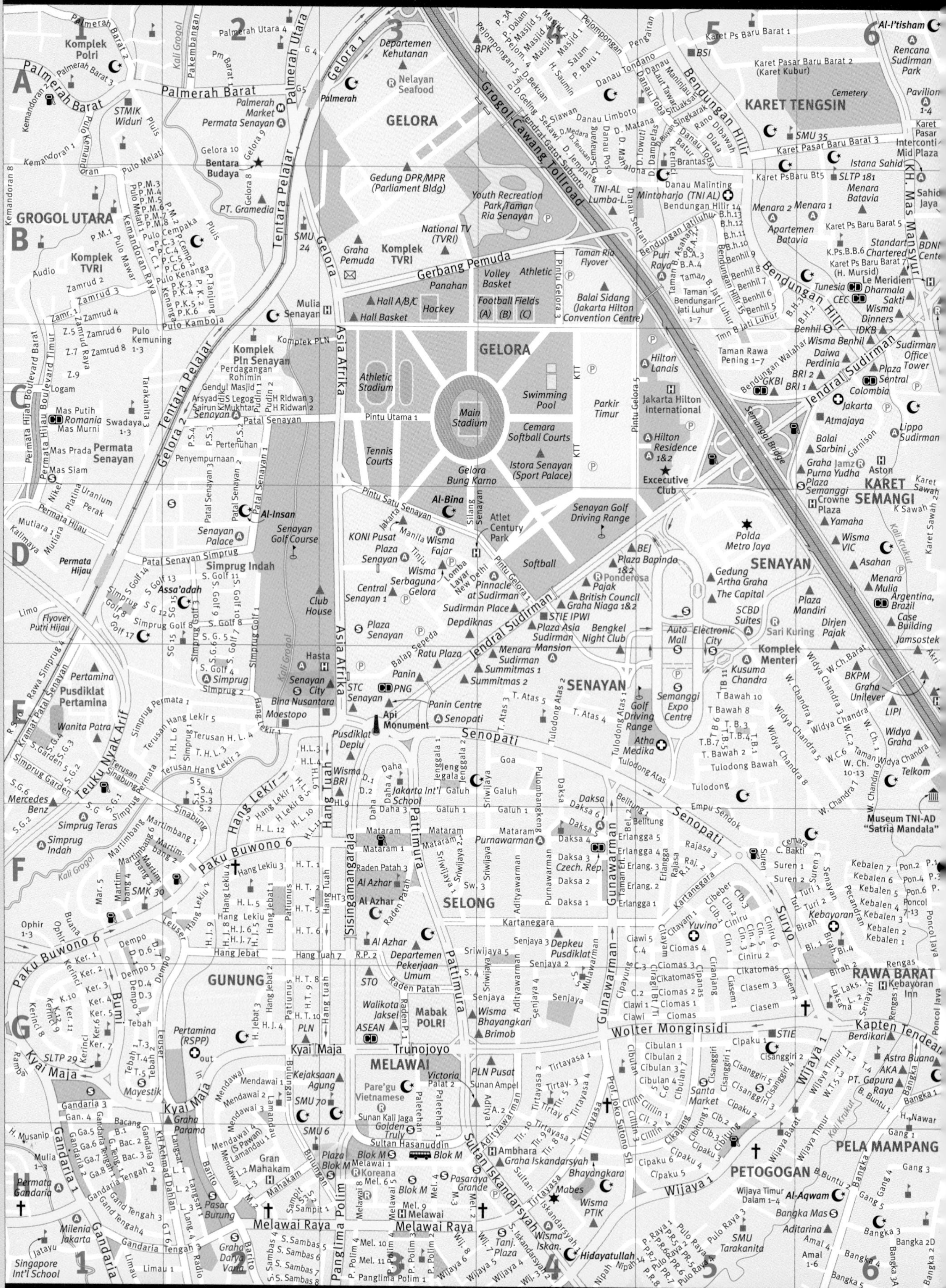

CENTRAL JAKARTA

Medan Merdeka, or "Freedom Square", is an expansive, open field lying in the heart of Jakarta. It is bordered on four sides by broad boulevards and government buildings that form the nation's administrative nucleus. Originally used as a military training ground and a field for cattle-grazing, in the 19th century it became **Koningsplein** (King's Square), the symbolic centre of Dutch Batavia.

The centrepiece of the field is **Monas** (short of "Monumen Nasional") **National Monument**, a towering obelisk commissioned by Soekarno to commemorate the soaring spirit of Indonesian nationalism. Rising to a height of 137 m and topped by an illuminated bronze flame sheathed in 35 kg of gold, it is Jakarta's most conspicuous landmark and unofficial symbol.

From Monas, it is a short walk to the **National Museum** on the western side of the square. This is the oldest and best museum in Indonesia, containing fascinating stone, bronze, and ceramic collections. The most interesting displays are the treasure and bronze rooms on the second floor.

Adjoining one another on the northern side of **Merdeka Square** are two imposing presidential palaces. The **Istana Negara**, which faces north onto Jl. Veteran, was erected as a private residence in the late 1700s by a Dutch businessman and is now used for important state functions. It served as the official residence of the Dutch Governors-General until the larger **Koningsplein Palace** was constructed in 1879.

East of the palaces on Jl. Veteran is **Istiqlal Mosque**. Officially opened in 1978, the enormous marble edifice is East Asia's largest mosque. Behind the mosque rises the black spires of the neo-gothic **Catholic Cathedral** on Jl. Katedral, built in 1901. South of the corner of Jl. Pejambon, opposite Gambir railway station, is the **Immanuel Church** — a curious but appealing mixture of Graeco-Roman and classical European theatre architecture. After its completion in 1835 by Dutch Protestants of Batavia it was known as Willemskerk. Further south on Jl. Prapatan, opposite the Hyatt Hotel, is the **Anglican All Saints Church**. Built in 1829, it has beautiful hand-painted glass windows.

The field between the Catholic cathedral and the Hotel Borobudur is called **Lapangan Banteng** ("Buffalo Square"). The Freedom Memorial, the grimacing statue in the centre of the field — a muscled figure breaking his chains of bondage — was erected by Soekarno in 1963 to commemorate the "liberation" of Irian Jaya from the Dutch. In colonial times the square was known as **Waterlooplein** and was the site of a magnificent governors' mansion. Nothing is left of it now, but a second palace begun by Daendels in 1809 still stands to the east of the square. Next to it stands the Supreme Court building which dates from 1848.

Leafy, laid-back **Menteng** is a residential and diplomatic district composed of colonial mansions and posh new villas, located to the south of Freedom Square. A thick canopy of angsana trees shades streets lined with fine colonial houses — many containing hidden gardens and other delights. Jl. Jendral Sudirman, is Jakarta's "money mile," lined with gleaming, steel-and-glass towers housing banks and corporate offices. The vast Senayan sports and office complex also includes a convention hall.

INDEX

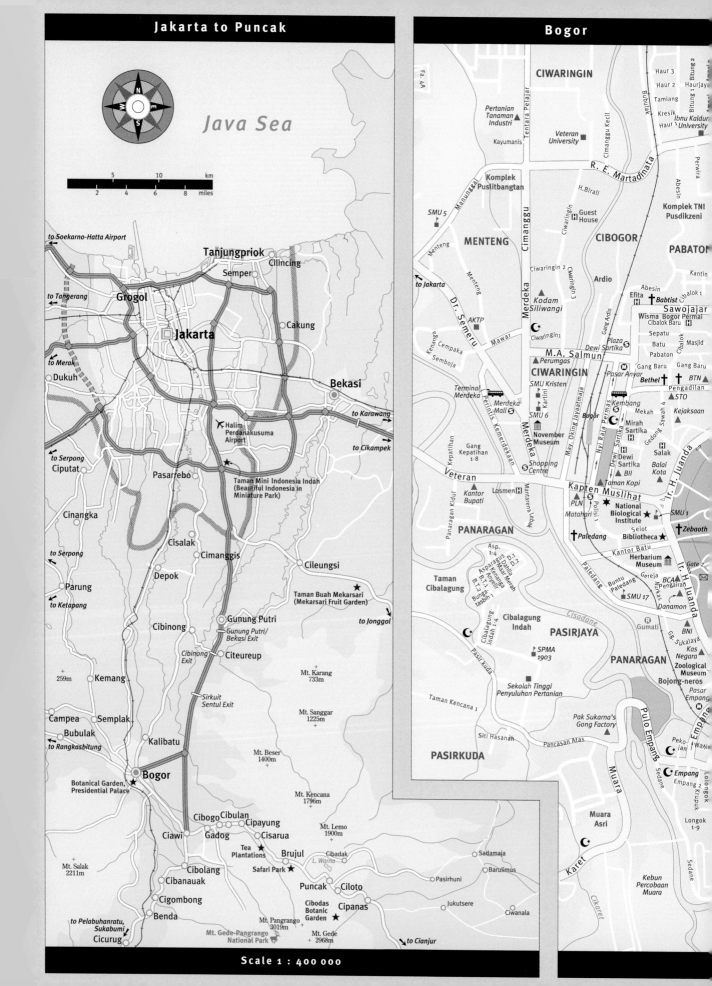

BOGOR

One of Indonesia's earliest known kingdoms — the 5th-century Hindu-Javanese state of Tarumanegara — was probably based in the vicinity of present-day Bogor. There are a number of stone inscriptions in the area, including a particularly striking one that is still in situ at Ciampea, 15 km west of the city.

In 1745, Dutch Governor-General van Imhoff had a private retreat constructed 60 km south of Jakarta, at the foot of **Mt. Salak** at an altitude of 260 m. Cooler than the coast, the retreat named Buitenzorg (literally "free of cares"), provided a welcome respite from the sweltering heat and chaos of Jakarta. The town of Bogor grew up around this country home and soon became popular with the Dutch. From 1870 until 1942, the rebuilt and expanded palace became the primary residence of the Dutch Governors-General of the East Indies. Since independence, the Presidential Palace has been one of five official homes of the Indonesian president. President Suharto declines to use it, but Soekarno spent a good deal of time here and his spirit is said to inhabit the place. A herd of spotted deer imported from Holland roam the grounds.

Bogor's pride, and one of the world's great biological treasure troves, is the **Kebon Raya Botanic Gardens**. The Kebon Raya was officially established by the Dutch in 1827 under the directorship of D.B.D. Reinwardt. He and subsequent generations of botanists performed the herculean feat of assembling over 15,000 species of tropical plants from around the world. There are over 400 palm species, 5,000 trees and an orchid house with 3,000 varieties within the carefully landscaped 87 ha. Kebon Raya actually has five branches in Java, Sumatra and Bali — the largest of which is the important Cibodas Park just to the southeast of Bogor. The gardens were designed to serve as a research institute — a function which continues today. Institut Pertanian Bogor (IPB), Indonesia's leading agricultural institute on the east side of the gardens, works to develop new strains of rice and other important crops.

Near the entrance to the gardens is a **Zoological Museum** with an immense collection (300,000 specimens) of land and sea creatures from throughout Indonesia. The museum also boasts a fine library, the skeleton of a blue whale, and the last rhino (stuffed) found on the Bandung plateau.

PUNCAK

To the south of Bogor rises a towering volcanic massif which boasts some of the most beautiful scenery on Java. The highest peaks, **Mts. Gede** (2,958 m) and **Pangrango** (3,019 m) stand side by side 40 km to the southeast of Bogor. Together with Mt. Salak (2,211 m), they have created a broad alluvial fan with rivers spreading down to the coast. One of the largest rivers, the Ciliwung, has carved a valley into the northern slope of Mt. Pangrango. It was here at the beginning of the 19th century that a narrow, winding road was built across the 1,450 m pass known as Puncak (lit. "the summit"). Today, the cool and spectacularly scenic area traversed by this road is a popular weekend resort.

Tea plantations blanket the upper reaches of the pass, while villages just below it supply Jakarta's kitchens with fresh fruits and vegetables. The nights here are invigorating, especially during the rainy season, with temperatures averaging 20–22°C. On a clear day, there are splendid views of the plains below. Hiking trails pass through terraced rice fields and dense forests. Numerous scenic country walks around **Cisarua** lead to picnic grounds and small waterfalls. There is also an African-style Safari Park, in which lions, tigers, zebras, and giraffes graze in open spaces and stare at passing motorists. The total area of 168 ha includes a campground, recreation area and caravan park.

Near the top of the pass, the highway enters the Gunung Mas Tea Estate, which is open to visitors. A coloured lake, **Telaga Warna**, is tucked into a mountain niche 500 m below the Rindu Alam Restaurant.

Once over the summit, the road descends through more resorts. In **Pacet**, 7 km beyond the pass, there is a poorly marked road to the right leading up to the **Cibodas Botanic Gardens** — a high-altitude branch of the Bogor Botanic Gardens. These 60 ha were laid out in 1852 for the study of temperate and montane flora from around the world, and pioneering work done here on cinchona (quinine) and coffee made Java the world's largest supplier of these commodities by the late 19th century.

Assembling Cibodas's collection of over 5,000 specimens was an even greater undertaking than the larger gardens at Bogor. There are pools, quiet walks, flowing streams, and great views of the volcanoes on a clear day. The park includes virgin native jungle and the starting point for mountain hikes.

A few kilometres further east along the main highway is the town of **Cipanas** (literally "hot waters"), site of a natural hot spring whose sulphurous waters, it is claimed, cure skin diseases and relieve rheumatism. Also in Cipanas is the Presidential Summer Palace, **Istana Cipanas**. This colonial mansion, built in 1750, sits on a large manicured estate fronting the highway and is now rarely used. The grounds extend into the jungle and contain their own hot springs.

32

Java

Grid columns: 1 2 3 4 5 6
Grid rows: A B C D E F G H

PAJAJARAN
Tamanmilenia
Sukawarna Wetan
PT. Dirgantara Indonesia
Al-Fajar
Kapten Tata Natanegara
Cipedes
Sukawarna 3
Sukawarna 1
Baladewaasri
CICENDO
Simpang Raya
Saung Kabayan
Raja Rasa
Cipedes 1
to Jakarta
Pancoran
Cibarengkok
Dr.Djundjunan
Garunggang
Garunggang Sukaati Sukabungah
BRI
BNI
Cat 17
Premier
Dai Soghon
The Promenade
Elizabeth
S.E.A.
Sapulidi
Prinnggodani
Samyudo
Cikapayang
TAXI Media
Cihampelas
Cihampelas Jeans
Pelesiran
Pelesiran
Perahu Jeans
Kebonbibi
BOOM
ASTEX
Studio Jeans
OZ Wonder
Candy
Edward Forrel
Bandung Jeans
West
IBC
Melodi-Pub
Ampera
Bongkaran
Pulosari

Hüsein Sastranegara Airport
Baladewa
PAMOYANAN
Pandu Cemetery
Pandu
Kembar
Hamid Mahmud 5
Mochamad Mahmud 4
Pancoran
Dursasana
Sukatenang Pamoyanan Sukasintir Sukabakti
Sunda Kelapa
Ahmad 4 Ahmad 3 Ahmad 2 Ahmad 1
Biofarma
Mandiri
RSU Dr. Hasan Sadikin
Rumah Sakit
Rancabadak
Ayam Goreng Jakarta
Pasteur
Swike Walid
Curie
Joyci
Rajiman
Dr.Otten
Dr.Sukiman
Oncom Raos
Dr.Hatta
TAMANSARI
Sawunggaling
Tamansari
BANDUNG WETAN
Tamansari Bawah
Cimaung
Trocadero
Universitas Islam Bandung
Wastukencana
Kampoeng Kuring
Merdekalio
Sekolah Tinggi Hukum Bandung
Bandung Centre Electronic
BABAKANCIAMIS

Komplek PJKA
Al-Ikhlas
ANDIR
Abdurahman Saleh
BCA
Permata
Baso Malang Pajajaran
Komodor Udara Supadio
City Square
Jatayu
Andir
Jatayu Dalam
Sirnaraga Cemetery
Artos Parahyangan
Pajajaran Laksmana Satrugna Barata
SMK Penerbangan
Pandu
Pajajaran
Kartika
Pulen
Panorama Tour
Purabaya
Somawinata
Ekonomi
STADION PADJADJARAN
Pabrik Kina
Babakan Cintawargi
Griya Indah
Kebonkawung
Kartikasari
Patradissa
Permata
Selekta
Dumah Mutiara
Cemerlang
Kebonkawung
Rumah Sakit Mata Cicendo
Cicendo
Gedung Pakuan
Astra Graphia
Inter Link
Bethel

Halteu Utara
Swadaya
Cicukang
Kebonsawo
Kebonsayur
Terminal Ciroyom
Pemotongan Hewan
Kesatriaan
ARJUNA
Gedungdalapan
Industri
Gedong 9
Gedong 8
Sate Karjan
Taxi 4848
PT.DAMRI Guntur
Artos Danamon
Bandung
Kantor Pusat PJKA Bandung
Kebonjukut
Kedaton
Suniaraja
BCA
Landmark

DUNGUSCARIANG
Komplek Lugina
RI.Winata
Rajawali Timur
CIROYOM
BCA
NISP
BRI
Rajawali Timur
Kebonjati
RS Kebonjati
Pusat Textile Bandung
Stasiun Barat
Stasiun Timur
Jasa Artha
Kebonjati
BRAGA
Pusat Elektro Cikapundung
ABC
Naripan

to Cimahi
Dunguscariang
Pusat Penelitian Pengembangan Teknologi Mineral dan Batubara
Aksan
K.L.1
K.L.3
Kebonjukut
Waringin
Andir
Waringin
Jambal
Gabus
Kakap
Tanda Bakti Tiga Saudara
Sukamanah
Sukamanah Dalam
Kebonangkil
KEBON JERUK
King Garden
Trio
Sukamanah
RadenBrata
Saritem
Rio
Surabaya
Belakangpasar
Pasarbaru
Pasar Barat
Pasar Baru
Kartabrata
Enceajis
Lestari
Durma
Babatan
Executive Hotin
Oriental
Asia Plaza
Pecinanlama
Matahari
Blk.Factory
BRI
Mandiri
Cikapundung

Jend. Sudirman
Paramount
Laut Utara
Cibadak
Menara Mayapada
BNI
Prima Expres
Sasmintaputra
Hongkong TjoenKie
Kebonsalak
Jend. Sudirman
Budi
Kote
KARANGANYAR
Asia Afrika
Ramayana Robinson
Agung Bandung
TAMAN ALUNALUN
Parahyangan Plaza
King
Yogya
Pendopo Pangarang
REGOL
BALONGGEDE
Dewi Sartika
Ciguriang
Pasundan
Sasakgantung

BOJONGLOA KALER
Pagarsih
Ibu Aisah
Terang Hati
Citepus
Pagarsih
Pagarsih Barat
ASTANAANYAR
CIBADAK
Cibadak
Executive
Sukahaji
Sukasenang
JAMIKA
Empok
Karjan
Kamijan
Siti
Aki Maja
Kebonsalak
Pamarset
BABAKAN CIPARAY
Sukapakir
Pasirkoja
Pasirkoja
Babaktan Trigasi
A Widung
Mastabir Trigasi
B Inji
Tresnaasih
Saluyu 3
Kebonmanggu
Kalipahapo
Awiwulung
Basamalah
Kebon Manggu
PASUNDAN

Pratistatamansakura
As-Shiddiqien
Sakura Hegar
Sakura Indah
BABAKANTAROGGONG
Tanjung
Bab.Tarogong
Radendewi 6
Babaktan Trigasi
AMD 8
Pungkur
Kebonkalapa
Terminal Kebonkalapa
ITC
PUNGKUR
Asmi

to Pasir Koja
Terusan Pasirkoja
Pasirkoja
Taman Liligarden
Limosa
Taman Sakura
Babakan Irigasi
Blok Tempe
PANJUNAN
Pabaki
NYENGSERET
Giri Tubia Hidayah
Astana Anyar
Pajagalan
Wirya
Kebonkalapa

SUKAHAJI
Situgunting
"Carrefour", Mollis Periplus
Padepokan Seni
BABAKANASIH
Sukaleueur
Sukarma
Sitimunigar
Jaksa
Ibu Inggit Garnasih
Tegallega
Dewisartika
Moh.Toha
Pasundan

LAPANGAN TEGALLEGA

to Caringin
to Sayati
to Tegallega
to Cigareleng

0 0.2 0.4 0.6 km
0.2 0.4 miles

BANDUNG

Bandung, Indonesia's third largest metropolis, is the administrative and commercial capital of West Java. Planned in the 1920s by Dutch urban planners as the first "modern" city in the Indies, it is today perhaps the most "European" of all Indonesian towns.

Lying 187 km southeast of Jakarta in the midst of the lovely **Priangan** highlands, Bandung enjoys a surprisingly mild climate, with temperatures averaging a pleasant 22.5 ℃. The city is situated on a high plateau at an altitude of 768 m, surrounded on all sides by brooding volcanoes and lofty mountain ridges.

Bandung was founded only at the beginning of the 19th century, with the establishment of a tiny Dutch outpost. At that time, the area was still heavily forested and sparsely populated. Patches of swampland were remnants of a huge lake—the legendary **Situ Hiang**, or "Lake of the Gods", which once covered the entire basin.

Due to meticulous urban planning and large profits generated by the local economy, Bandung developed into the most modern of cities in the Indies— billed by local civic boosters as the "Parijs van Java," because of its gracious, tree-lined boulevards and fashionable shops and houses. The 1920s were Bandung's "Golden Age."

Bandung is no longer the gracious "Paris of Java" of the pre-war era. Urban archaeologists can nevertheless glimpse remnants of Bandung's faded glory. The **Savoy Homann Hotel** and the **Bank Jabar** building are classic art-deco confections. The tree-lined neighbourhoods of Jl. Juanda and Jl. Cipaganti are showcases of colonial suburban life. And the imposing Gedung Sate (lit. "Sate Building," named for the resemblance of its spire to a skewer of meat) is a paragon of Indo-European architecture.

The main shopping district of colonial Bandung in its heyday was around the Jl. Asia-Afrika and Jl. Braga areas. **Gedung Merdeka** ("Freedom Building"), at the northwest intersection of the streets, is where the 1955 Asia-Africa Conference was held. Built in 1895, it was the **Societeit Concordia**, an elegant high society club. A museum inside displays documents of the Bandung Conference. To the east along Jl. Asia-Afrika stand two hotels dating to the 1930s, the art-deco Savoy Homann and the Preanger. In the other direction, across a bridge spanning the **Cikapundung River**, lies the town square (alun-alun) that was the site of the original settlement at the beginning of the 19th century.

Moving north along Jl. Braga from Jl. Asia-Afrika, there are many proud old Dutch shops. On the left is the **Majestic Cinema**, built in the "Indo-European" style that was pioneered here in the early 1920s. Next to it is a building that formerly housed Au Bon Marché, a purveyor of haute couture.

Shaded suburban streets lined by magnificent colonial houses lead from the Gedung Sate to the **Bandung Institute of Technology** (ITB) — the oldest technical institute in Indonesia. The extraordinary university buildings designed by Maclaine Pont, one of the first and most influential proponents of the "Indo-European" architectural style that attempted to fuse traditional Indonesian forms with modern Western techniques. The up-turned roofs of the buildings are modeled on traditional Batak and Minang houses, while the library is a spectacular honeycomb of wooden beams.

Rice is farmed all around Bandung, while the mountain slopes are blanketed with plantations of tea, rubber, coffee, and cinchona. Bandung is also the home of the nation's nascent high tech industries, including computer assembly factories and an aircraft manufacturing plant.

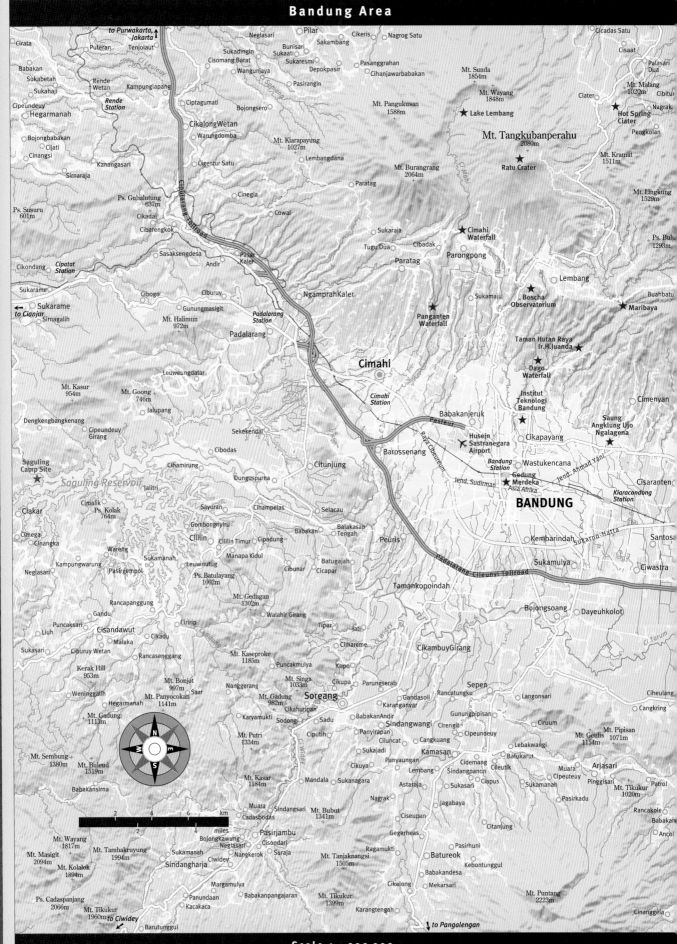

to Purwakarta, Jakarta

Cirata
Babakan
Sukabetah
Sukahaji
Cipeundeuy
Hegarmanah
Bojongbabakan
Cijati
Cinangsi
Sirnaraja

Puteran
Rende Wetan
Kampunglapang
Rende Station

Kanangasari

Neglasari
Cisomang Barat
Sukadingin
Wangunjaya
Bojongsero

Pilar
Bunisari
Sukaati
Sukaresmi
Depokpasir
Pasirangin
Ciptagumati

Sakambang
Pasanggrahan
Cihanjawarbabakan

Cikeris
Nagrog Satu

Mt. Sunda
1854m
Mt. Wayang
1848m
★ Lake Lembang

Cicadas Satu
Cisaat
Pasalari Dua
Mt. Malang
1020m
Cibitur
Ciater
Nagrak
★ Hot Spring Ciater
Pengkolan

Tenjolaut

Ps. Guhalutung
637m
Cikadal
Cibarengkok

Ps. Susuru
601m

Cikondang
Cipatat Station

Sukarame
← Sukarame
to Cianjur
Sirnagalih

Cikalong Wetan
Warungdomba
Cigentur Satu
Cinegla
Cowal

Mt. Kiarapayung
1027m
Lembangdana
Paratag

Mt. Burangrang
2064m

Sukaraja
Tugu Dua
Paratag
Cibadak

Mt. Tangkubanperahu
2080m
Ratu Crater

★ Cimahi Waterfall
Parongpong
Sukamaju

Mt. Lingkung
1529m
Mt. Kramat
1511m

Ps. Buh
1293m

Lembang
Buahbatu
★ Maribaya

Cibogo
Ciburuy
Gunungmasigit
Mt. Halimun
972m
Padalarang Station
Padalarang
Ngamprah Kaler

★ Panganten Waterfall
Boscha Observatorium

Taman Hutan Raya Ir.H.Juanda

Saguling Camp Site
★
Saguling Reservoir
Jalitri

Leuweungdatar

Mt. Kasur
954m
Mt. Goong
746m
Jalupang

Sekekendal

Cibodas

Mt. Dago Waterfall

Institut Teknologi Bandung
★
Cikapayang
★ Saung Angklung Ujo Ngalagena
★
Cimenyan

Dengkengbangkenang
Cipeundeuy Girang

Cihamirung
Dunguspurna

Cihampelas
Cimalik
Ps. Kolak
764m

Citunjung

Cimahi
Cimahi Station
Babakanjeruk
Pasteur
Husein Sastranegara Airport

Raya Cibeureum

Barossenang
Bandung Station
Wastukencana
Cisaranten

Ciakar
Cimega
Cinangka

Sayuran
Gombongnyiru
Clilin
Cililin Timur
Cipadung

Balakasap Tengah
Babakan
Peuris

Gedung Merdeka
Asia Afrika
★
BANDUNG
Jend. Ahmad Yani

Jend. Sudirman
Kembarindah
Sukarno-Hatta
Santosa

Kiaracondong Station

Wareng
Sukamanah
Pasirgempol
Leuwinutug
Manapa Kidul
Cibunar
Cicapar
Batugajah

Tamankopoindah
Padalarang Cileunyi Tollroad
Sukamulya
Ciwastra

Neglasari
Kampungwarung
Ps. Batulayang
1002m
Mt. Gedugan
1302m
Walahir Girang

Bojongsoang
Dayeuhkolot

Rancapanggung
Gandu
Puncaksari
Cisandawut
Liuh
Malaka
Cikadu
Ciririp
Tipar
Jati

Cimareme
Cikambuy Girang
Langonsari
Ciruum
Cangkring
Ciheulang

Sukasari
Ciburuy Wetan
Rancasenggang
Mt. Kaseproke
1185m
Puncakmulya
Kopo
Cikupa
Parungserab
Sepen
Rancatungku

Kerak Hill
953m
Mt. Bonjot
997m
Nanggerang
Saar
Mt. Singa
1033m
Gandasoli
Karanganyar
Gunungpipisan
Cipeundeuy
Lebakwangi
Mt. Pipisan
1071m

Weninggalih
Hegarmanah
Mt. Panyocokan
1141m
Mt. Gadung
982m
Cikahuripan
Soreang
Karamukti
Sodong
Sadu
Babakan Andir
Sindangwangi
Cirengit
Cangkuang
Cidemang
Batukarut
Mt. Geulis
1154m

Mt. Gadung
1113m
Mt. Putri
1334m
Ciputih
Panyirapan
Ciluncat
Kamasan
Lembang
Sindangpanon
Cileutik
Ciapus
Sukamanah
Muara
Cipeuteuy
Pinggisari
Arjasari

Mt. Sembung
1380m
Mt. Buleud
1519m
Babakansirna
Mt. Kasar
1184m
Mandala
Sukanagara
Cikuya
Sukajadi
Panyaungan
Astaraja
Jagabaya
Sukasari
Ciapus
Pasirkadu
Mt. Tikukur
1020m
Rancakole
Babakan

Mt. Wayang
1817m
Mt. Masigit
2094m
Mt. Kolalok
1894m
Mt. Tambakruyung
1994m
Sukamanah
Muara
Cadasbodas
Sindangsari
Mt. Bubut
1341m
Ciseupan
Gegerheas
Ragamukti
Pasirhuni
Batureok
Kebontunggul
Ancol

Ps. Cadaspanjang
2066m
Mt. Tikukur
1960m to Ciwidey
Sindangharja
Neglasari
Nangkerok
Suraja
Pasirjambu
Cisondari
Mt. Tanjaknangsi
1505m
Citanjung
Babakandesa
Mekarsari

Margamulya
Panundaan
Kacakaca
Babakanpangajaran
Mt. Tikukur
1399m
Karangtengah
Cikalong
Mt. Puntang
2223m
Cinanggela

Barutunggul
↓ to Pangalengan

Nagrak
Mulya
Cimega

N
W **E**
S

0   2   4   6   km
0   2   4   miles

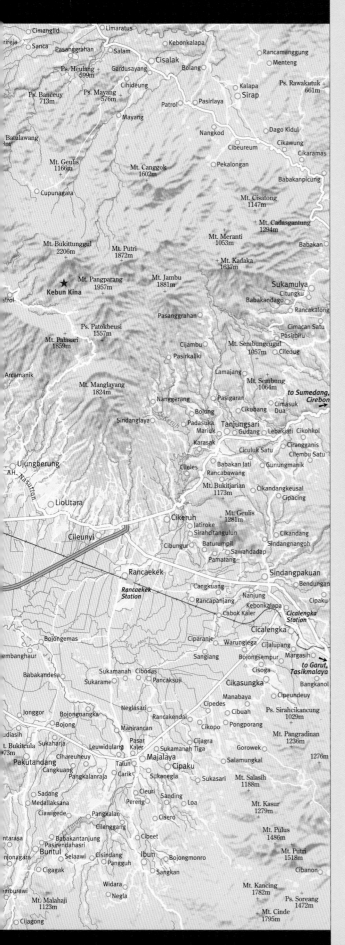

BANDUNG AREA

The highlands around Bandung are collectively known as the Priangan or Parahyangan (from para, "many" and hyang, "gods"). This is the sacred Sundanese homeland — a tangled and once-isolated series of peaks and valleys.

Thousands of years ago a cataclysmic eruption of **Mt. Tangkubanperahu** dammed the Citarum River, forming a vast lake. Two millennia later, an earthquake opened a crack in the side of the valley and allowed the lake to slowly drain, leaving behind fertile alluvial deposits and swampy ponds that have since been filled. Ringing the valley is an array of dramatic volcanoes, many of them bubbling with sulphurous hot springs, solfataras, and fumaroles.

The old Dutch resort town of **Lembang**, 16 km north of Bandung, is the first stop on a trip up to the crater of Tangkubanperahu ("Up-turned Boat") volcano that dominates the northern side of Bandung basin. From Lembang, the road skirts the eastern flanks of the volcano past a turn-off to **Maribaya**, passing through verdant tea plantations. The gate marking the entrance to the **Tangkubanperahu Nature Reserve** is about 9 km down, and a narrow but well-surfaced road winds 4 km right up to the crater's edge. There are a series of craters to walk around and even down into, where a sulphurous steam gurgles out of muddy fissures in the earth. When the mountain mists roll in, as they generally do in the late morning or early afternoon, the entire area, with its jagged, brown-black ridges and stunted shrubbery, takes on an eerie, other-worldly atmosphere.

The highway east of Bandung to **Cirebon follows** the route of the "Great Post Road" built between 1808–1810. It winds down a narrow valley through a range of mountains drained by the **Cipeles** and **Cimanuk Rivers**. The upper stretch of this picturesque road was carved into the walls of a steep cliff at the cost of many lives. The highway then descends into the small mountain village of **Sumedang**, 40 km east of Bandung. This delightful town lies flush against the encircling hillsides in a natural fortress that was the last capital of a powerful kingdom which reigned in West Java for a thousand years.

The glories of Parahyangan's last kingdom are on display in the **Museum Prabu Geusan Ulun** in Sumedang. Consisting of five buildings on the south side of the town square, this is one of the finest museums in Java. The museum's greatest treasures are the original gold crown and jewelry of Pajajaran's rulers, brought from Pakuan to Sumedang in 1578. Alongside these priceless relics are several keris daggers with gold and diamond inlaid sheaths.

PANGANDARAN

Pangandaran is both a nature reserve and a beach resort — 530 ha teardrop-shaped peninsula tethered to Java's south coast by a slender isthmus. The beach on the eastern side of the isthmus is a base for the local fishing industry; the one on the western side is said to be the safest on Java's southern shore.

The **National Park** has plenty to explore: limestone cliffs rear up unexpectedly, dotted with narrow, winding caves which lead, like true pirate caves, down to secluded beaches; the remains of an ancient Hindu temple; a swimming hole at the top of a waterfall that plunges 50 m over a cliff into the Indian Ocean. And there is wildlife everywhere: athletic squirrels, pugnacious grey macaques, patrician crested leaf monkeys, and gossamer-fine black and white butterflies.

Pangandaran

Scale 1: 330 000

36

Java

MAGELANG

CENTRAL JAVA

to Ambarawa, Semarang
110° 15'
Pakis
Sekayu
Gatak 110° 30'
to Salatiga, Semarang
Ampel
Badran
Kaliwungu

Beseran Bandongan
Kyai Langgeng Park ★
Tegalrejo
+ Mt. Merbabu 3150m
Gubug
Kaliwungu

7° 30'
Candimulyo
Selo
Banyuanyar
Jolodrian
Kradenan

Mertoyudan
Ngablak
Penggung

Sawangan
Mt. Merapi 2925m +
Cepogo
Mliwis
Winong

Blondo
Dukun
Musuk
Tempelrejo
Tlangu
Mojosongo
BOYOLALI

Mungkid
Madu
Lejing
Tulung

Pabelan
Ngablak
Plawangan Volcano Observatory ★
Mountain Resort ★
Temuireng
Kauman
Tangkil

Srumbung
Kaliurang
Dompol
Kemalang
Jatinom

Salaman
Muntilan
Turi
Pakem
Gampar
Krajan
Karanganom

★ Mendut
Soko
Cangkringan
Karangnongko

Borobudur
Tegalrejo
Salam
Ngaglik
Tempel
Ngemplak
Banyuaeng
Kebunarum

Pawon ★
Klangon
Ngluwar
Wates
Manisrenggo
Klaten

Sendangsono ★
Kalibawang
Tegalserut
★ Plaosan
Jogonalan

Samigaluh
Sleman
Beran
Hyatt
Randusari
Gondangwinangun

Kaliapak
Balangan Seyegan
Jumeneng
Tajio ★ Sewu
Tangkisanpos
Danguran

7° 45'
Paras
Cebongan
Beran
Melati
Prambanan Temple Complex
Prambanan
Wedi

Kedokan
Minggir
Jogja Kembali Monument
Depok
Tanjungtirto
Ratu Boko Palace
Gantiwarno

Kenteng
Ngijon
Selmo
Godean
YOGYAKARTA
Kalasan
Kalasan ★ Banyunibo
Dengkeng River

Girimulyo
Tulusan
Sambisari
Berbah
Ijo ★
Karangnongko
Pacing

Nanggulan
Gamping
Adisucipto Airport
Berbankrikilan
Mojosari
Karangmunggu

Banjaran
Moyudan
Pedes
Sultan's Palace, Batik Production
Kotagede
Sampang
Pace

Pangasih
Banaran
Art Colony ★
Losari

Gebongan
Sedayu
Brongkol
Kasongan Traditional Pottery
Silver Smithing, Royal Grave ★
Piyungan
Mt. Blencong 686m

Wates
Kasihan ★
Plered
Bangunpapan
Nglampar
Kedangpoh

to Purworejo, Purwokerto
Kalimenur
Pajangan
Sewon
Gondowulung
Putat
Bunder
Nglipar

Bendungan
Nglabu
Selarong Cave ★
Gondangwulung

Panjatan
Demangan
Bantul
Jetis
Mt. Sudimoro 507m +
Gading

Lendah
Pandak
Imogiri Royal Cemetery
Wanagama Forest ★
Piyaman

Pleret Galaran
Brosot
Srandakan
Kaumanlipuro
Imogiri ★
Kembangsore
Seropan
Playen

Patuk
Sewugalur
Panggang
Pundong
Sawanan
Karangmojo
Dungdowo Wareng
Wonosari

Tambakboyo
Sanden
Kretek
Nawungan
Dlingo
Karangrejek

Trisik Beach
Jagadayoh
Mt. Brengguk 450m +
Gembol
Sangkar
Karangasem
Kepil
Duwet

8°
Pandansimo Beach
Samas
Banyumeneng
Gebang
Temuireng
Paliyan
Mengger
Karangmiri
Mulo

Samas Beach
Puyahan
Parangrejo
Panggang
Bandung
Sodawetan

Parangkusuma Beach
Grogor
Gabug
Klepu
Ngluweng
Blimbing
Jemblong
Karangasem

Parangtritis
Parangtritis Beach
Langse Cave ★
Klampok
Tungu
Matianmati
Pucung
Joyok

INDIAN OCEAN
Parangendog Beach
Warak

Girikerto
Cabe
Sentul
Glagah
to Baron, Kukup

Progo River, Elo, Pabelan River, Tangsi River, Blongkeng River, Pegu River, Boyong River, Krasok River, Code, Gajahwong River, Bedog River, Tepus River, Winongo River, Opak River, Oyo River, Mujung River, Sudu River, Strong River, Tinduh River, Dengkeng River, Kambuyudo River

N
W E S

2.5 5 7.5 10 km
2.5 5 miles

110° 15'
110° 30'

YOGYAKARTA-SOLO AREA

Lying at the heart of a fertile crescent of ricelands that is overshadowed to the north by smouldering **Mt. Merapi** and bordered to the south by the churning Indian Ocean, the graceful old cities of Yogyakarta, or Yogya (commonly pronounced JOG-ja), and Surakarta, or Solo, are the two traditional court centres of Java's ancient hinterland.

The earliest-known kingdom in the area is mentioned on a stone linggam dating from A.D.732 and discovered at **Canggal**, just north of present-day Yogya. It describes a just and peaceful Sivaite king, Sanjaya, whose descendants ruled the area known as **Mataram** until the early 10th century A.D. A Mahayana Buddhist dynasty known as the Sailendra, or Kings of the Mountain, also occupied the region at the same time, and between them these two families left an impressive heritage of inspiring statements in stone—including the world-renowned Buddhist **Borobudur**, which lies to the west of Yogya, and the Hindu **Prambanan** complex, lying just east of Yogya.

The centre of political and economic activity shifted east to the Brantas river basin suddenly in A.D. 928, and it was not until the end of the 16th century that the Mataram region was revived politically with the establishment of a new and powerful kingdom at **Kotagede**, now the southeast corner of Yogyakarta. The royal cemetery and the grave of Panembahan Senopati is a revered pilgrimage site. Senopati's grandson, Sultan Agung, Mataram's greatest ruler, extended the domain to include most of central and east Java during his reign (ca. 1613–46) and built the royal cemetery at **Imogiri**, 17 km Southeast of Yogya, where he and all his descendents of both ruling houses are buried.

The capital was moved several times to the east, first to Plered, then to Kartasura, and by 1743 was established in the village of **Solo** with the new name, Surakarta. A long and convoluted series of rebellions and wars of succession in the middle of the 18th century culminated in a Dutch-negotiated settlement between the ruler of the Surakarta palace and his rebellious uncle. In 1755, the kingdom was split into two separate domains ruled by rival courts. Mangkubumi was granted half of the realm and established himself in the new capital of Ngayogyakarta Hadiningrat, or Yogyakarta.

Nature's statements in this densely populated part of Java — whether in the form of smouldering volcanoes, jagged limestone cliffs or violently pounding surf — are unquestionably powerful. **Mt. Merapi** (literally "Fire Mountain"), just to the north of Yogya, is Java's most active volcano — a towering behemoth that periodically spews forth clouds of smoke and ash. On its southern slope lies the quiet highland resort of **Kaliurang**, 24 km north of Yogya.

Along the southern coast, shallow waters near the shore drop suddenly into a deep undersea trench, creating a strong undertow. Although dangerous for swimming, the numerous beaches to the south of Yogya and Solo, are scenic and alluring. Of these, the nearest is **Parangtritis**, a glistening black sand beach with its raging surf, 28 km south of Yogya.

From Solo, the short trip out to **Sangiran**, 15 km north, is an excursion back in time. The area first became famous in 1936, when a team headed by paleontologist G.H.R. von Koenigswald, unearthed a fossilised Homo erctus ("Java Man") jawbone here. The Sangiran area is rich in fossils of all types, some of which date back 1.8 million years.

1 **2** **3** **4** **5** **6**

to Borobudur,
Magelang,
Semarang,
Dieng Plateau

to Kaliurang
Mountain Resorts

Sagan

38

Java

Pakuningratan

Valentino's

Parsley R

Kranggan

Phoenix
Heritage

Terban
Colt/Bus
Terminal

Java
Palace

Army
Museum

Novotel

Galleria
Mall

A

Kyai Mojo

Bus-stop
(to Borobudur)

Asem Gede

Danamon

Poncowinatan

Diponegoro

Gita Anjana
Steak

Merpati

Minibus
Agents

Garuda
Airline

Tugu
Monument

Niaga Santika

Mandiri

Rajawali
Putra Travel

Jend. Sudirman

Gramedia
Bookstore

Bethesda
Hospital

BCA

B

Pingit Kidul

Pesta
Perak

Tentara Rakyat Mataram

Tentara Pelajar

Bumijo Lor

Bumijo Tengah

Bumijo

Gowongan Lor

BCA

Arjuna
Plaza

New Batik
Palace

Syuhada

RRI Kota Baru

BII

Sunaryo

Patimura

Ungaran

A. Jazuli

Nyoman Oka

Kota
Baru

St. Anthony's

Sabirin

Supadi

F.M. Noto

Sajiono

Suharto

Telkom

Suroto

Hadidarsono

Juadi

Trimo

Wahidin Sudirohusodo

Koesbini

Gowongan Kidul

Suryonegaran

Wonosudirjan

Tugu

Kridosono
Stadium

Yos. Sudarso

Wardani

Atmo S Sikarto

Pembela Tanah Air

Ilagran

Pasar Kembang

Asia
Afrika

Natour
Garuda

Superman I

Lempuyangan

Kom Pol

Kota

Mendut
Batik Palace

Superman II

Ana's Rest. R

Gandhi Losmen R

Sosrowijayan

Aziatic

Niaga

Legian
Rest.

Perwakilan
Malioboro
Mall

Zamrud

Sosrokusuman

Bouraq

LEMPUYANGAN

C

Pringgokusuman

Kemetiran

Kemetiran Kidul

Joyonegaran

Batik Palace
Cottages

Sari Ilmu
Bookstore

DANUREJAN

Mas. Suharto

Tukangan

Tegal
Kemuning

Macanan

Hayam Wuruk

Pengok Kidul

Wora Wiri

Cempaka

Tunjung

Soko

Dr. Sutomo

**GEDONG
TENGEN**

Dagen

Peti Mas
Guest House

Sri
Wibowo

Matahari
Dept. Store

Malioboro

Mutiara

Pajeksan

Suryatmajan

Jeminahan

Bausasran

Gayam

D

Winongo River

Let. Jen. Suprapto

PATOK

Aipda KS Tubun

NGAMPILAN

Bhayangkara

Beskalan

Gadean

Terang Bulan
Batik Shop

Melia
Purosani

Mandala

Ketandan

Mayor Suryotomo

Jagalan

Purwanggan

Gajah Mada

Hariowinatan

PAKUALAMAN

Paku Alaman
Palace

KI Mangunsarkoro

Sokanandi

Amri Yahya's
Gallery

Margomulyo
Mirota Batik
Reksobayan

Remujung

Beringharjo

Pabringan

Jayengprawiro

Beji

Mesjid

Kusumanegara

to Purworejo,
Kebumen

A. Yani

Fort Vredeburg
(Benteng Budaya)

Guerilla Monument
(Monumen Serangan Oemoem)

Sultan Agung

E

Wirobrajan

K.H. Ahmad Dahlan

Senopati

Nitour

Sono Budoyo
Museum

BNI

St. Francis
Xavier

Cetiya
Buddha
Prabha

GONDOMANAN

Biology Museum

Bintaran

Sasmita Loka
Panglima
Jendral Sudirman

Bintatan Kidul

Surokarsan

State
Guest House

Gedong
Senisono

Trikora

Ibu Ruswo

Kenekan

WALL

Le dok Gondomanan

Dalem
Notoprajan

Grand
Mosque

**ALUN-
ALUN
LOR**

William

Mangunnegaran
Kulon

Brigjend. Katamso

MERGANGSAN

Wahid Hasyim

Notoprajan

Kauman

WALL

Kadipaten Lor

Kareta Kraton
Museum

Pagelaran

Kemitbumen

Code River

F

Kadipaten Kulon

KRATON

Rotowijayan

Polowijan

Sultan's
Palace
(Kraton)

P. Mangkurat

Panembahan

Suryomentaraman

Ireda

Djava R

Purawisata
(Ramayana Dance
Drama Performances)

Tiara

Letjend. S. Parman
(Taman Sari)

Kadipaten Kidul

Nogosari Kulon

Ngasem
Bird Market

Magangan Lor

Suryoputran

Mantrigawen
Lor

Pasindenan

Mantrigawen
Kidul

Gamelan Lor

Brigjen Katamso

Taman Siswa

Water Castle
(Taman Sari)

Taman

Sasono
Hinggil

Gamelan

Gamelan Kidul

Dalem Pujokusuman
Dance School

Nogosari

TAMAN

Mesjid Soko
Tunggal

Ngadisuryan

**ALUN-
ALUN
KIDUL**

Langensuryo

Langenastran
Lor

Langenastran
Kidul

Namburan
Lor

Namburan
Kidul

Siliran Lor

G

Sugeng Jeroni

Nagan Lor

Nagan Tengah

Nagan Kidul

Patehan Tengah

Patehan

Patehan Kidul

Gading

Langenarjan
Lor

Langenarjan Kidul

Siliran Kidul

WALL

Dalem Pujokusuman
Dance School

Gedongkiwo

Letjend. M.T. Haryono

Mayjend. Sutoyo

Kol. Sugiyono

Menteri Supeno

**GEDONG
KIWO**

Bantul

PUGERAN

ISI Music
Faculty

Panjaitan

Swasthigita
Wayang Kulit
Workshop

Perjuangan
Museum

Sisingamangaraja

Mbarakan

H

Prapanca

Suryodiningratan

Kedai
Kebun R

Tirtodipuran

Dutch
Cafe

Borobudur
Sriwijaya

Hanoman's Rest.

to Samas, Glagah,
Bantul & Kasongan

Batik
Shop

Indrakila

Tulips R Batik
Factories
to Parangtritis

Prawirotaman

Rose

Palm
House Rest. Duta

Galunggung

1 **2** **3** **4** **5** **6**

YOGYAKARTA

In 1756, Sultan Hamengkubuwono I carefully selected the site for his new palace, **Ngayogyakarta Hadiningrat**, at the southern foot of **Mt. Merapi** and north of the mysterious Southern Seas. The palace (kraton) represented the spiritual, political and cultural centre of the new kingdom. The processional leading north from the kraton was planned as a ritual path to clear one's mind in preparation for union with the Creator and is symbolised by the **Tugu** monument at the northern end. The processional is now the busy heart of the city, Jl. Malioboro.

The kraton, built between 1756 and 1790, is a splendid example of traditional Javanese court architecture. Conceived not only as the royal residence, but as the focal point for the entire kingdom, the kraton is constructed as a miniature model of the Hindu-Javanese cosmos. Each gateway, pavilion, courtyard, tree, and field (alun-alun) has a symbolic meaning. It was thought that by structuring the kraton in this way, the court and kingdom could be harmonised with the divine forces of the universe — thereby ensuring the ruler's continued success.

Southwest of the palace proper, within the fortress walls, is the remarkable **Taman Sari** complex, known also as the "Water Castle." Planned in 1758 as an elaborate retreat, it included not only an impressive two-storey mansion built on an elevated mound arising out of an artificial lake, but also underground and underwater tunnels, sunken bathing pools, secluded meditational chambers, and 18 lavish gardens planted with flowers, vegetables and fruit trees. Hundreds of families have since taken up residence amidst the ruins of the Water Castle, many of whom have taken to producing batik paintings. At the northern end of this complex lies the large **Ngasem Market**, a regular daily market with a section specialising in tropical birds.

The city of Yogya has since grown up around the ceremonial boulevard extending 2.3 km north from the kraton which was the route taken by the royal cortege and is now known as Jalan Malioboro (although the official name changes several times along its length). The sidewalks are lined with stores and an array of street vendors, hawkers and artisans. After 9 pm, the stores close and the vendors pack up, and then the night food stalls roll out mats along the sidewalk and set up the makeshift gas burners for late-night eating, a Yogya hallmark.

A monument on the northeast corner of the intersection of Jl. A. Yani and Jl. Senopati commemorates the guerilla attack of revolutionary forces fighting the Dutch on March 1, 1949. North of the monument stands **Fort Vredeburg**, built for the Dutch troops in 1756–1787. Vredeberg has since undergone renovation and is now a museum featuring spacious air-conditioned galleries with dioramas depicting key moments in the struggle for Indonesian independence.

The **Sono Budoyo Museum** at the northwest corner of the north square (alun-alun lor) was founded by the Java Institute in 1935. The permanent exhibit features a small, but exquisite collection of ancient bronze bells, batik, a variety of puppets and masks from Central and West Java, Madura, and Bali, gamelan musical ensembles, and a carved teak house partition from Jepara.

Yogya is also famous as a centre for batik. Small stores in the Ngasem area supply the local artists with the necessary supplies for both traditional and modern techniques. The **Batik Research Centre** on Jl. Kusumanegara, was opened in the early 1960s to stimulate documentation on traditional methods of wax and dye application, as well as experimentation into new dyes and techniques.

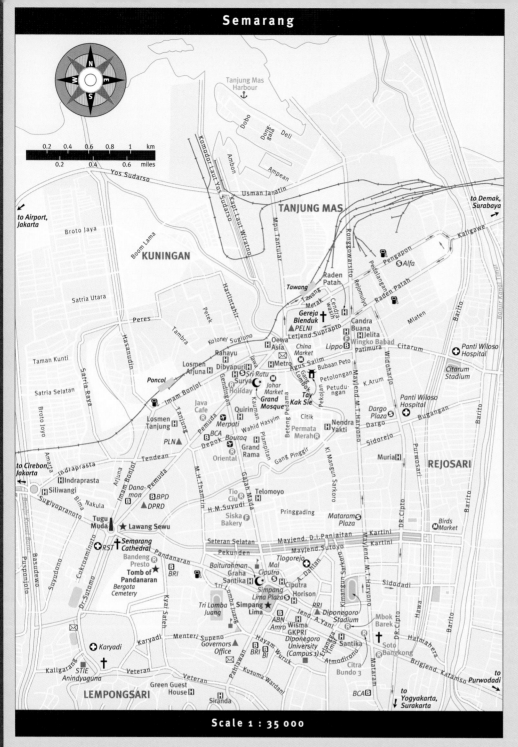

Scale 1 : 35 000

SEMARANG

Since the 18th century, the premier port along the central north coast of Java has been Semarang, now the provincial capital of Central Java and the island's fourth largest metropolis. **Tanjung Mas** harbour is a smaller version of Jakarta's Sunda Kelapa and Surabaya's Tanjung Perak. South of this area lies the old European commercial district around Jl. Jendral Suprapto. The major landmark here, standing amidst 200-year-old warehouses and offices, is the copper-domed **Gereja Blenduk**, a Dutch church dating from 1753.

To the west, across the river, lies Semarang's shopping and hotel district, while colourful Chinatown is south. The maze of lanes tucked inside a bend in the river at the end of Jl. Pekojan offers a fascinating glimpse of bustling shops and old "Nanyang" row-houses with carved doorways and latticed balconies. The area also features a number of dimly-lit temples and clan houses. Just before the bridge on Jl. Pekojan, stands the **Tay Kak Sie**, Semarang's largest Chinese

temple. The main deity here is the Buddhist goddess of mercy, Kuan Yin, but there are a host of other gods and saints in alcoves all around the complex.

The **Grand Mosque**, with its multi-tiered Javanese roof, is on Jl. Kauman. In front of it is the former town square, which has now been taken over by **Johar Market**, Semarang's sprawling central market filled with stalls selling brasswares and bric-a-brac, in addition to the usual foodstuffs and textiles.

West of Johar Market is the busy intersection with **Jalan Pemuda**, Semarang's main shopping street. In colonial times this was called Jl. Bodjong—a broad, broom-swept boulevard bordered by leafy tamarind trees, shops and elegant villas. A Dutch writer at the turn of the century glowingly referred to it as the most fashionable street on Java—the island's "Champs Elysée."

At the very end of Jl. Pemuda, facing a fountain and the **Tugu Muda** obelisk commemorating youths who died here in the early days of the revolution, is the home of Resident Nicolaas Hartingh, built between 1754–61, and the "Indo-European" style offices of the former Netherlands Indies Train Company, dating

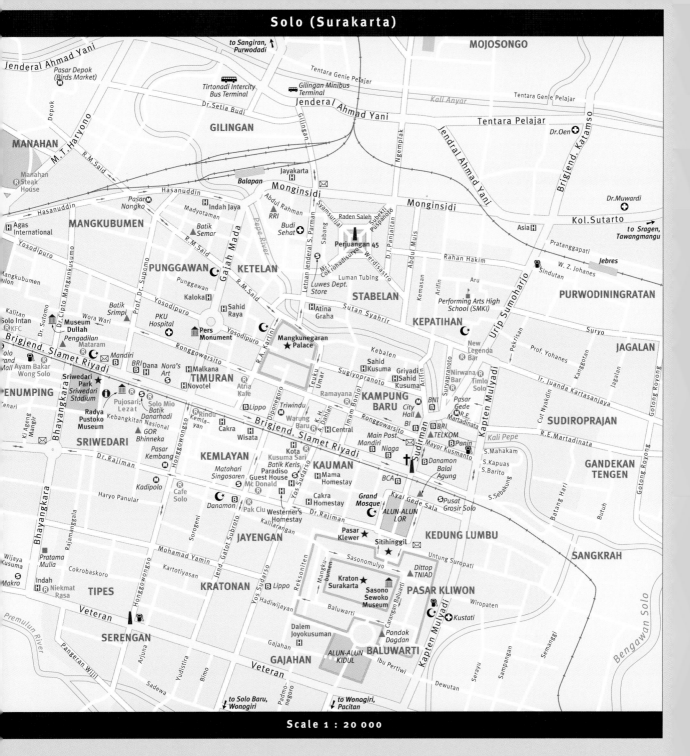

Scale 1 : 20 000

from the 1920s. The latter has been dubbed Lawang Sewu (lit. "Thousand Doors") because of its many outward-facing doors.

SOLO (SURAKARTA)

The Surakarta kraton was relocated from Kartasura to the village of Solo, on the banks of the Solo River, in 1745. On the north side of the kraton, is the alun-alun lor, or north square, which has a pair of sacred banyan trees in the centre. On the west side of the square stands the **Grand Mosque** which was built in 1750 by Sunan Pakubuwana III.

A bit further west of the alun-alun and the mosque is **Klewer Market** — a three-storey concrete block housing Java's biggest textile emporium. Cloth of every imaginable description is for sale in aisle after aisle of tiny stalls piled high with woven and printed cottons, linen, silks — and, of course, batik.

Across Jl. Slamet Riyadi to the north lies the **Pura Mangkunegaran** — Solo's "other" palace. The Mangkunegaran was founded by a dissident prince, Raden Mas Said, who was given a portion of the Sunan's fiefdom as the price of his submission to the latter's authority.

Just south of Pura Mangkunegaran lies the small but fascinating **Triwindu Market**. Anything and everything is for sale here, as long as it's old, or at least used. The front stalls sell masks, paintings, photos, statuettes, wayang puppets, old coins and curios of all sorts. At the back of the market several stalls sell musical instruments alongside old car and motorcycle parts.

The huge **Sriwedari Park** complex lies west of Triwindu. The park features amusement park rides and food stalls, as well as a theatre with nightly wayang orang (dance drama) performances. The sports stadium is south of the park.

Just east of Sriwedari is the **Radya Pustaka Museum**, founded in 1890 by the kraton and the Dutch colonial government. It is a small, but fairly well-endowed museum with displays of Javanese, Balinese and Thai puppets, weapons and intricate models of the kraton and the royal cemetery at Imogiri. The library contains a fascinating collection of old books, most in Dutch or Javanese.

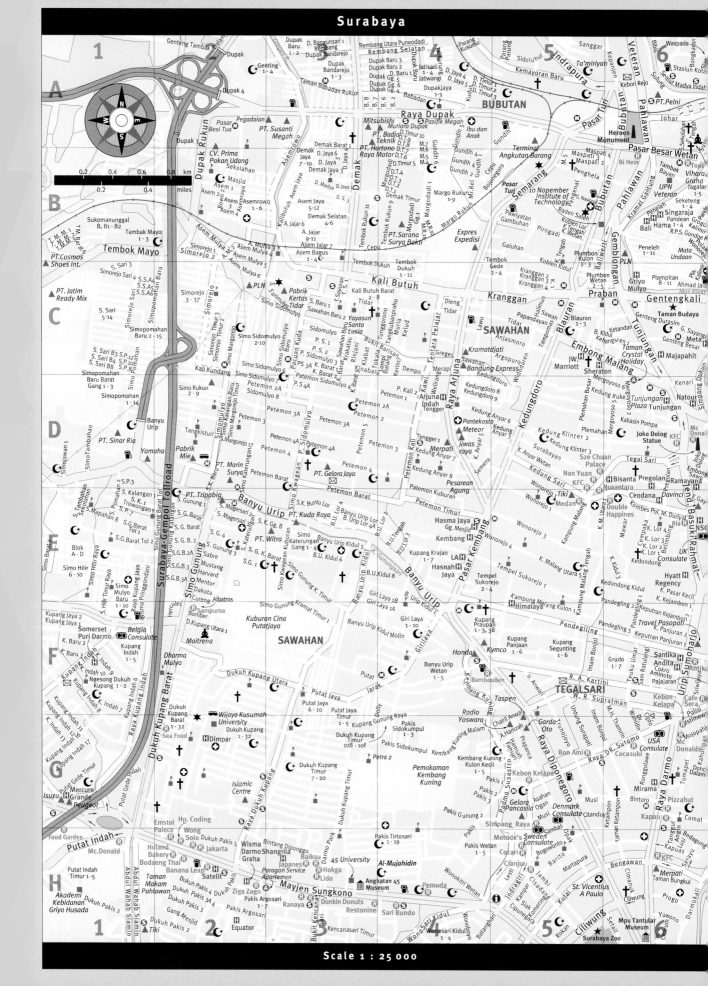

SURABAYA

As the burgeoning commercial and industrial region of Java, the island's north coast is anchored at its eastern end by Indonesia's second largest city, Surabaya. A blue-collar canton, the so-called "City of Heroes" has developed into the economic capital not only of East Java, but of all of Eastern Indonesia. Its port, **Tanjung Perak** (lit. "silver promontory") is a crossroads of trade between the archipelago's eastern islands and points west — a role that Surabaya has in fact played for centuries.

Unlike Jakarta, which is a catch-all of cultures from Indonesia and beyond, Surabaya's ethnic identity is Javanese. However, unlike Solo and Yogya of the central Javanese heartlands, the people of Surabaya are coastal. The city runs at a faster pace and has a more cosmopolitan outlook than the hinterland — cultivated through hundreds of years of contact with trading peoples from across the sea. Here there is little fascination with courtly life and etiquette; Surabaya is more commercially oriented and more egalitarian.

The commercial and administrative centre of the city is on Jl. Tunjungan and Jl. Pemuda. Tunjungan's landmark is the old **Oranje Hotel**, now called Hotel Majapahit. In tandem with the **Hotel Sarkies**, diagonally across the street on Embong Malang, it creates a corner of a faded colonial glory flanked to the east by the former Das Deutsche Verein — a private club now known as Balai Sahabat.

Taman Budaya on Jl. Genteng Kali, is a cultural centre for art exhibits and performances. The complex served as the regent of Surabaya's official residence and office until the 1970s, when the regency's capital was moved to Gresik.

South of Jl. Pemuda, on Jl. Dolog, is a statue of King Kertanagara in his incarnation as the Buddha Aksobhya. The statue bears the date A.D. 1289 at the base and was brought to Surabaya by the Dutch from the vicinity of Malang. Locally known as **Joko Dolog** (lit. "fat boy"), it is still worshipped by Javanese syncretists.

Just to the east on Jl. Pemuda is **Grahadi**, the official residence of East Java's governor — a mansion once used by colonial Residents. Across Jl. Pemuda from the mansion, is a park with a statue of Governor Soerjo, East Java's first governor.

Further to the east is the **Balai Pemuda**, which was built in 1907 as the Simpang Club. It has been turned into a luxury cinema complex and exhibition gallery of the Surabaya Arts Council. North of it in the middle of a traffic island, stands a statue of General Sudirman, commander of Indonesia's revolutionary forces, and the Dutch-built City Hall, facing Taman Surya park.

Surabaya's older quarters lie north of the Tunjungan-Pemuda-Kaliasin triangle. On Jl. Pahlawan stands another symbol of Surabaya, the **Heroes' Monument**, built in the 1950s to commemorate the bravery of Surabayan youths during the Battle of Surabaya. It is from this famous battle that Surabaya derives its epithet, "City of Heroes." East of the square is the colonial Governor's Office.

Jembatan Merah, the "Red Bridge," lies north on Jl. Veteran, at the centre of the city's early 19th century colonial business district. The bridge has always been that colour; a folk tale attributes it not to paint, but to the blood shed during a legendary confrontation between a shark and a crocodile.

At the southern city limits, along Jl. Raya Darmo is an elegant neighbourhood developed by the Dutch early this century. The **Mpu Tantular Museum** houses a small, but interesting historical and archaeological collection in the former residence of the Javaasche Bank agent. From the museum, it is a short walk to the **Surabaya Zoo**, one of Southeast Asia's oldest and largest zoos. Among its exhibits are somnolent Komodo dragons and Borneo river dolphins. Also in the Darmo area is the Centre Culturel Français, which sponsors occasional art exhibits, films, and musical performances.

Fueled by deregulatory measures introduced in the 1980s, Surabaya seems poised to regain its former status as the premier centre for commerce and industry in the archipelago — a position it held before World War II.

MOUNT BROMO

There are three routes into the **Tengger highlands** on Mt. Bromo. The most common approach to the Bromo caldera is from the northeast via a road that leaves the main highway near **Probolinggo** and climbs 44 mountainous kilometres up to **Ngadisari**. Another road runs south from Pasuruan up to Tosari and Wonokitri. From here, it's a longer climb up to the rim of the caldera, but it's less crowded. Finally, there is a steep track that runs up from Malang via Tumpang to Ngadas, a village in the forested region between Bromo and Semeru.

The mountain resort of **Tretes**, 60 km south of Surabaya, offers an escape from the urban heat. Near Pandaan, on the road to Tretes, is **Candi Jawi**, a 14th century temple built to enshrine King Kertanegara's ashes. During the dry season, the **Candra Wilwatikta** open-air amphitheatre presents massive dance-dramas.

Along the coastal road between Surabaya and Banyuwangi, lies **Pasuruan**, one-time sugar capital of Java. Pasuruan's renovated **Grand Mosque** is, without a doubt, one of Java's most beautiful. The **Madakaripura Waterfall**, accessible from Probolinggo, about 40 km east of Pasuruan, is reputed to be a sort of fountain of youth and the meditation site of legendary heroes. The road south from Pasuruan to Malang passes the **Purwodadi Botanical Gardens** which specialises in dry climate lowland vegetation mainly from eastern Indonesia and are second only to the gardens at Bogor.

MALANG

Situated 450 m above the oppressive heat of the lowlands, Malang is perched on a picturesque plateau ringed by volcanoes. The Malang area contains many interesting antiquities, but the modern city is a creation of the colonial era — its development fueled after 1870 by enterprising Europeans who set up coffee, rubber, and cacao plantations alongside the government sugar estates.

Malang's alun-alun (town square) took shape in 1882 along the usual Javanese lines: bordered by a market, mosque, and local ruler's residence. Colonial priorities dictated that it also have a home for the Dutch assistant resident, a Protestant church, and later a bank. In 1914, a new municipal centre was established across the **Brantas River**. The Balai Kota houses municipal offices; the original fountain in the the park was replaced by the present Tugu monument.

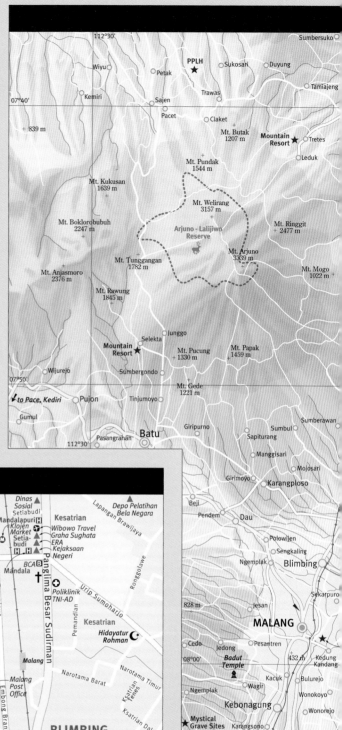

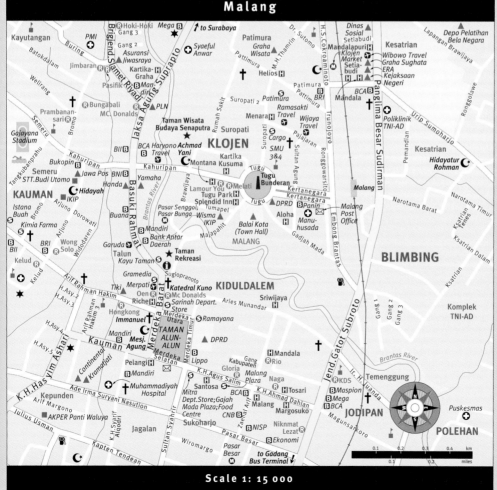

Malang

Scale 1: 15 000

Mount Bromo

Madura Strait

to Sidoarjo,
Surabaya
at (Sanctuary)

Candra Wilwatikta
Open-Air Theater
Pandaan
Candiwates

Pekoren
Rembang
Wonokerto

Kraton
Colonial Architecture,
Scenic Harbor

PASURUAN

Ngempit
Pohjentrek
Rejoso

Ledek

Watuprapat
276 m

Rowogempal
to Probolinggo,
Situbondo

Tampung
63 m
Budengan
Rabono

Kejayan

Gondangwetan
Gratitunon

Wotgalih

Klampok

Sukorejo
257 m
Sebandung
Wonorejo
19
Tamansari

Luwuk

36
Pasrepan

Winongan
Trewung
Ranu
Klindunggan
Plososari

Lawekyun

Gotehan

Jatiarjo

Karangtengah

Kedungsari
Jatisari
Purworejo
Kedemungan
+148 m

Bener
Sapulante

Umbulan
Sibon
Lumbang

Panditan

Karanglo

Sumberrejo

Purwodadi
Purwodadi
Botanical Garden
501 m

Bandut
Ngembal

Galih
Petung
Pancur

Hotel Niagara,
Guesthouse
Lawang
Kebon Teh
Wonosari
Cengkrakan

Sumberpitu

Ampelbanjar
Jimbaran

Puspo
719 m

Madakaripura
Waterfall

Wonogoro

24
28

Gerbo
Mendek
Rojapasang

Tutur
Ngawas
Keduwung

Lambangkuning

Trosono
Pondokterop

Sukapura

Singosari
ple
Singosari
Sumbersat
Tengo
1209 m
Nongkojajar

Hotel Bromo
(Cottages)

Sedaeng
Tosari
Hotel,
Guesthouse

Mt. Penanjakan
2775 m

2726 m

Cemara
Indah
2347 m

Sapikerep

Bobor

Hiking, Wonokitri
Hanggliding

Andonosari
Taman

Mororejo

Spectacular
Panorama

Cemara
Lawang
Wontoro

Guesthouse

PHPA
Office

Ngadisari
Guesthouse

Abdulrahman
Saleh
Airport
Jabung
Sidomulyo
615 m

Kletak

Mt. Batok
2240 m

Tengger Crater,
Sand Sea

Gunung Bromo
2329 m

Mt. Mungal
2480 m

Mt. Jantur
2706 m

Argosari
Pojok

Karanglo
Tirtomoyo

Bunut Kidul
Wendit
Spring/Pool
Pakis
Tambaksari

Sukopuro
Bogawant
Jajang

Mt. Keciri
2297 m

Mt. Kursi
2501 m

Gedok

Cokro
Malangsuko
Pandanrejo

Gunung Bromo

numents &
ch Architectures
Kebalon
Cokro
541 m

Ngadirejo

Ngadas
Scenic
Hiking

Bromo - Tengger - Semeru
National Park

Mt. Iderider
2527 m

Slamet

Jago Temple

Benjor
Duwet

Mt. Tanjung
2215 m

Ranu Pani
Ranu Regulo

Iheng-iheng

566 m
Pulungdowo
Tumpang
Kebonsari

Gubugklakah

Waterfall
Ranupani

Ranupani Guesthouse,
PHPA Office

Kambingan
Kidal
Kidal Temple
Poncokusumo
Rabyong

Besuki

Mt. Pangonancilik
2833 m

Mt. Butak
2039 m

Ranu
Kumbolo
Besuktompe

Mt. Gede
1270 m
1380 m

Ngingit
Ngrebruk

Nongkosewu
Wonorejo
Poncokusumo

Mt. Kukusan
2790 m

Shelter,
Fresh Water

Mt. Tompe
1944 m

Tajinan
Mt. Ronggo
680 m
Waduk
Tenggeran
Lanjuran

Pandansari Kidul

Mt. Jambangan
2030 m

Lesti

Pandanmulyo
Ngembal

Jajang

Mt. Keduwung
2334 m

Mt. Kepolo
3035 m

Mt. Jengel
1672 m

Base Camp 1

Jambekumbu

Pabrik
Dawuhan

Base Camp 2

Kuwolu
Kasri
Pringo
Sukoanyar
Sukolilo
Plaju
Wajak
Ngandeng
Sumberrejo

Mt. Siluman
1460 m

Mt. Mahameru
3677 m

Pasrujambe

Bakalan
Patokpicis

Basri
Bambang

Bendo

Mt. Gentong
1951 m

Gelapan Lor

Penanggal

Sudimoro
Codo
Bringin

Talangsuko

Kedok
Wonokasian
Sanankerto
Sanankerto

Garotan

Jambangan
Rejosari

to Turen, Tempeh,
Lumajang

Blubuk
Wringinanom

Mt. Widodaren
2000 m

Lava Flows

Besukikoboan

Kedungkandang Kulon

Rekesan
Joglo

Besuksemut

2.5   5   7.5   km
2.5   5   miles

Scale 1 : 250 000

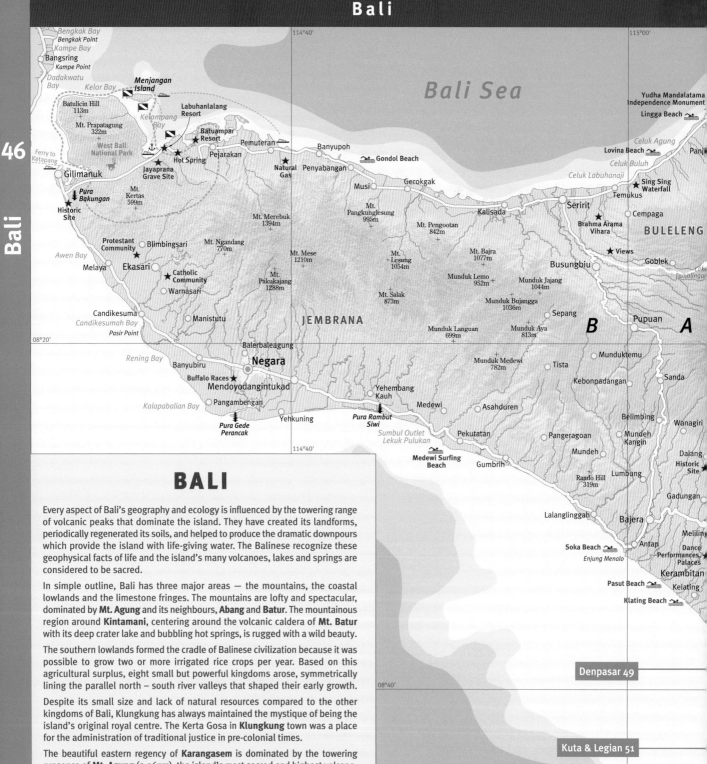

Bengkak Bay
Bengkak Point
Kampe Bay
Bangsring
Kampe Point
Dadakwatu Bay
Kelor Bay
Menjangan Island
Batulicin Hill 113m
Labuhanlalang Resort
Mt. Prapatagung 322m
Kelompang Bay
Batuampar Resort
West Bali National Park
Pemuteran
Banyupoh
Gondol Beach
Ferry to Ketapang
Gilimanuk
Hot Spring
Pejarakan
Natural Gas
Penyabangan
Musi
Gerokgak
Jayaprana Grave Site
Pura Bakungan
Mt. Kertas 599m
Mt. Pangkunglesung 995m
Mt. Pengootan 842m
Kalisada
Seririt
Temukus
Historic Site
Mt. Merebuk 1394m
Brahma Arama Vihara
Cempaga
Awen Bay
Protestant Community
Blimbingsari
Mt. Ngandang 770m
Mt. Lesung 1054m
Mt. Bajra 1077m
Busungbiu
Goblek
Melaya
Ekasari
Mt. Mese 1210m
Munduk Lemo 952m
Munduk Jajang 1044m
Catholic Community
Mt. Pakukajang 1288m
Warnasari
Mt. Salak 873m
Munduk Bujangga 1036m
Sepang
Pupuan
Candikesuma
Manistutu
JEMBRANA
Munduk Languan 699m
Munduk Aya 813m
Candikesumah Bay
Pasir Point
Balerbaleagung
Munduktemu
Rening Bay
Banyubiru
Negara
Munduk Medewi 782m
Tista
Buffalo Races
Mendoyodangintukad
Kebonpadangan
Sanda
Kalapabalian Bay
Pangambengan
Yehembang Kauh
Medewi
Asahduren
Belimbing
Wanagiri
Yehkuning
Pura Gede Perancak
Pura Rambut Siwi
Pekutatan
Pangeragoan
Mundeh Kangin
Dalang Historic Site
Sumbul Outlet
Lekuk Pulukan
Gumbrih
Lumbung
Gadungan
Medewi Surfing Beach
Rando Hill 319m
Lalanglinggah
Bajera
Melilin
Soka Beach
Antap
Dance Performances, Palaces
Enjung Menalo
Kerambitan
Pasut Beach
Kelating
Klating Beach

Bali Sea
Yudha Mandalatama Independence Monument
Lingga Beach
Celuk Agung
Lovina Beach
Panji
Celuk Buluh
Celuk Labuhanaji
Sing Sing Waterfall
BULELENG
Views
Tamblingan
B
A

Denpasar 49

Kuta & Legian 51

INDIAN OCEAN

Labuansait Beach
Suluban Beach

BALI

Every aspect of Bali's geography and ecology is influenced by the towering range of volcanic peaks that dominate the island. They have created its landforms, periodically regenerated its soils, and helped to produce the dramatic downpours which provide the island with life-giving water. The Balinese recognize these geophysical facts of life and the island's many volcanoes, lakes and springs are considered to be sacred.

In simple outline, Bali has three major areas — the mountains, the coastal lowlands and the limestone fringes. The mountains are lofty and spectacular, dominated by **Mt. Agung** and its neighbours, **Abang** and **Batur**. The mountainous region around **Kintamani**, centering around the volcanic caldera of **Mt. Batur** with its deep crater lake and bubbling hot springs, is rugged with a wild beauty.

The southern lowlands formed the cradle of Balinese civilization because it was possible to grow two or more irrigated rice crops per year. Based on this agricultural surplus, eight small but powerful kingdoms arose, symmetrically lining the parallel north – south river valleys that shaped their early growth.

Despite its small size and lack of natural resources compared to the other kingdoms of Bali, Klungkung has always maintained the mystique of being the island's original royal centre. The Kerta Gosa in **Klungkung** town was a place for the administration of traditional justice in pre-colonial times.

The beautiful eastern regency of **Karangasem** is dominated by the towering presence of **Mt. Agung** (2,567m), the island's most sacred and highest volcano, whose dramatic foothills and lava flows provide some of the most breathtaking landscapes found anywhere in Bali. High up on Mt. Agung's southern flanks perches the great "Mother Temple," **Pura Besakih** — the most sacred and powerful of the island's innumerable temples.

There is excellent diving on the coastal reefs off **Tulamben**, where the sunken wreck of a WW II ship provides a home for a host of colourful marine life. Six kilometres west of **Singaraja**, the popular beach resort of **Lovina** is a long stretch of black sand bordering five coastal villages. The pace of life at Lovina reflects the calmness and safety of the sea. This is an excellent spot for swimming and snorkelling, particularly near the reef.

On the westernmost tip of the island, extensive montane forests, coastal swamps and marine waters comprise the West Bali National Park.

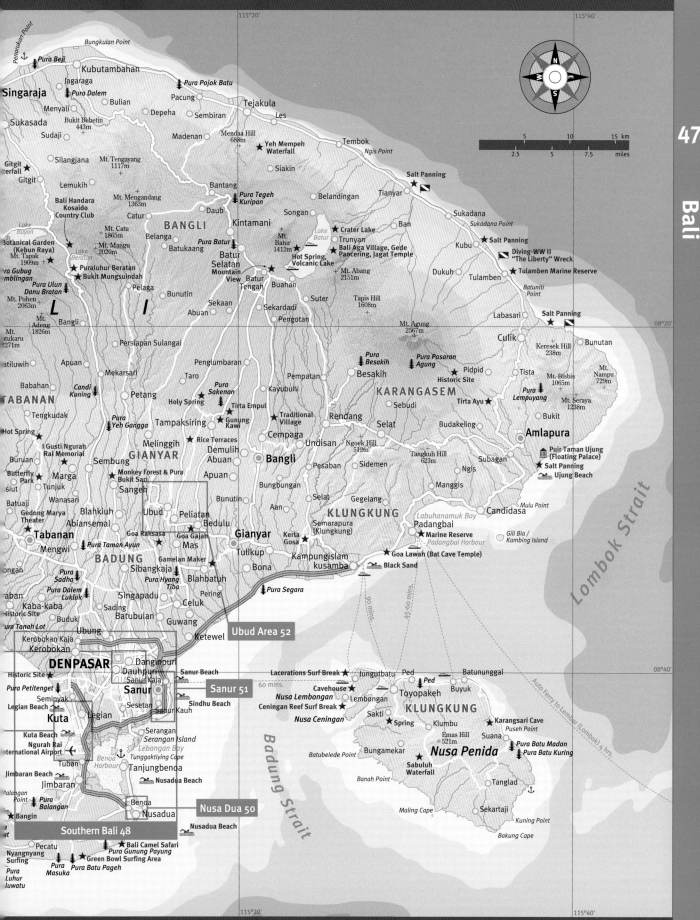

Scale 1 : 400 000

Bali

↑ to Beraban, Tanah Lot
↑ to Muncan, Kapal, Mengwi, Tabanan
↑ to Sibanggede, Sangeh
↑ to Batubulan

Datengan Umakepuh Lebak Tengah Sempidi Tegalkauh Paang Tengah Pengambangan
Nyanyi Gambang Jerowan Gunungbuduk Kung Liligundi Tegallinggah Pengukuh Ambengan Pengurukuh Kalah Telabah
Pancean Bandung Padangtawang Dukuh Pendem Pohgading Anyaranyar Peninjoan Sema Tohpati
Baleagung Kerobokan Babakan Dawas Umaklungkung Darmasanti Purnamaasri Kayangan Saba Tambau Kaja Buaji
Keliki Tibubeneng Tegallingagah Batur Binoh Kelod Kertasari Tanggunititi Bantas Kayangan Tambau Tengah Tegebe
Sengguan Kangkang Kalibul Kangin Petangan Dakdakan Tagtag Kaja Teguhkuri Batanancak Menguntur
Batu Kayutulang Kalibul Kawan Silayukti Gunung Sanghiang Binoh Kelod Tegehsari Tanguntiti Sasih
Mengening Pipitan Aseman Kangin Batuculung Alamsari LUMBUNGSARI Gatot Subroto Timur By Pass Kesambi
Sogsogan Tandeg Gadon Petingan Mudingsari DENPASAR Tangtu

DENPASAR

Gatot Subroto Barat By Pass
Puncaksari Batanbuah to Gianyar, Klungkung
Abiankapas Kaja Kesumajati
Pura Dalem
Selasih Beach Canggu Kesambi Gunung Agung Balun Supratman Kedaton Perada Padanggalak
Pererenan Beach Pelambengan Peliatan Padang Balun Kreneng Ketapian Kelod Kebonkurikelod
Batu Mejan Beach Mekarbuana Mertasari Pagan Kelod Buanaanyar
Tegalgundul Brawa Semer Muliawan Celagigendong Yangbatu Kangin Sanur Beach
Historic Site Saptabumi Pekambingan Chandra Hayam Wuruk Tanjungbungkak Kelod
Berawa Beach Umalas Kauh Pengubengan Kauh Ki Hajar Dewantara Sanur
Batubelig Beach Bali Sani Suites Pengubengan Kangin Sanglah Utara Raya Puputan Pekandelan SANUR
Villa Lumbung Lebaon Jabapura Batannyuh Beraban Kangin Hang Tuah Belong Radisson Bali
Pura Petitenget The Legian Diponegoro Peken Pande Tengah Taman
Resor Seminyak Margaya Geladag Kaja Longan Segara Village
The Oberoi Seminyak Dalem Kelod Panti Sindhu Kaja
Imperial Bali Villa Lalu Pegok Medura Batujimbar
Seminyak Beach Suwung Kangin Penyaringan Hyatt
Jayakarta Bali Legian Kaja Rumah Manis Legian Karyadharma Pengayasan Semawang
Bali Padma Legian Tengah Dukuhtangkas Tamansari Grahakerti Belanjong Sativa
Legian Beach Panorama II Tarunabhineka Batankendal Kertausada Puri Santrian
Legian Beach Intan Legian Legian Kelod Sakah Ambengan Suwungbatankendal Raddin Sanur Beach
Alam Kul Kul Rangkansari Makro Bugissuwung
White Rose Kuta Beach Aneka Kuta SOS Medika Inyah Point Kaja Sakenan Temple
Hard Rock Hotel & Cafe Ramayana Dewa Ruci Statue Bugis Dukuh
Natour Kuta Beach Pura Luhur
Kuta Paradiso Bali Jabajero Serangan Island
Kartika Plaza Parangan Point Tirtaarum Point
Tuban Beach KUTA Bali Sari Tunggaktiying Cape
Ramada Bintang Bali Segara Benoa Harbour
Rama Beach
Holiday Inn Balihai Pesalakan Ngurah Rai Statue
Patrajasa Beach Prani Gatotkaca Seraya Statue
Tubangerya Pancabineka Taman Sari Marine Sport
Ngurah Rai International Airport Nusa Pudut Purwasanti Nusadua Beach
Kelanabian Tanjungbenoa Century
Toyota Rent-a-Car Rasa Dua Arirang Beach
Kubualit Novotel Novotel Benoa
Kerthayasa Grand Mirage
Jimbaran Beach Menega Bali Benoa Resort Tengkulung Vila Bintang
Puri Bamboo Udang Puri Panca Setra Peninsula Resort
Jimbaran Benoa Bay Aston Bali
Vila Hanani Matahari Terbit
Keraton Bali Terora Bali Royal
Bali Intercontinental Resort Conrad Bali Resort
Pura Tegalwangi Simpangunud Nusadua Beach
Ritz Carlton Four Seasons Resort Mumbul Bali Tropik NUSA DUA
Pura Balangan Tamanmumbul Melia Benoa
Balangan Point Club Mediterranee
Bena Estuary Balidesa Suites
Bali Hill Celuk Nusa Dua Beach
Bangin Kesambimekar Bualu Sheraton Nusa Indah Resort
Kesumasari Pande Cengiling Gonzaga Sheraton Laguna
Bungalow Ayu Guna Inn Villa Taman Bali Grand Hyatt Bali
Bangin Bangket Ancak Swiss Belhotel Resort Baliaga Putri Bali
Pura Goa Gong Siligita Bali Hilton
Garuda Wisnu Kencana (G.W.K.) Kajajati Penyarikan Amanusa Bali Golf & Country Club 18 Holes
Ungasansimpang Menesa Pemunge Baru The Bale
Raya Bualu Ungasan Sekar Nusa Nusadua Beach
Santhikarya Bousen Villed Pura Geger
Kaja Gegar Point
Bungalow Ayu Guna Inn Kesumasari Sawangan Kaja
Dauhpuseh Bakungsari Wanagiri Sarikaya Ungasan Kauh Petengan Panthigiri Sawangan Kelod Nikko Bali Resort
↑ to Pura Luhur Uluwatu

Bali Strait

Badung Strait

Jimbaran Bay

1 2 3 km
1 2 miles

N S E W

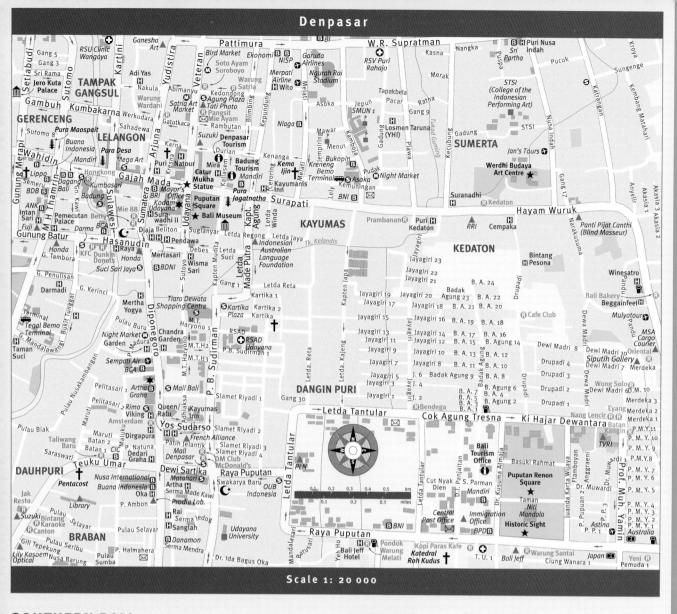

Scale 1 : 20 000

SOUTHERN BALI

Badung, the southernmost regency of Bali, is the most heavily populated area of the island. This is partly because **Denpasar,** the island's capital and principal metropolis, is here. Also, Bali's major tourist resorts are all in Badung — the **Kuta** and **Legian** beaches to the west, **Sanur** on the east, and the **Bukit** peninsula, with the **Nusa Dua** and **Jimbaran** complexes, to the south.

The **Bukit** peninsula is connected to the rest of Bali by a narrow isthmus, upon which lies the village of **Jimbaran.** The beach to the west is the broad expanse of Jimbaran Bay and the Indian Ocean, while to the east is a tidal mudflat enclosing the shallow and sheltered **Benoa Harbour.** The plateau which constitutes most of the peninsula rises abruptly to about 200 m above sea level, and is ringed on all sides by steep cliffs.

Pura Ulun Siwi (or Ulun Swi) is Jimbaran's best-known site. This large temple lies at the northwestern corner of the principal crossroads, across the street from the market. It is the principal temple in Bali dedicated to the welfare of both wet and dry rice fields. Farmers and farming groups regularly come to Pura Ulun Siwi to get water, which they then take back home and sprinkle on their fields either to protect them from pests or rid them of those already present.

Tanjung Benoa, which appears isolated at the northeastern tip of the peninsula, was a trading port for Badung and the eastern town of Bukit, and has an outlook extending right across the archipelago.

Serangan is a small island lying just off Bali's southern coast near Sanur. It has an area of only 173 ha and is known principally for its turtles and its important **Sakenan Temple.**

DENPASAR

Denpasar is a "village-city" with an aristocratic past. Born from the ashes of the defeated Pemecutan court following the puputan massacre of 1906, Denpasar became a sleepy administrative outpost during Dutch times. Since independence, and especially after it was made the capital of Bali in 1958, it has been transformed into a bustling city that provides administrative, commercial and educational services not only to Bali, but to much of eastern Indonesia as well.

Originally a market town — its name literally means "east of the market"— Denpasar has far outgrown its former boundaries, once defined by the Pemecutan, Jero Kuta, and Satriya palaces and the brahman houses of Tegal, Tampakgangsul and Gemeh. Presently, urban growth is enveloping the neighbouring villages and obliterating the surrounding ricefields. To the east, urbanization spills across the **Ayung River** into the village of **Batubulan;** to the south, it reaches **Sanur** and **Kuta;** and to the west, it sprawls as far as **Kapal.**

In the very heart of **Denpasar,** just behind the main artery of the city, Jalan Gajah Mada, one can see many traditional compounds with their gates, shrines and pavilions, in among the multi-storey Chinese shopfronts. The most ancient temple is **Pura Maospait,** in the middle of the city on the road to **Tabanan.** It dates back to the early Javanization of Bali in the 14th century. Pura Jagatnatha is on the central square of the city next to the museum. Its tallest building is a large "lotus throne" shrine that symbolizes the world (jagat) as the seat of Parama-Siwa, the "Supreme Siwa."

Examples of traditional Balinese architecture can be found at the **Bali Museum** on Taman Puputan square. At the northwest corner of **Puputan Square,** the Catur Mukha, "God of the Four Directions," gazes impassively through one of its four faces at the statue of the fallen heroes of the puputan.

Bali

Nusa Dua map

to Tanjung Benoa
(Watersport Facilities)
Daksina
Pratama Raya
Dieba Cafe
Bukit Sari
BENOA
Car Rental
Pratama
Fitness
Billiards
Dive Centre
KUTA
Celuk
Warung Agung
Pratama
Chinese
Cemetery
Japanese
Lotus Garden
Koki Loka
Peken
Village Market
to Denpasar, Sanur,
Kuta and Airport
Balekembar
Horse Stable
Srikandi
Penyarikan
Bali Nusa
Dua Clinic
BTDC
Office
Tennis
Court
Koki Bali
Nyomans Beergarden
Ujam
Bale Banjo
El Pirata
Netayan
Steamboat
Poco
Loco
Ming Garden
Swiss
Belhotel
Resort
Baliaga
to Sawangan
PEMINGE
Bualu
Village
Kocak
South
Gate
Pantai Mengiat
Bali Hilton
to Sawangan
Pratama Fitness
Pura
Dewata
Gonzaga
Balidesa
Suites
Bali Gonzaga
BTDC Staff
Housing
Nusa Dua
Beach
North
Gate
Dive School
Pura Samuh
Club Mediterranée
Pura Samuh
Bali International
Convention Centre
Sheraton Nusa
Indah Resort
Sheraton
Laguna
Nusa Dua
Main Gate
Bali Golf &
Country Club
Wirayuda
Melia Bali
Spanish
Consulate
Roundtable Pizza
Miyabi
Central Parking
British Tavern
Uno's
Payok
Tragia
Supermarket
Bali Millenium
Shopping
Centre
Garuda
Airlines
Nusa Dua Gallery
Gallery
Mandiri
Matsuri
Roundtable
Pizza
Eria
Keris
Keris
Cafe
Bali Nidori
Pundi Pundi
Sea
Galth
Breeze
Bidari
Nusadua
Kura
Kura
Amphitheatre
Duty Free Shop
Jukung
Pura
Lamun
Pura
Segara Nata
Putri Bali
Grand
Hyatt Bali
Pura Bias
Tugel
Mengiat Fishing
Boat Station

Scale 1 : 18 000

Badung Strait

Kuta–Legian map

Tekor Bali
Puri Naga Cottage
Evergreen Puri
Cafe Warna
Jayakarta Bali
Puri Tantra
Beach Bungalows
Bhaskara
Maharta
Sari Beach Inn
Cafe Espresso
Legian Beach
Bali Mandira
Hulu Cafe
The Legend
Karang Mas
Cafe Espresso
Intan Legian
Papa's Cafe
Alam Kul Kul
Alam Kul Kul
Kuta Jaya
Southern Cross
La Cobana
Komala
Indah II
Bali Nina
Istana Rama
Tourist Police
Sahid Raya Bali
Poppies
Cottages II
Indah Beach
Maharani
McDonald's
Aneka Kuta
Kuta Beach
Masa Inn
Hard Rock Hotel & Cafe
Mr Ba
Natour Kuta Beach
Jenggala Ceramic
Kuta Art
Sol Paradise
Kuta Paradiso Bali
Melasti Beach
Karthi
Benny's
Bali Garden
Cafe Taman
Mysro Disco
Kartika Plaza
Impala Seafood
Monalisa Spa
Bali Dynasty Resort
Santika Beach
Ramada Bintang Bali
Nelayan Kuta
Bakung
Tuban Beach
Zero Six
Rama Baruna
Holiday Inn Balihai
Sa Cafe
Maesa
Bali Segara
Patrajasa
Beach
Bali Prani
Historic Site
Surati
Kumala
Blue Eddy's
Sing
Ken Ken
Zanzibar
Mira
Opal Legian
Bali
Wina
Bali
Niksoma
Tanjung
Bali
Poco Loco
Melasti
Swiss
Consula
Bagus Terum
Puri
Anggrek Prasanth
Nakula
Legian Clin
Puri Raja
Balisa
LEGIAN
Padma
Warung Padma Indah
La Monde
Loji
Yudist
Bali Qui
Dolmin
Melast
Legia
Garde
Camplur
Brun
Spa
Skegs
Lu
Adr
Darn
Garde
M
Raja
Seafoo
Bali
Bagus
Warun
Ny. Su
Risata Bali Resort
Jatra
Kartika Pla
Sekar Sari
Ayu Nadi
Supermar
Samudra
Sandi Phala
Resort
Palm Cafe
Wana Segara
Lotus
Tavern
Kaisar
Pan Enter
Kuta
Seafoo
Bali
Pantri
Bali
Bali Village
Thai Bakery
Chai Bakery
Dwir
Bali Strait

Scale 1 : 25 000

International
Terminal
Domestic
Terminal
Historic Site
Ngurah Rai International Airport

NUSA DUA

Nusa Dua is a government-run dreamland of coconut palms, white sand beaches and pristine waters located near the island's southern tip. Making Nusa Dua into a tourist paradise was a consciously implemented government policy, designed with the help of the World Bank. Two main concepts underlie the project: to develop an accessible up-market tourist resort, while keeping the disruptive impact on the local environment as low as possible. The village of **Bualu** was chosen both for its scenic location as well as for its relative isolation from densely populated areas. The hotels are landmarks of the new Balinese architecture: the design committee specified that buildings be no higher than the coconut trees and that their layouts be based on Balinese macro and microcosmic models.

KUTA–LEGIAN

This bustling beach resort has in the short space of just two decades burst onto centre stage in the local tourist scene. The main attraction here was, and still is, one of the best beaches in Asia — and the trickle of cosmic surfers and space age crusaders in search of paradise, mystical union, and good times has turned into a torrent. Kuta's beach and back lanes have filled up with homestays, restaurants, and shops galore. New affluence has spawned flashy villas and a life of sultry tropical evenings beneath moonlit palms.

SANUR

This was Bali's first beach resort; a place of remarkable contrasts. **Sanur** today is a golden mile of Baliesque hotels that has attracted millions of paradise-seeking globetrotters. It is also one of the few remaining brahman kuasa villages in Bali — controlled by members of the priestly cast—and boasts among its charms some of the handsomest processions on the island, Bali's only all-female keris dance, the island's oldest stone inscription. The **Prasasti Belanjong**, an inscribed pillar here dated AD 913, is Bali's earliest dated artifact and is now kept in a temple in **Belanjong** village in the south of Sanur.

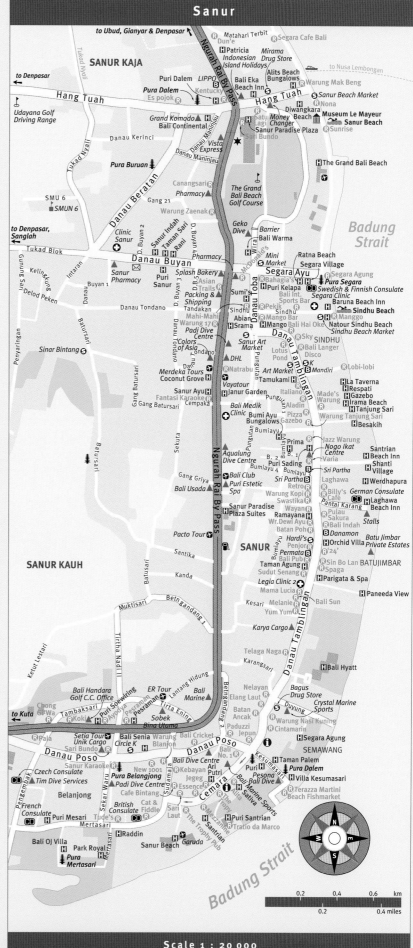

Scale 1 : 20 000

52

Bali

to Payangan, Chedi, Bagawan Giri ↑

to Pujung & Kintamani ↑

Plumerta
Puri Bunga
Bunga Permai
Payogaran
Petulugunung
to Pujung & Kintamani ↑

White Water Rafting
Cahaya Dewata
Villa Indah
Blind Masseur
View

Citra Minang Titi Garden
Warung
Ubud Indah
Garden

Tegalkuning

Sayan Ridge
Raya Sanggingan

KELIKI
Anom
Ulun Ubud Cottages
Bangkiansidem
Bentuyung
Petuludesa

TEGALLALANG

KEDEWATAN
Amandari
BRI
Adi Asri

TEGAL LALANG
Sunari
Wakadiume Resort
Bintang Pesona
Bintang Lima
Bintang Pari
Pondok Kecil 2
Tegallantang
Villa Pacung
Yani Craft Center
Trio Cafe
Puri Asri
Ratih
Gentong Sari
Swara Mandera

Finish Rafting
Kadewatananyar
Sobek Rafting
Suargan Temple

Say May Cafe
Dewatan Anyar
Sunny Blow
Villa Jepong
Nuri
Cantika Beauty Parlour
Agung Rai
Kori Ubud
Antonius Kho
Mozaic
Bali Video
Ananda
Bukit Asri
Agung
Dennis

FedEX Courier
Villa Bukit Ubud
Neka Museum
Sanggingan
Anom Cottage
Tama
Pita Maha
Indus
Villa Bagawan
Danamon
Taman Indrakida
I. M. Yang
Wisata Cottages
Sika

Pondok Sakti
Taman Sakti
Nyoman Ada
Globetrotter
Studio 13
Puri Naga
Loka Sari

Kutuh Kaja
Viceroy Resort
Bayan Tree Kamandalu
Nagi

Warung Bunga
Villa Puricamas
Gaya
Sayan Ayu

Samdadad Village
Agris Homestay
Ketut
Rahmat
Merpati Inn
PETULU
Nagi
Arya
Laplapan

Ayung River
Tanggayuda
Warung Red Rice
Sayan Resort
View
Ngurah KK Studio
Puri Raka
Tankis

UBUD
Sembahan
Pondok Bulan Mas
Ketut's Place

Komala
Yamasari
Made Kertonegoro's Future Art
Ambengan
Gunung Merta
Batik Workshop
Sukawati
Courts
Nature Resort & Spa
Raya Laplapan

Taman Bebek
Sayan Terrace
Four Seasons
Cafe Sayan
Sayan Dewata
Kutuh
Breadworks
Penestanan Kaja
Leke Leke
Siddharthas
Penestanan Bungalows
Made Bawa Bungalows
Bali-Ubud Cottages
Tjampuhan
Pura Campuhan
Beggar's Bush
Ibah
Blancos
Bridge Cafe
Murni's Warung
Roof Garden
Miros Garden

Ubud Kaja
Lecuk Inn
Siti Bungalows
Sekar Ayu Inn
Puri Lukisan Museum
Puri Saraswati
Ubud
Suci Inn

Taman Kaja
Kutuh Kelod
Tirta Taman
Andong
Jero Ganding
Pura Gunung Sari
Gunung Sari
Rambut Indah Wig Factory
UBUD
Maya Ubud Resort

Marajig
Penestanan Young Artists
Ketut Soki
Panestaan Kelod
Sri Ratih Cottages
Animale
Tino DS
Pringga Juwita
Okawati's
Ubud Palace
Neka Museum
Cok Putra S.
Lempad Gallery
Bamboo
Oka Kartina
Siwa Ratih Dance Stage
BRI
Telkom
Tebesaya
Pande
Tirtasari Dance Stage

Baung
Penestanan Kelod
Puri Sani
Anna Sari
Whitney
Wayan Toni
Dirga Rahayu
White Lotus Lodge
Ina Inn
Nick's
Camden
Night Market
Ibu Rai
Do Drop Inn
Cafe Bali
Komaneka Resort
Dewi Sita
Astiti
Nyoman
Warta
Family
Matahari
Teruna
Rona's
Utama
Mudita Inn
Agung Rai

SAYAN
Mas
Djagra's Inn
Purpas Silver Ubud Village
Cafe Wayan
Pertiwi Spa
Lotus Lane
Ibunda Inn
Seraphim Art
Pande Permai
Camplung Sari

Cafe Api Api
Jani's
Jati Titib
Komaneka Resort
Ubud Inn
Fibra Inn
Padangtegal Kelod
Shah Losmen
Dewa Windia
Agung Rai

Sinteg Bungalow
Ketiklantang

Monkey Forest
Dewi Sri Cottage
Kura-Kura
Flying Elephants
Puri Padi
Crafts
Sahadewa
Hore hore
Tengah Kauh
Puri Agung
Ibu Arsa Homestay & Rest.
PELIATAN
Yanglon
Bali Jingga
Kelep

Hungry Tiger
Nuriani's
Ubud Raya
Greenfield Bungalows
Abian
Panorama
Kagemusha
Artini Cottages 3
Legong
Made Budiasa
Nyoman Sumerta Art
Pering
Jawa Timur
Yamaha
Honda
Cafe Bali

Alam Indah
Saren Indah
Laka Leke
Garden View
Chili Cafe
Putri Dewata
Agung Raka
Pondok Impian
Warung Balima
Arma Agung Rai Museum of Art
Puri Indah
Sado
Kokokan
Agung Rai
Pura Puseh
Ruci
Sugaia
Massari
Open Air Stage
Teges Kanginan

Swasti Homestay
Villa Kerti Yasa
Indra Villa
Alamjiwo
Guci Guesthouse
Pengosekan Kaja
Widya Kusuma Wood Carvings Museum
Panili Vanilla
Bharata
Mas
Peliatan Raya
Exiles
"Dewa Nyoman Batuans" Community of Artists
Lumba-Lumba
Suma
Kalah
Nyoman Astanas Inn
Nandia Art Studio
Sawah Alam Lodge
Sari
Siti Arsana
W. Hardja
Nya. Sugaia
I W Bawa
Warung Barva
Teges Kawan

Bamboo Foundation
Nyungkuning 1
Nyungkuning 2
Villa Wana Kedi
Danginlabak
Raya Singekerta
Bali Taksu Spirit
Murni Art Studio
Bali Tourist Service
Nyungkuning
Batik Workshop
Pengosekan Kelod
Raya Pengosekan
MAS
Rudana Museum & Gallery
Djelita Handicrat Center
Nyoman Togog
Nasi Campur
Warung Lawar
Puri Bukit Mas Art
Agung Raka
Ida Bagus Putra Cafe
The Cafe
Suly Resort and Spa
Tiok Rai Pudak

SINGEKERTA
Tengah
Tunjung
Cafe Sanbo
Lobong

Raya Buduk
Astina
Ayodya
Batuh
Tebongkang
to Denpasar, Bali Bird Park

LODTUNDUH

Abiansemal
to Silungan, Singapadu

Brama's Bandil

UBUD

Far from the madding crowds, **Ubud** has long been a quiet haven for the arts. Set amidst emerald green rice paddies and steep ravines in the stunning central Balinese foothills, some 25 km north of **Denpasar**, the village was originally an important source of medicinal herbs and plants. "Ubud," in fact, derives from the Balinese word for medicine — ubad.

It was here that foreign artists settled during the 1920s and '30s, transforming the village into a flourishing centre for the arts. Artists from all parts of Bali were invited to settle here by the local prince, Cokorda Gede Sukawati, and Ubud's palaces and temples are now adorned by the work of Bali's master artisans.

According to an 8th century legend, a Javanese priest named Rsi Markendya came to Bali and meditated in **Campuhan** at the confluence of two streams — an auspicious site for Hindus. He founded the **Pura Campuhan** (Gunung Lebah Temple) here, on a narrow platform above the valley floor, where pilgrims seeking peace came to be healed from their worldly cares.

The **Puri Saren** palace, with its maze of family compounds and richly carved doorways, is at the main crossroads. The royal family temple, **Pura Pamerajaan Sari Cokorda Agung**, is next door — a storage place for the family heirlooms. To the west behind a lotus pond by the **Puri Saraswati** palace (now a hotel), lies the superbly chiseled Pura Saraswati temple of learning. Ubud's "navel" temple, **Pura Puseh**, with its delightful sculptures, lies to the north.

The Museum Puri Lukisan features paintings, sculptures and a peaceful garden. The museum was founded in 1953 by surviving members of Ubud's famed Pita Maha art movement. Painted panels that I Gusti Nyoman Lempad executed 40 years ago depict the Balinese agrarian cycle.

Ubud's best commercial galleries are at the eastern end of town, about one km away. Munut Gallery belongs to a former pupil of Dutch painter Bonnet. Suteja Neka, whose father was a painter, is the foremost dealer and collector on Bali. His collection is displayed at the **Neka Museum**. The most famous artist of Ubud, however, was Lempad, whose work is on exhibition in the Lempad Gallery.

To the west, in **Penestanan Village**, is the home of many "Young Artists." Though each has his own distinctive style, the influence of the surrounding landscapes can be seen in all their works. Further west, spectacular views are offered along the Sayan Ridge which overlooks the **Ayung River**.

Half an hour's walk or a 10-minute drive from central Ubud, due south along the shaded main street of **Padang Tegal**, past open rice paddies, art shops and homestays, is **Pengosekan**, which despite its small size, has over the past 20 years become a major player on the Balinese art scene. Pengosekan paintings are seldom seen in shops and galleries, and must be hunted down in the village.

Peliatan is best known for its legong — a graceful dance performed by two pre-pubescent girls in glittering costumes. **Teges Kanginan** is one of the few places on Bali where the dancers are still trained in the traditional manner. Regular performances of dance and music are held on both the Gunung Sari and Tirtasari Dance Stages. The **Agung Rai Museum of Art** not only has one of the best collections of Balinese art, but also sponsors cultural events on a regular basis.

Just 2 km east of the Teges intersection, is the complex known as **Goa Gajah** — the famous "Elephant Cave." It overlooks the **Petanu River** and consists of a Siwaitic rock-cut cave, a bathing place, a monk's chamber, a number of Buddhist rock-cut stupas and statues, and several foundations.

The antiquities of Yeh Pulu, dating from the late 14th century, consist of reliefs cut out of the rock and a sacred well. The reliefs are in a naturalistic style. Horsemen, men carrying animals hanging from a pole, a sitting brahman holding an offering spoon, sitting women, an ascetic, and a man carrying two large pots on a pole over his shoulder are among the figures which are depicted.

The area north of **Bedulu**, around **Pejeng** and **Intaran**, contains many antiquities. The most important is the **Pura Penataran Sasih**, which forms part of a group of three temples. Sasih means "moon" and refers to the "Moon of Pejeng" — a giant bronze kettle drum kept in a shrine in the temple. This area was also once considered the "Navel of the World" and there is a temple bearing this name, the **Pura Pusering Jagat**.

Another temple in Pejeng, the **Pura Kebo Edan**, possesses the statue of a standing giant 3.6 m tall. He is called Kebo Edan, the "Mad One," and may represent a demonic manifestation of Siwa as a dancer. There is another statue representing a fat, crouching demon holding a big skull upside down in front of his chest. The style of these statues points to a 13th–14th century origin.

The **Museum Gedong Arca** features displays of several stone sarcophagi, neolithic axe heads, bronze jewelry and figurines, and Chinese ceramics.

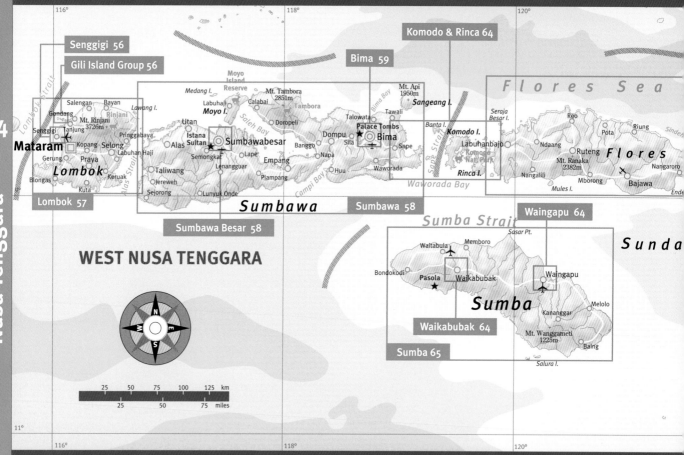

Senggigi 56

Gili Island Group 56

Komodo & Rinca 64

Bima 59

Lombok 57

Sumbawa Besar 58

Sumbawa 58

Waingapu 64

Waikabubak 64

Sumba 65

WEST NUSA TENGGARA

25   50   75   100   125   km
25   50   75   miles

Scale 1 : 3 500 000

NUSA TENGGARA

In the modern Indonesian state, the group of islands east of Bali are called Nusa Tenggara, the "Southeastern Islands." To geographers, they are the **Lesser Sundas**, at least partially because they are smaller than the **Greater Sundas** — Sumatra, Java and Borneo. There is nothing "lesser" about the region's charms, however, with a variety of physical and cultural attractions.

From Lombok to Timor, the islands have deserted white sand beaches, transparent waters, and beautiful coral reefs. The three water-filled craters of Keli Mutu on Flores provide an almost surreal sight, as minerals have tinted each of the lakes a different hue. Tiny **Komodo**, nestled between Sumbawa and Flores, is the home of the largest lizard extant.

Lying just a few degrees south of the equator, the **Lesser Sundas** stretch 1,300 kilometres east to west, forming a central link in the 5,600 kilometre Indonesian archipelago. There are 566 islands in Nusa Tenggara, of which 320 are so small they don't even have names. Of the 42 inhabited islands, four loom largest on the map — **Lombok, Sumbawa, Flores**, and **Timor**.

The western islands, Lombok and Sumbawa, are in many places covered with the luxuriant vegetation characteristic of the humid tropics. Further east, however, the dry season lengthens and parts of Timor are the driest in all of Indonesia.

The region as a whole is Indonesia's driest. It lies at the edge of the influence of the northwest monsoon, and the southeast monsoon brings rain-bearing winds only to the southern coasts. These islands, relatively dry and rocky, do not harbour dramatic rainforest ecosystems or a large variety of odd endemic species. They are, in fact, rather sparsely populated with large animals.

The islands of **Nusa Tenggara** form two distinct arcs. The long northern arc — Lombok, Sumbawa, Komodo, Flores, Lembata — is volcanic in origin. The islands of the shorter, southern arc — Sumba, Savu, Rote, Timor — are formed of raised coral reef limestone and sedimentary rock.

The islands in the volcanic arc are potentially quite fertile, lacking only reliable rain in the east. But the southern islands exhibit barren limestone plains and sparse savannahs, which in places can barely support cattle. Overall, the islands are much less populated than Java and Bali, and villages and cultivated land are widely scattered.

VOLCANOES Dominating the northern chain are volcanoes of all shapes and sizes, ranging from the massive **Tambora** caldera, 7 km across, to isolated cones a mere 100 m high. Most, such as Rinjani, Tambora, Sangeang, Ebulobo, and Ile Ape display classical conical outlines. Their precipitous, finely scored upper slopes descend to gentler middle slopes, slashed by deep ravines, and then broaden out to almost level footslope fans.

Mount Tambora, on the island of **Sumbawa**, produced the greatest eruption of modern geological times on April 5–7, 1815. The force of the explosion was far greater than the better-known eruption of Krakatau, off western Java, in 1833. The Tambora explosion produced an astounding 150 cubic km of ash and pumice, reducing the height of the volcano overnight from 4,200 to 2,851 m.

Several of Nusa Tenggara's volcanoes tower to more than 3,000 m in height and some contain deep crater lakes. The most famous of these are the mystically coloured trio of lakes in **Mt. Kelimutu** in central Flores. The colours derive from dissolved minerals in the lakes, and the varying content of the minerals and shifting light causes the lakes to assume a range of colours; although usually described as light green, turquoise and black, they have been known to appear as sea green, deep blue, even red.

Other crater lakes, like the magnificent 5-km-long caldera lake of **Rinjani** on northern Lombok, **Danau Segara Anak**, contain miniature volcanic landscapes of their own, in the form of new daughter cones, complete with many and varied fresh lava flows.

LOWLANDS The shorelines in the northern island chain contrast sharply with those of the southern islands. The coasts of the northern islands are markedly irregular, twisting in and out of small and large sheltered sandy bays, curving around exposed rocky headlands and liberally sprinkled with clusters of attractive reef-bound islands. The southern islands, on the other hand, possess more regular coastlines. They have long stretches of coastal cliffs alternating with narrow sandy beaches, guarded by ramparts of inshore or offshore coral reef.

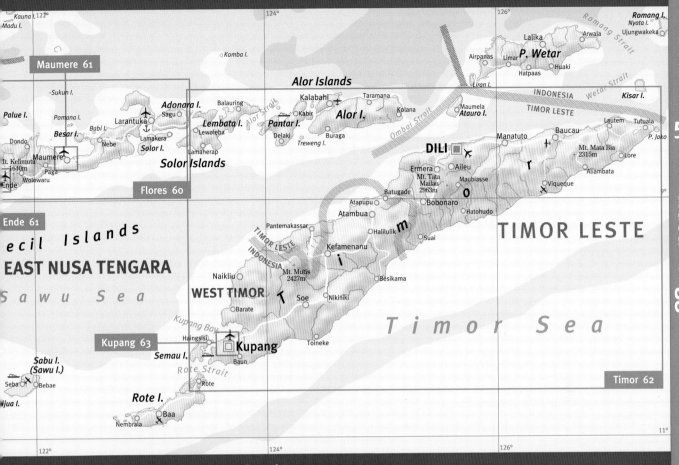

Scale 1 : 3 500 000

WILDLIFE The most dramatic creature found in the islands is the Komodo dragon, the largest lizard extant. Endemic to Komodo and Rinca islands and nearby eastern Flores, Varanus komodoensis is the largest known monitor lizard.

The scrublands of Nusa Tenggara support wild deer and pigs, as well as bats and numerous species of lizards and snakes. Few mammals, however, are native to the islands; just one species of wild pig, one shrew and a cuscus. The sulfur-crested cockatoo, as well as parrots, sunbirds, bee-eaters, and the unusual mound-building megapode bird, can also be found on these islands.

Underwater, the scene changes, and the coral reefs of Nusa Tenggara are one of the richest ecosystems in the world. No place on earth has greater numbers of diversity of aquatic species. A single large reef in Nusa Tenggara can contain almost 1,000 fish species, more than can be found in all the creeks, rivers, lakes, and streams of Europe.

LOMBOK

Lombok's area (4,739 sq km) and population (2.5 million people) are both just slightly smaller than Bali's. The island measures about 80 kms north to south and about 70 km east to west. A prominent peninsula extends west from the southwest corner and a smaller peninsula juts out from the southeast.

The name "Lombok" is said to come from a fiery red chili pepper, used as a condiment. The natives of Lombok, the Sasak population, call their island **Bumi Gora**, which means, "Dry Farmland," or **Selaparang**, which is the name of an old East Lombok kingdom.

Lombok is dominated by 3,726-m **Mt. Rinjani**, Indonesia's highest volcano and one of the highest points in the archipelago. Rinjani crowns a group of mountains that dominate the north-central section of the island. Most of the rainfall striking these mountains flows south, irrigating a large, rich agricultural area. Elsewhere on the island, the landscape is more barren and planting is only possible during Lombok's rainy season, the October–March northwest monsoon.

The coastal hills to the south, with average elevations around 500 m, do not form a watershed, but drop spectacularly into the sea. These cliffs frame beautiful bays and sandy coves. Other than the harbours at Lembar, in the crook of the southwestern peninsula, and **Labuhan Lombok**, in the northeast, only the south coast has any large bays.

The population centre of Lombok is an urban sprawl in the west made up of three contiguous cities spreading inland from the coast: the old port town of **Ampenan** blends into the administrative city of **Mataram**, which melds into the commercial town of **Cakranegara**. Mataram is the capital of **West Nusa Tenggara** province (incorporating Lombok and Sumbawa), as well as the capital of the West Lombok district.

Heading north from this central city cluster, the road rises over two small hills and then drops down to the coast to long, curved **Senggigi Beach**.

There are several clusters of small islands off Lombok's coast, all called "Gili", from the Sasak word for island. Some are just inhabited by fishermen and stray cattle. The best-known for their white sand beaches and clear waters are **Gili Air**, **Gili Meno**, and **Gili Trawangan**, off the northwest coast.

THE GILI ISLANDS

Gili Air is the closest to **Bangsal** and the "mainland," and has the highest local population of the three: 1,000 people. Most of the people live in the south of the island and the bungalows are concentrated in this area as well. Here, and on all the Gilis, the principal economic activities other than tourism are coconut growing, fishing, and small-scale cattle and goat raising. The beach runs all the way around Gili Air's 100-plus hectares, and the best sunbathing and snorkelling areas are located on the southern shore. The waters off Gili Air are crystal clear; the best snorkelling is at the edge of the reef which encircles the island.

Only 350 people live on **Gili Meno**, the middle island. Just inland from the west coast is a large salt lake, its surface marked off into sections for collecting salt during the dry season.

Gili Trawangan, the furthest offshore, is also the largest, covering 3.5 sq km. In 1891, Gili Trawangan was a penal colony housing Sasak rebels, but today, activities centre around the fine snorkelling and diving sites for both novice and experienced divers.

Gili Island Group

Bali Sea

56

Nusa Tenggara

Gili Trawangan

Lighthouse
Nusa Tiga
Sudi Mampir
Coral Beach II
Creative II
Blue Marlin Dive Centre
Blue Coral Diving
Paradise Pub
3 Caves Area
Rinjani
Sunset
Mawar II
Ekky
Alex
Simple
Mountain View
Danau Hijau
Pasta Masjid
Jenny Beach
Talina
Sigilarius
Rainbow
Mawar I
Bintang Terawangan
Pondok Santai

Blue Coral Area
Coral Beach I
Snorkeling
Good Heart
Salt Pans
Art Market

Blue Coral
Bungalow
Snorkeling
Coral Garden Area

Gili Meno
Meno Lake
Casablanca
Pondok Wisata
Rawa Indah
Bonkas
Lumba-lumba
Rust Restaurant
Matahari
Bungalows
Mallia's Child
Bungalows
Restaurant
Kon Tiki
Gazebo Hotel &
Bouganvil Resort
Gogo
Anjani
Salabose
Lucky
Safari
Sunset Bungalo

Pondok Meno
Zoraya Pavilion
Pondok Lombok Indah
Legenda
Coconut
Sandi
Gusung Indah
Reefseekers
Dive Shop
Bunga
Gili Air
Kirakira
Fantastik
Mata Hari
Hing

Gili Air
Bupati's
New Han
Gili Gili Cottages
Puteri Bungalo
Pino
Corner
Scuba Shop
Resorta
Pondok Gili
Pearl Farm
Gili Indah
Surfing

Sira Point
Nusa Tiga
Sira
Sira Beach
Lendangberura
Cupek
Muara

Lombok Strait

Small Ferry Boats
to Gili Islands
Bangsal

N

0.5   1   1.5 miles
1   2   km

Scale 1: 85 000

Senggigi

KELUI
to Bangsal, Gili Islands,
Additional Cottages
Nusa Bunga
(Bunga Beach Cottages)
Windy Beach Cottages
Sentosa
Sentosa
Holiday Inn
MANGSIT VILLAGE
Pondok Damai
Puri Mas
Santai Beach Inn
Alang-Alang
Puri Mas Village
KARANGDANGAN

N
0.5   1   1.5 km
0.25   0.5   0.75 miles

Lombok Coconut
Puri Saron
Pacific Beach
Pura Kapusan
Sonya Homestay
Pasar Seni
Pondok Shinta Cottages
Lombok Intan Laguna
Souvenir Market
Wayan Gallery
Albatross Dive Centre
Senggigi Beach
Pool Villa Club
Maskot Cottages
Dharmarie Senggigi
Lina Cottages
Graha Beach
Sahid Tamara
Cafe Alberto
Pura Batubolong
Sambhu
Wayan Cafe
Sasak Garden
to Senggigi Palace Hotel, Mataram

Sheraton Senggigi
Kebun Rohani
Anjani Photo Shop
Princess of Lombok
Elen
Sudirman Antiques
Raja's Bungalows
Bukit Senggigi
Marina Pub
Graha Beach
Pondok Senggigi
Melati Dua Cottages
Palma Raja
Galeria
Soyang-soyang Disco
Sun Shine
Tropical Bay

Senggigi Beach

Lombok Strait

Scale 1: 50 000

Bali Sea

Gili Trawangan   Gili Meno   Gili Air
Surfing & Pearl Farm
Sorongjukung
Sunday Market
Jenggala
Tanjung
Pura Medana
Sira
Bangsal
Sokong
Montong
Lendangbila
Pemenang
Bengkoang
Onggong
Terangan
Pandanan
Baturuku Hill 406m
Malimbu Hill 460m
Malimbu
Pandan Hill 694m
Sangkanesebiu Hill 702m
Monkey Forest
Sambiak Hill 130m
Setangi
Duduk Hill
Kelui   Mt. Pusuk 851m
Kedongdong Hill 587m
Semaya
Senggigi
Krandangan
Pura Batubolong
Batubolong
Palm Sugar Production
Kekait
Batu Layar
Sandik
Bamboo Crafts
Menining
Wooden Crafts
Pura Segara
Ampenan
Dayen
Mt. Sabiris 893m
Kedongdong
Mt. Pelola 593m+
Gunungsari
Midang
Kekeri
Sesela
Tinggar
Pejeruk
Mambi
Penimbi
Mambalar
Dasangeria
Dumar
Sigerongan
Rembiga
MATARAM
CAKRANEGARA
Sweta
Karangbedil
Pagesangan
Pagutan
Dasancermen
Mapakbelatung
Kuranji
Bajur
Nyamarai
Sweta Market
Karange cicang
Sembung
Bengkel
Bagikpolak
Telagawaru
Banyumulek
Kedir
Rumak
Gunung Pensong Temple
Taman
Gapuk
Kuripan
Endok
Kebonayu
Dasangeres
Gerung
Buncit
Nyiurlembang
Lendangiahe
Jembatankembar
Berora
Lembar
Pottery
Beleke
Jagaraga

Nanggu Cottages
Snorkelling
Gili Nanggu
Gili Sudak
Medang Utara
Sekotong Timur
Pelah
Sekotong Barat
Medang
Tanjungbelik
Lendangie
Mt. Mereje 713m
Batubuwih
Mt. Raruna 357m
Mt. Kosong 244m
Jago
Montongsapah
Mesembur

Gili Anyaran
Surfing
Bangko
Selegong
Labuan Poh
Gubuk Bali
Mt. Gua 149m
Ketapang
Gili Rengit
Gili Layar
Gili Asahan
Asahan
Gili Gede
Gili Lontar
Pandanan
Orongbukal
Labuancenik
Temeran
Pelangan, Bathing Beach
Berambang
Selindungan
Permula
Pelangan Barat
Mt. Embit 418m
Gebangtebal
Rambutpetung
Mecanggah
Mt. Marmadi 490m
Gaok
Giligenting
Sekotong Indah
Scenic Area
Lekongsamah
Gelumpang
Sekotong Tengah
Repokgapok
Mt. Blongas 299m
Blongas
Sepi
Timbal
Mt. Bremi 272m+
Pengantap
Numpang
Selong Blanak Beach
Selong Blanak
Batu Rujaan
Scenic Area
Surfing
Belanggung Point
Gili Sarangburung
Ujunglangit Pt.
Sameti Pt.

to Padangbai, Bali (3-5hr)

Lombok Strait

Batubuton Pt.
Batukun Pt.
Labuankuwe Bay
Tg Kerandangan
Mekaki Bay
Marmadi Pt.
Batujonggat Bay
Batujonggat Bay
Sepi Bay
Blongas Bay
Penantap Bay
Panggang Bay
Mt. Panggang 329m

INDIAN OCEAN

Scale 1: 350 000

Scale 1 : 350 000

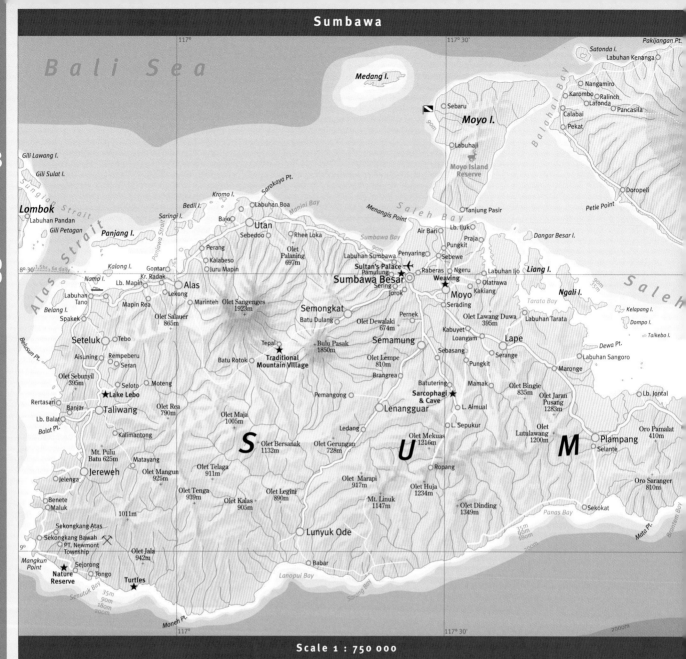

Scale 1 : 750 000

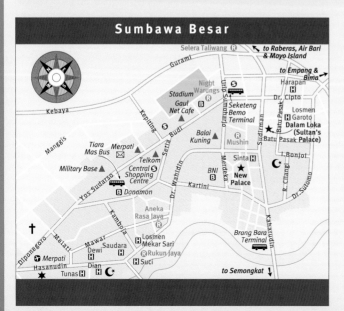

Sumbawa Besar

SUMBAWA

Although **Sumbawa** is three times the size of Lombok, it has just one-third the population. The island's terrain is rough and mountainous, and Sumbawa has no fertile plains. The outline of the island is contorted by capes, peninsulas and deeply cut bays. The 15,600 sq km island stretches 280 km east-west, but its width varies from 15 km to 90 km.

Sumbawa is part of the volcanic northern chain of Nusa Tenggara and while activity took place over the eras, no single explosion seems to have been as dramatic as the **Mt. Tambora** eruption of 1815.

Sumbawa is really two cultural islands: **Sumbawa Besar** in the west and **Bima** in the east. In fact, although outsiders call the whole island "Sumbawa," on the island this term is only used for the west. The two parts of the island are divided by both geography and language — that spoken by the Sumbawanese being more like Sasak (the language spoken on Lombok), while that spoken by the Bimans being more like the languages of Flores and Sumba. This division has been further reinforced by the historical influence of the Balinese in the west and the Makassarese of South Sulawesi in the east.

Some 85 % of **Sumbawa** is too mountainous to farm, but the rich volcanic soil of the river valleys yields bumper crops. These valleys were the sites of many petty states, the island's first political units.

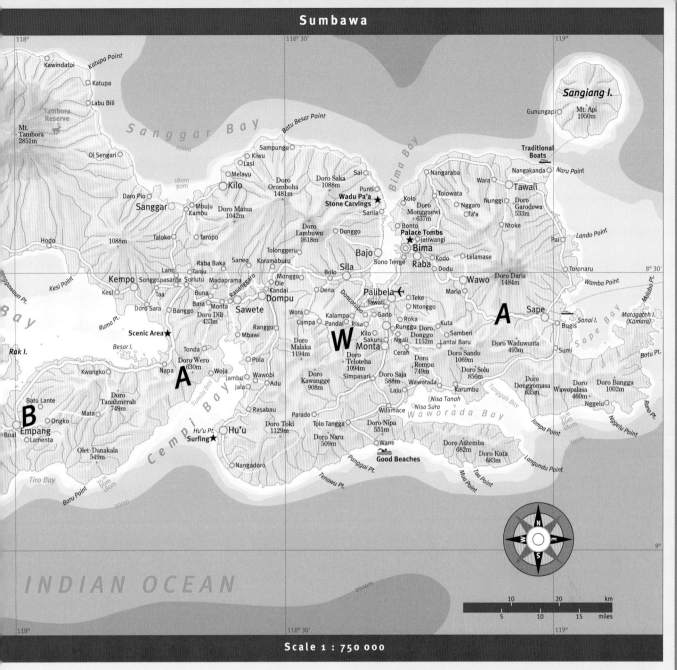

Scale 1 : 750 000

The area around **Taliwang** in the west and along the south coast has superb, deserted beaches and quiet little fishing villages. **Moyo Island** in the north has a state nature reserve — a haven for birders — and some of the finest undisturbed reefs in the region. **Tepal**, in the highlands southwest of Sumbawa Besar, is one of the few remaining traditional villages on the island.

SUMBAWA BESAR

The district capital of the western part of the island is a large town which boasts a beautiful beach at **Labuhan Sumbawa** and an old palace, built in 1885 and partially restored a century later.

BIMA

With its large, hourglass-shaped bay, protected year-round from the monsoon winds, **Bima** has always been the island's preeminent town. This harbour was the logical place for traders to stop to take on water, rice and other foodstuffs, and to buy local cloth and sappanwood, which is used in dye-making.

The port in Bima is usually a beehive of activity with graceful wooden freight schooners and ungainly iron ships tied up at the docks. During the dry season, bright blue bags of salt destined for Java and Kalimantan are stacked on the docks. Truckloads of garlic, soybeans and especially shallots — the Bima district's chief agricultural export — are shipped to Java.

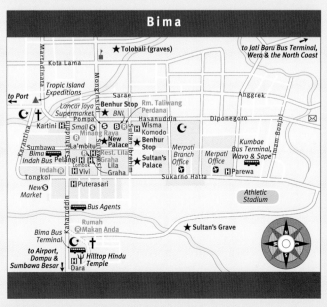

Bima

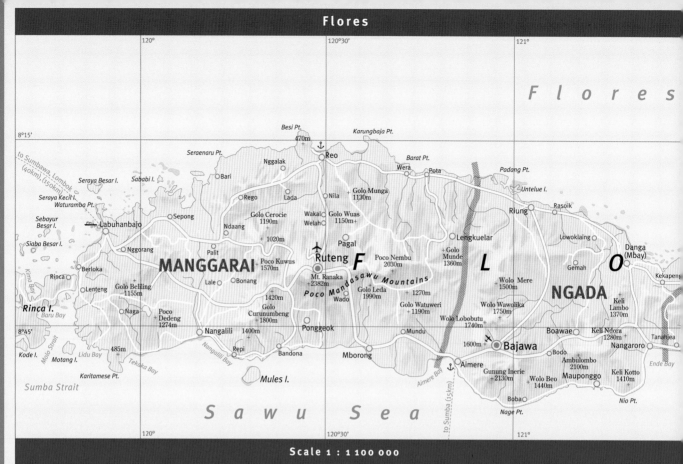

Scale 1 : 1 100 000

FLORES

Flores is a long, narrow rugged island with dramatic volcanoes, beautiful mountain lakes, grassy savannah, and mountain forest. The landscape is beautiful in an untamed way. Flores is 360 km long, and varies from 12 to 70 km wide. Although the rains here are often irregular, the high mountains ensure a fairly constant supply of water.

On the far west coast of Flores is **Labuhanbajo**, a quiet fishing village which is also the port for ferries to and from **Sape** on the east coast of **Sumbawa**. **Ruteng**, the district capital of the **Manggarai** district on Flores, lies at the base of a tall mountain range and at the head of an intricate network of valleys that makes up the island's largest rice-producing area. The district is also one of the largest coffee-growing areas in Indonesia.

The **Ngada** district, with its capital at **Bajawa**, has retained its traditional ways more than any other part of Flores. Although the population is almost entirely Roman Catholic, they maintain their megaliths and ancestral shrines. **Riung**, on the north coast, boasts beautiful coral gardens, and thousands of flying foxes on the north coast of **Untelue Island** in the **Seventeen Island National Reserve**.

Keli Mutu, in southern Flores about 40 km from Ende, consists of three volcanic craters, each filled with a lake of different colour. The base camp for approaching the crater lakes is **Moni village**, on the main Ende-Maumere highway.

ENDE, nestled in the crook of a small peninsula on the south coast, is the largest town on Flores. There is a port on either side of the narrow peninsula; most of the shipping activity is concentrated at **Pelabuhan Ende**, which faces west and offers a good view of the wide **Ende Bay**. The new dock, **Pelabuhan Ipi**, is on the east side and it is here that the large ships call. The area south of the old port is Ende's most lively with lots of shops crowded together into narrow streets.

MAUMERE lies at the island's hub of communications and attractions. The city is on the north coast, near the narrowest part of the island. Just southeast of the town, Flores thins out to only 18 km wide.

The villages south and west of Maumere offer a gamut of attractions: the only real museum in the province (the **Bikon Blewut Museum** at Ledalero), splendid views onto the Flores and Savu seas (at Koting-Diler, just past Nitta on the road to Ende), ikat weaving (Sikka village), and a sacred spot reserved for ancestor worship (Lekabai).

TIMOR

Timor, the largest of the islands east of Bali, is a rugged, dry land that once was best known for its valuable sandalwood. It stretches along a southwest-northeast axis. The 33,615 sq km island is about 500 km long and 80 km wide. The southwestern tip is just 500 km from Australia.

This Timor island was, before, politically divided into two provinces (when it was a part of Indonesia). But, as of now, the eastern section of the island, including the enclave of Oecussi, situated within West Timor is as a new nation of the world which is formally known as Timor Leste. The people there had formally celebrated its independence on 20 May 2002 after the majority of the people (78.5 percent) in that area voted in favour of independence in a referendum sponsored by the U.N. and Indonesian Government.

WEST TIMOR

West Timor covers 19,000 sq km. Its capital, **Kupang**, is the largest city in the southeastern islands. It is the capital of the **East Nusa Tenggara (NTT)** province and the largest town in the region. The city stretches along the sea and climbs a low hill before spreading inland. Only a large, flat curved stone remains of **Fort Concordia**, built by the Dutch in 1653, but still serves as the site of a garrison , now for the Indonesian army. The oldest church in town is **Gereja Kota Kupang**, near the downtown bus terminal. Originally built in 1873, the church was reconstructed in 1987. Kupang's Provincial Museum features an excellent display of ikat cloths from the region, scale models of the traditional houses of East Nusa Tenggara, and weapons, musical instruments, and carved wooden and stone ancestor figures.

The island of Timor is 60 percent mountainous; Mt Fatuleu is the highest point in West Timor at 1,115m. Unlike many other Indonesian islands, the soils of Timor are not enriched by volcanic ash. Rainfall is unpredictable and unevenly distributed making agriculture a risky proposition.

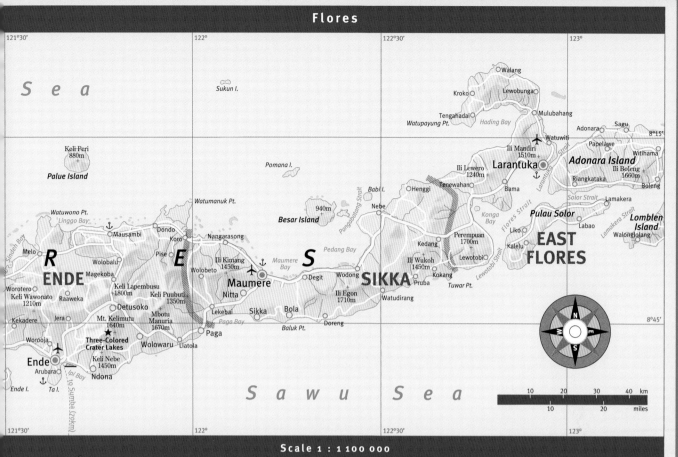

Scale 1 : 1 100 000

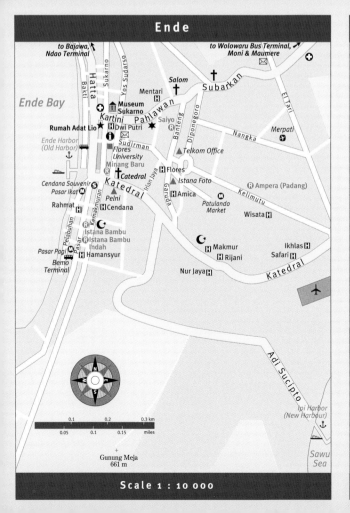

Ende

Scale 1 : 10 000

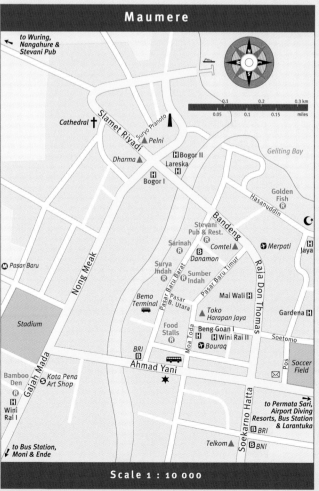

Maumere

Scale 1 : 10 000

124°

125°

Boleng Strait

Tobiwutun
Riangeba
Balauring
Muruona
Hadakewa
Lewolein
Lewoleba
Mt. Kabau
1170 m
Lembata Island
Bauberepa
Waiteba
Mt.
Labalekang
1650 m
Lamaherap
Tobilolong
Atande Point

Alor Strait

Leur
Point

Lapang Island
Batang Island

Marisa Island
Rusa Island
Kambing Island
Biangono
Kayan

Blangmerang Bay

Kabir
Teba
Abangiwang
Tama
Pantar Island
+ Mt. Topaki
1370 m
Delaki
Delaki Point

Tamuang Bay

Hukoleen
Reta I.
Pura I.
Lanliki

Pantar Strait

Treweng Island
Margeta Point

Ternate I.

Pasir Putih
Kokar
Kalabahi
Benlelang
Moru
Kahalwo
Sibelah
Point

Buraga
Kui

Sika Point

Bantelang Bay
Limbur
Taramana
Babi Point
Takala

A l o r

Mt.
Potomana
1899m

Werula

Augamin
Point

Manamani Point
Niakena
Kolana

Maritaing
Lisomu
Point
Batulolong

Ombai Strait

Maubara
Carimbala Point
Mt.
Vatoboro
1009 m
Atabae
Quima
Cailaco
Mt. Loelaco
1929 m
Batugade
Maliana

EAST NUSA TENGGARA

S a w u   S e a

9°

10°

Atapupu
Tuameseh
Point
Mena
Atambau
Weluli
Nobelu
Fatululic
Lolotoi
INDONESIA
TIMOR LESTE
M

Wini
Manumean
Halilulik
Fohorem
Suai

Pantemakassar
Lifau
OECUSSI
Nitibe
Oesilo
Kuafeu
Supun
Boas
Tafara Point

TIMOR LESTE
INDONESIA

Nasikonis
Point
Eban
Kefamenanu
Oelolok
I
Betun
Besikama
Wetoh Point

Gumuk
Point
Naikliu
Mt. Mutis
2427 m
Musi

Mas Point
Naibonat
Lelogama
Mt. Human
+ 1296 m
Kapan
WEST TIMOR
Nikiniki
Kie
Putain
Nunkolo

Kurus
Point
Noimena
Barate
Batuitam
Point
Olisina
Point
Sulamu
Camplong
Mt. Fatu Leo
1115 m
T
Soe
Oekamusa
Ngilmina
Mt. Penkase
750 m

Mt. Tapan
975 m
Kolbanu

Kupang Bay
Babau
Kupang
Tarus
Tenau
Haingsisi
Semau Island
Oebowa
Oesalin
Natoni
Baun
Mt. Kofnoe
657 m
Panite
Toineke
Oetune
Tewe Point
Kera I.

Oisina
Mali
Point
Tarba
Point

Rote Strait

Rote
Mandoi Point

Rote I.
Batuidu
Pokobatu

124°

125°

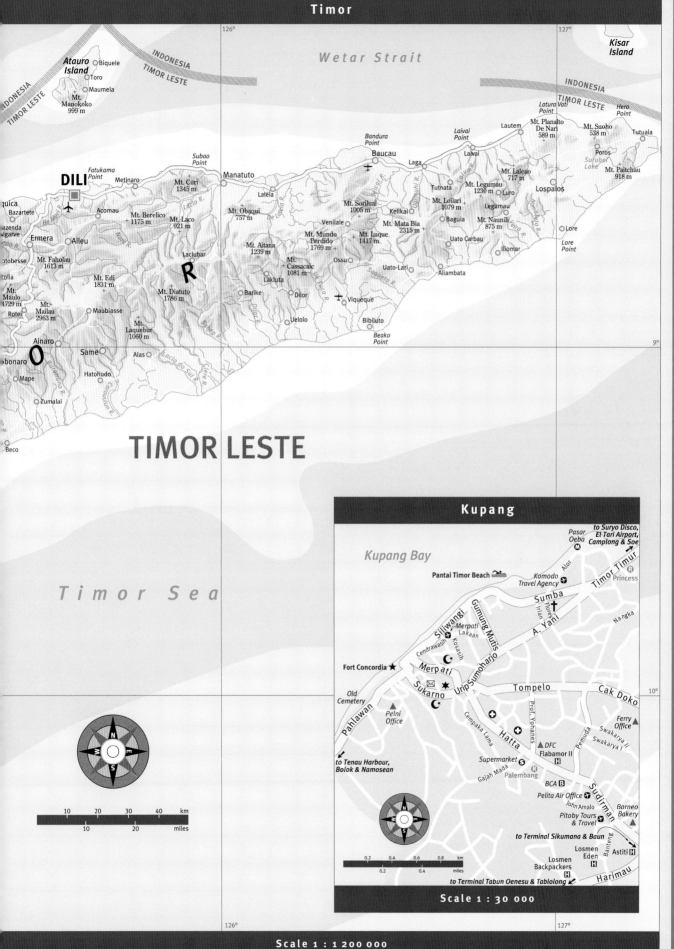

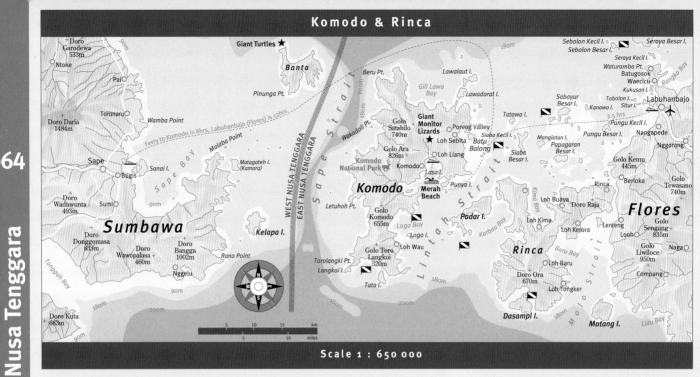

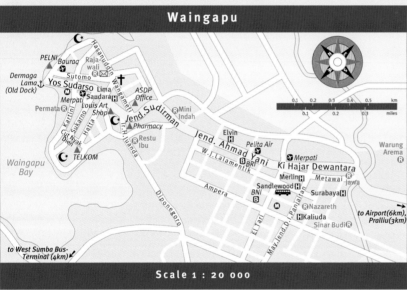

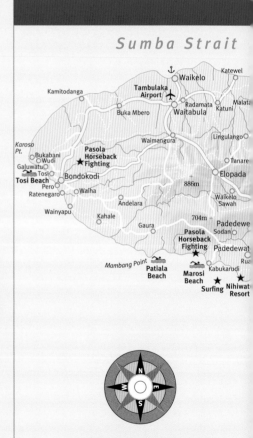

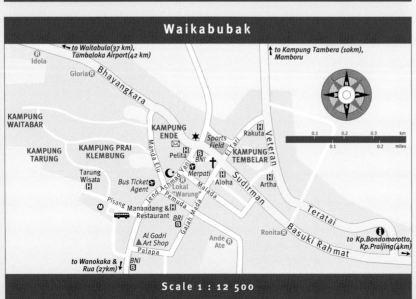

KOMODO & RINCA

Komodo Island and neighbouring **Rinca** are between Sumbawa and Flores, approximately 500 km east of Bali. The shape of the island is very irregular, its 340 sq km spread over a number of peninsulas and promontories. The dry hills, which rise to 735 m, sprout skinny lontar palms. The plankton-rich seas around Komodo and Rinca support amazing reefs and a range of large marine life, including whales and dolphins.

There is just one village on Komodo and the approximately 600 islanders cling precariously to the eastern shore. They make their living by fishing at night from graceful, twin-hulled catamarans.

The Komodo dragon is found only on the islands of **Komodo**, **Padar** and **Rinca**, and parts of western Flores. Locally called ora, the dragons are most numerous on Komodo, which together with nearby Rinca has been set aside as a National Park. There are many walks — along designated trails and always accompanied by a ranger — through dragon's territory. The views of the emerald blue seas and coral reefs off Komodo, especially from **Mt. Ara** are incredible. The snorkelling and swimming around **Pantai Merah** — "Red Beach" — east of **Loh Liang** and **Pulau Lasa**, an island near Komodo village, are superb.

SUMBA

By Indonesian standards, 11,150 sq km Sumba is relatively small, with a bent, irregularly oval shape. The island stretches 210 km along a northwest–southeast axis and is 40–70 km wide. The southeast is the most mountainous region, crowned by the island's highest peak, **Wanggameti**, at 1,225 m. Much of the interior is made up of grassy plateaus, punctuated by deep valleys and scattered hills.

The island and its approximately 350,000 inhabitants are divided into two administrative districts: **East Sumba**, in an area of about two-thirds of the island holds just one-third of the population; **West Sumba**, which receives notably more rainfall and is thus more fertile, sustains the majority of the Sumbanese.

East Sumba is rocky and mountainous and the **Massu** mountains here drain into the Watumbaka, the Payeti, the Kambaniru, and the Kamberu basins, all reaching the **Sumba Strait** near **Waingapu**, the eastern capital.

The cultural life of Sumba is distinguished by spectacular rituals, huge megalithic grave sites, unusual peaked houses, and beautiful ikat cloths. The island is one of the most culturally interesting places to visit in East Indonesia. Some of the island's beaches are excellent, and the rocky highlands provide great panoramic views of the coastline — but the traditional culture is one of the best reasons to visit.

WAINGAPU is the largest town on Sumba, the island's seaport, and the administrative capital of the East Sumba district. The bulk of the population is concentrated in the harbour area and about a kilometre inland, around the bus terminal and adjacent shops. The old pier, usually with a fair variety of inter-island craft docked, juts out across a little bay.

The capital of West Sumba is **WAIKABUBAK**. The area's ritual centre, **Tarung**, a hillcrest village just west of the commercial centre of town, is one of the headquarters of the **Marapu** religion and the site of some spectacular rituals.

In **Bondokodi** (or just Kodi), on the island's southwestern tip, you can see the tallest peak-roofed houses on Sumba, and **Anakalang** has the island's finest megalithic tombs.

Sumba

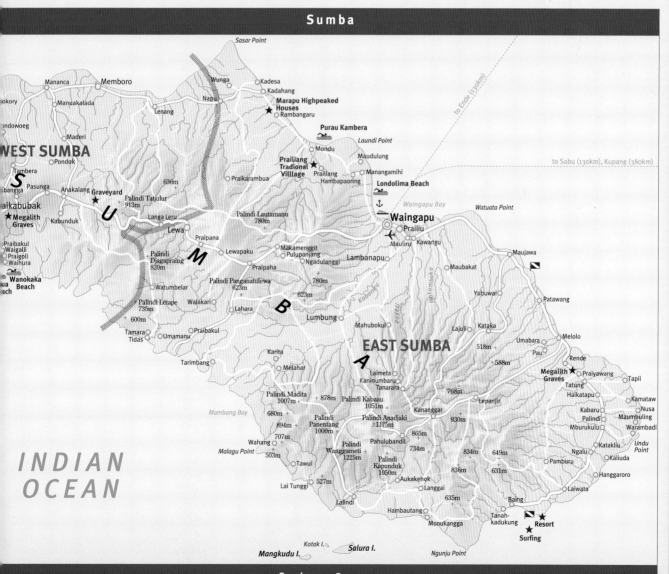

South China Sea

110°   115°

Kimanis B.

Kuala Penyu

**BRUNEI
DARUSSALAM**

Labuan I.   Kg. Mempakul

Beauf
Weston

BANDAR SERI BEGAWAN   Muara   *Brunei
Bay*   Labu

Seria   Kludang

Lawas
Trusan

50   100   150   200 km

50   100   miles

Laut I.

Lutong   Kuala Belait   Sukang   Mt. Mulu
1571m

Miri   Marudi   Longseridan

Salor I.   Teluk Butun

Natuna Besar I.   Binjai

Panarik   Niah   ★ Goa
Niah   Long Lama   Mt. Murud
2438m   Bareo

Longbawan

Lagong I.

Labang   Long Lellang

Natuna Islands

Bintulu   **MALAYSIA**

Mida I.   *Subi I.*

Subi Besar I.   Mukah   Balingian   Tatau   Tubau   *Sungai
Kayan-
Mentarang*

Panjang I.   *Sirik Pt.*   Dalat   Kejaman

Serasan I.   **Bruit I.**   **SARAWAK**   *Hose Mts.*

Serasan Strait   Sibu   Keranji   × Rumah Kulit   Datadian

Sarikei   Bitangor   Song   Kapit

Natuna Sea   *Datu Pt.*   *Datu Bay*   Kabong   Juliau   **MALAYSIA**   Longapung

Hutan
Sambas   Sematan   Betong   **INDONESIA**   Mt. Liangpran
2240m   Metulang

Paloh   **Kuching**   Mt. Lawit
1767m

Blawak   Bako National
Park   Simunjan   Gedong   Pantu   Bandar Sri Aman
(Simanggang)

Sambas   Bau   Siburan   Putusibau   Datah Dawai

Seluas   Serian   Entikong   *Luar L.*   Semitau   *Muller Mts.*   **K A L I M A N**

Pemangkat   Mt. Niyut
1701m   Mount Niyut
Reserve   Balaikarangan   *Ketungau R.*   **(B O R N E**

Singkawang   Bengkayang   Semang L.   Putisibau

Tambelan Besar I.   Mandon Reserve

Benua I.   Pinang   Ngabang   **WEST KALIMANTAN**   Semitau

Mempawah   Sosok   Sanggau   Longiram

Pontianak   Sintang

0°   *Kapuas R.*   Nanga Pinoh   *Padang Luwai
Nature Reserve*

Pontianak 68

Kertamulya   Tumbangkunyi   Purukcahu   Muaralahung   Lamben

Bengkolan Bay   Balaiberkuak   Mt. Raya
2278m   Benamang
Benangin

Teluk Tikar I.   Telukbatang   *Schwaner Mts.*   Seihanyu   Tumbanglahung

Nuri Bay   *Mount Palung*   Tumbangheran   Kualakurun   **Muarateweh**   Lampung

Penebangan I.   *Maya I.*   Sandal   Tumbangsenamang   Tumbangmiri

Pelapis I.   Sukadana   Tumbangmanjul   **CENTRAL KALIMANTAN**

Karimata Islands   Nangahtayap   Tumbangsamba   Tumbangtujuh   Pendang   Tabakkanilan

Karimata I.   Kudangan   Muarakayang   Buntok   Ampah   Mt. Sarempa
1380m

Serutu I.   Tapinbini   Kasongan   Tangkiling   Timpah   Tanjung   Kupangnunding
Kelua   Pangelah

**BANGKA
BELITUNG**   Ketapang   Nangabulik   Cempakamulia   Pilang   **Palangkaraya**   Amuntai   Baraba

Karimata Strait   Balairiam   Kotawaringin   Baamang   Pulangpisau

Kendawangan   Sukaraja   Kotawaringin   Sampit   Sanuda   Margasari

Tanjungpandan   Badau   Sukarama   × Pangkalanbuun   *Sembulu
Lake*   Telagapulang   Kualakapuas   Rantau

Liat I.   Manggar   Kumai   Sungaibaru   **Banjarmasin**

Lepar I.   Gantung   **Belitung**   *Bawal I.*   Kualajelai   Kumai Bay   *Sampit Bay*   Martapura   *Meratus Mts.*

Membalong   Dendang   *Gelam I.*   *Sambar Pt.*   *Air Hitam Bay*   *Tanjung Puting*   Kuin
Floating
Market   Banjar Baru   Lasung

Sebangau R.   *Damar I.*   Mt. Panggilingan
1101m   Mt. Aurbung
1150m

Keluang Pt.   *Kumai Bay*   *Sebangau Bay*   *Malacu Pt.*   Pelaihari   Kinta
Martapura   Jorong

Puting Pt.   *Selatan Pt.*   Babakan

Banjarmasin 68–69

110°   115°

Scale 1 : 5 400 000

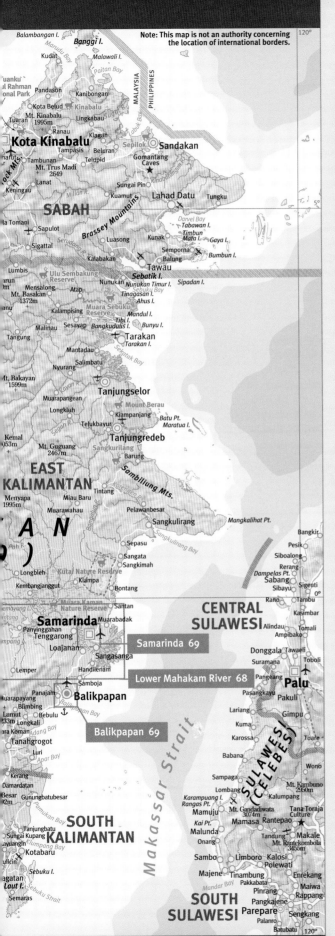

KALIMANTAN

Borneo is the world's third largest island (after Greenland and New Guinea) with a land of area of 746,309 sq km. The northern section of the island is not part of Indonesia, but forms the East Malaysian states of Sarawak and Sabah, as well as the tiny, oil-rich, independent sultanate of Brunei.

Kalimantan, which means "River of Diamonds" in Indonesian, is the name Indonesia gave to her two-thirds of the huge island of Borneo. It is a rugged land, through which flow tremendous rivers: including the **Kayan**, the **Mahakam**, the **Barito**, and the **Kahayan**. The region has abundant natural resources, many of which are still untapped, and is covered by one of the world's largest stretches of tropical rainforest. Although the region is home to just 5 percent of Indonesia's population, Kalimantan's 549,032 sq km represents 28 percent of the nation's land mass.

SAMARINDA

Samarinda, the capital of the East Kalimantan province, was founded by Buginese warrior-merchants who migrated from South Sulawesi at the beginning of the 18th century. It has grown to a city of some 50,000 and serves as both the government and commercial centre of the province. It is the point of departure for all river travel inland on the **Mahakam River** and its tributaries, as well as for flights to the interior — to the upper Mahakam and to the Apokayan region.

The **Mahakam River**, which is almost one kilometre wide here and as much as 90 metres deep, splits the town in half. A bridge now spans the river, a busy highway filled with log raft and ships of all sizes and types.

LOWER MAHAKAM RIVER

The Mahakam River and its tributaries reach far inland in **East Kalimantan**, providing access to relatively remote **Dayak** villages, including those in the area around and above Long Iram on the Mahakam, the area around **Long Segar** on the Kedang Kepala River, and to the Apokayan.

The city of **Tenggarong**, the former capital of the Kutai sultanate, now serves as the administrative headquarters of the huge **Kutai** district. The chief attraction here is the **Mulawarman Museum**, which is located on the site of the old palace of the Sultan of Kutai. The town of **Muaramuntai** is the regional centre for all trade, market activities and communications. **Tanjung Isuy**, the Dayak village most frequented by visitors, is also one of the last places in Borneo where traditional vegetable fibre cloth is still woven. **Muarapahu**, the next upriver town from Muaramuntai, sits at the confluence of the Mahakam River and the Pahu River. The **Kersik Luwai Orchid Reserve**, 16 km past Melak, boasts 110 species of orchids, including the unique "black" orchid.

BALIKPAPAN

East Kalimantan receives the greatest number of visitors, thanks to an infrastructure built for the oil industry. **Balikpapan** is an oil town — big, modern and relatively expensive. This city is Kalimantan's centre for transportation to and communications. The big refinery is next to the deep-water harbour, with the town proper covering the hills at the back of the bay.

BANJARMASIN

Banjarmasin is just 22 km from the Java Sea, and since portions of the city are below sea level, the city rises and falls with the tides. Originally, the city was completely river-oriented, and much of this is still evident today. Houses on stilts line the waterways which crisscross the capital. The **Martapura River** snakes through the city, a busy "main street" for a bewildering variety of boats. The floating vegetable and fruit market is a colourful bustle of boats. Banjarmasin has one of the best mosques in Kalimantan. The **Grand Mosque**, Sabilal Muhtadin, is set on a 10-hectare plot in the centre of the city, facing the Martapura River. The **Tanjung Puting Nature Reserve** in Central Kalimantan is relatively easy to reach and is a rewarding place to view wildlife. The reserve maintains two rehabilitation centres where orangutans which have been kept as illegal pets are readapted to jungle life.

PONTIANAK

A few kilometres from the sea, away from the coastal mangrove swamps, the city of **Pontianak** lies on the junction of the Kapuas and Landak Rivers. The **Jami Mosque** was erected a couple of centuries ago and reconstructions have remained faithful to the original layout. The sultan's palace, an impressive wooden structure, is just 100 metres away, and like the mosque, was built by order of Syarif Rahman. Around the market area and old Chinese quarter, there are several Taoist temples. Freighters berth at the **Dwikora** docks just downstream from the market area, while the more exotic Bugis schooners tie up opposite the sultan's palace. The **Provincial Museum** has a wealth of items relating to the local Malay culture and a fair number of Dayak pieces.

Kalimantan

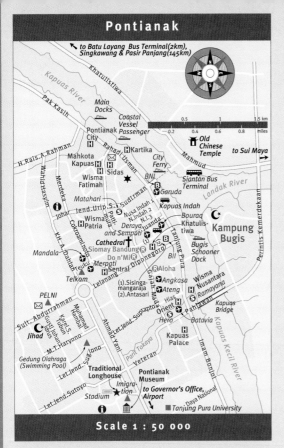

Pontianak

Scale 1 : 50 000

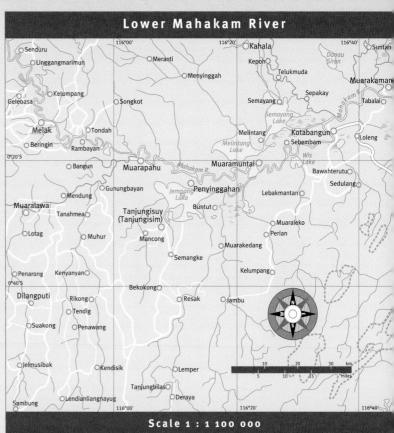

Lower Mahakam River

Scale 1 : 1 100 000

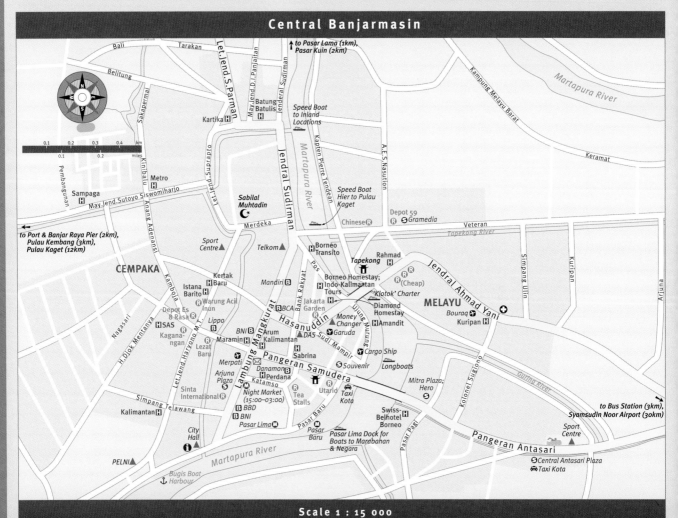

Central Banjarmasin

Scale 1 : 15 000

Lower Mahakam River

117°00'   117°20'   117°40'

Pancepoh
Sidomukti
Sumbersari
Sidomulyo
Sidomakmur
Sukamaju
Mulawarman
Gerenggung   Santan Point
Kersik Point
Sebuntal
Benuapahan
Beloro
Sebulu
Separi
Sambera
Bulukesi
Marangkayu Point
Loatebu
Bangunrejo
Manunggaljaya
Muarabadak
Simpangbadakbontang   0°20'S
Mangkurawang
Tenggarong
Telukdalam
Tanahmerah
Sungailantung
Saliki
Lerong Point
Kaeli Point
Muarakaeli
Lerong Island
Loakulu
Loabakung
Samarinda
Anggana
Mangkok Island
Tunu Island
Kebonsari
Loakulu
Margasari
Loajanan
Palaran
Perantang Island
Rempanga
Wargatunggal
Tumbanglungun Point   0°40'S
Sangasanga
Perangatan Island
Timbangbapasir Point
Tanimaju
Tanijaya
Nubi Island
Hutan Lindung Bukit Soeharto
Muarakembang
Handilenam
Kanyuran Island
Bayur Point
Sokeyan Point
Sungaimerdeka
Km.48
Muarajawa Ilir
Perangatan Island
Gunungpasir
Pamedasdalam   Ainung Pt.   Sembilang Point   Tanggi
117°00'   117°20'   117°40'

Scale 1 : 1 100 000

Samarinda

to University, Bontang Bus Terminal and MAF Office

0.2 0.4 0.6 0.8 km
0.2   0.4 miles

Panjaitan
S. Parman
A. Yani   Panjaitan
A. Vina S. Sutoyo
Mesra
Kesuma Bangsa
Lamin Indah
Andhika
Katak Tua
Pegunungan Maratus
Bitaharangata
Cempaka
Stadion
D. Senayang
Yarmidi
Dahlia
D.D.Mahinau
D.Poso
KH.A.Dahlan
D. Jempang
Bukit Barisan
Basuki Rahmat
D. Toba
D.Sartika
Merapi
Tirta Kencana
Milono
Basuki Rahmat
Musi
Barito
A. R. Hakim
Arjuna
Rahayu
Kayan
Brantas
Merapi
Semeru
W.R Supratman
Mas Mul Lara
Kapuas
Aminah Syukur
Wisma Pirus
Abdul Hasan
Hayani
Diponegoro
Imam Bonjol
Sudirman
Sewarga Indah
Hidaya
Sula-wesi
Kattini
Merpati
Jakarta I
P. See
batik
Hidayatullah
Gajah Mada
Veteran
Panglima Batur
Pelabuhan Flores
Niaga Timur
Pondok Indah
to Longboard Pier and Brigde to Balikpapan (Further Upriver)
Citra Niaga
Dibermaga
Mulawarman
P. Samosir
Speedboat Terminal
Yos Sudarso
Shakhodavatan
Mahakam River
Pelni Harbour
Taxi and Bus Terminal
Bendahara
to Balikpapan
Hasanuddin
Cokroaminoto
SEBARANG

Scale 1 : 30 000

Banjarmasin Area

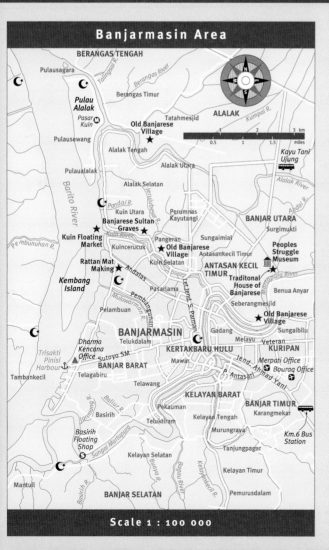

BERANGAS TENGAH
Pulausagara
Talingai R.   Berangas River
Berangas Timur
Pulau Alalak
Pasar Kuin
Tatahmesjid
Kumpai R.
ALALAK
Old Banjarese Village
1 2 3 km
0.5   1.5   miles
Pulausewang
Alalak Tengah
Kayu Tani Ujung
Pulaualalak
Alalak Utara
Alalak Selatan
Alalak River
Andai R.
Barito River
Kuin Utara
Perumnas Kayutangi
BANJAR UTARA
Pandai R.
Banjarese Sultan Graves
Pangeran
Sungaimal
Surgimukti
Kuin Floating Market
Kuincerucuk
Old Banjarese Village
Antasankecil Timur
P embunuhan R.
Rattan Mat Making
Kuin Selatan
ANTASAN KECIL TIMUR
Peoples Struggle Museum
Kembang Island
Andatas
Pasarlama
Traditonal House of Banjarese
Pembunuman R.
Pelambuan
Benua Anyar
BANJARMASIN
Telukdalam
Gadang
Seberangmesjid
Old Banjarese Village
Trisakti Pinisi Harbour
Dharma Kencana Office
Sutoyo SM
KERTAKBARU HULU
Melayu
Sungaibilu
Tambankecil
BANJAR BARAT
Telagabiru
Mawar
Veteran
KURIPAN
Jend. Ahmad Yani
Merpati Office
Telawang
P. Antasari
Bouraq Office
KELAYAN BARAT
Pekauman
Km.6 Bus Station
Basirih
Kelayan Tengah
Karangmekar
Basirih Floating Shop
Teluktiram
Murungraya
Sungai Martapura
Kelayan Selatan
Tanjungpagar
Buoya R.
Kelayan Timur
Mantuil
Basili R.
Baltiur R.
Kelayengkecil R.
Pemurusdalam
BANJAR SELATAN

Scale 1 : 100 000

Balikpapan

to Kilometer 5 Intercity Bus Station and Samarinda
Samarinda
Suprapto
Art Shop
Balikpapan
Blue Sky
Supermarket
Karang Anyar
Negara
Fire Station
0.5 1 1.5 2 km
0.5   1   miles
Attaka
Bemo to Intercity Bus Station
Bongas 1
Bongas 2
Wonokromo
Minyak
Mama
Karang Rejo 1
Pertamina Oil Complex
Aida
Balikpapan Bay
Karang Jawa
Bumi
Karang Bugis
Gunung Kawi
Long Iks
Tirta Plaza
Gunung Guntur
Prabumulih
Gunung Pancur
Martadinata
Passenger Dock
TVRI
S. Parman
Harbour Bemo Station
to Airport
Gunung Dubbs
Sengir
Dumai
Banda
P. Tendean
Budiman
Antasari
Pelayaran
Prapatan
Sutoyo
Mirama
Benakutai
Sport
V & W
Sentosali
Sudirman
Sentosa
Sederhana
Balikpapan
Bahtera
Yos Sudarso
Achmad Yani
Klandasan Market
Gajah Mada
Makassar Strait

Scale 1 : 70 000

Celebes Sea

Manadotud

Bunaken

Manado City 75

Manado Region 74

Pelawanbesar

Sangkulirang

Mangkalihat Point

Sangkulirang Bay

Binar Pt. Santigi

Binontoan Dako Pt.

Mt. Dako 2304m

Bukaan

Dako I.

Dondo Bay

Bilang Bay

Kwandang Bay

Amuran

NORTH SULAWESI

Ogotua

Bilo

Tolitoli

Bonobogu

Paleleh Bolontio

Boroko Inobonto

Ongkaw

Bangklr

Bambapuang

Mt. Malino 2499m

Mt. Tentolomanian 2065m

Blawu

Kwandang

Molombulahe Issimu

Limboto

Lake Limboto

Dumoga Bone National Park

Maelang Mount Ambang Reserve

Kotamobagu

Pesik Mt. Sonjal 2525m

Siboluton

Ongka

Marisa Tabulo

Bilungala

Pinogu Mt. Bulawa 1970m

Imandi

Siboa

Palasa

Lamito

Taluda Negerilima

Rerang

Tinombo

Moutong

Tanjung Panjang Reserve

Gorontalo

GORONTALO

Dampelas Pt.

Sibayu

Sigenti

Tambu

Rano

Kasimbar

Unauna I.

Togian Islands

Malenge I.

Waleabahi I.

Molucca Sea

Tomali

Talatakoh I.

Togian I.

Boalemo

Alindau

Ampibabo

Tomini Bay (Gorontalo)

Batudaka I.

Puah I.

Walea Strait

Mayapap

Siuna Teku

Donggala

Tawaeli Toboli

Tanjung Api Reserve

Dondo

Ampoa

Bunta

Poh Sirong

Poh Bay

Balo

Surumana

Palu

Torue

Uebonti Bay

Masapi Tobelombang

Baloa

Luwuk

Peleng Strait

Sabang

Pangeang

CENTRAL SULAWESI

Lore Lindu National Park

Pakuli

Podi

Kintom

Batui

Toili

Luksagu

Peleng I.

Pasangkayu

Mapane

Poso

Poso Bay

Tobamawu

Mt. Katoposa 2835m

Salea

Dongin Kembani

Bulagi

Tinagkung

Banggai I.

Todeli

Lariang

Sedoa

Tongku

Uekuli

Malino

Morowali Reserve

Pola

Labobo I.

Bangkurung I.

Taduno

Matanga

Masoni I.

Wayhay

Kuma

Gimpu

Wosa

Tentena

Mt. Tenamatua 2563m

Watambayoli

Baturube

Marowo

Salue Timpaus Strait

Melilis I.

Timpaus I.

Karossa

Doda

Toare

Taripa

Kolonodale

Tolo Bay

Salue Besar I.

Salue Kecil I.

SULAWESI (CELEBES)

Lake Poso

Pendolo

Peruhumpenai Mts. Reserve

Tompira

Salonsa

Bawokan Islands

Babana

Tana Toraja 73

Wono

Kangkela

Mt. Baleasi 3016m

Tinompo

Watta

Nuha

Sampaga

Mt. Kambuno 2950m

Maleku

Lake Matano

Matano Reserve

Bungku

Karampuang I.

Lombang

Kalumpang

Masamba

Bonebone

Wotu

Saroako

Bahodopi

Rangas Point

Mamuju

Mt. Gandadiwata 3074m

Sabbang

Lorana

Malili

Lake Towuti

Ngalo Point

Mamasa

Tana Toraja Culture

Rantepao

Palopo

Lingkeh

Langkobale

Pombangi

Salabangka Islands

Malunda

Rantepao 73

Makale

Latowu

Padalere

Padeabesar I.

Bondebonde

Padangsappa

Abuki Mts.

Wawolandawe

Matarape Bay

SOUTH SULAWESI

Balopa

Malamala

Asera

Labengke I.

Manui I.

Somba

Kalosi

Polewali

Cimpu

Latimojong Mts. Reserve

Sanggona

Asolu

Bahubulu I.

Majene Tinambung

Enrekang

Maiwa

Siwa

Lasusua

Mt. Mengkoka 2790m

Tinobu

Toreo

North Banda Basin

Mandar Bay

Pakkabata

Rappang

Wawo

Latoma

Pinrang

Sidenreng

Anabanua Jalang

Twoimenda

Wawotobi

Kendari

Wowoni Island

Parepare

Sidenreng

Lake Sidenreng

Bone Bay

Kolaka

Raterate

Pulupanda

Batumea

Munse

Palanro

Batubatu

Sengkang

Lake Tempe

Padamarang I.

Maniang I.

Tambea

Embeipua

Benua

Kolono

Labuhantobelo

Buton Utara Reserve

Watansoppeng

Pampanua

Rawa Aopa Watumohae National Park

Punggaluku

Torobuku

Lambale

Pekkae

Taccipi

Lalebata

Watampone

Bajo

Bontobonto

Benrongeng

Ponreng

SOUTHEAST SULAWESI

Matausu

Daule

Tampo

Raha

Bonelipu

Pangkajene

Camming

Palattae

Taori

Bupinang

Kambara

Waogena

Buton Island

Maros

Palatta

Bugingkalo

Muna Island

Lasalimu

Kolowana Watobo Bay

Makassar

Waterfall & Cave

Sinjai

Kabaena Strait

Lambubalano

Napabale Lagoon

Bungi

Wangiwangi I.

Runduma I.

Makassar 71

Bantimurung

Mt. Lompobattang 2876m

Kassi

Dongkala

Lombe

Mawasangka

Wokole

Pasarwajo

Kamponaone

Sungguminasa

Bantimurung Reserve

Mt. Lompobattang Reserve

Bira

Baubau

Sampolawa

Lintea Tiwolu I.

Kaledupa I.

Tomea I.

Pattallassang

Bantaeng

Bissapu Waterfall

Liukanglu I.

Telagabesar I.

Kabaena Island

Kadatuang I.

Batauga

Siumpu I.

Marine Reserve

Binongko I.

Jeneponto

Bulukumba

Bontosunggu

Tanakeke I.

Tukang Besi Islands

Southwestern Sulawesi 72

Selayar Island

Bahuluang I.

Apatana

Benteng

Batuata I.

Moromaho

Makassar Strait

N E S W

25 50 75 100 125 km

25 50 75 miles

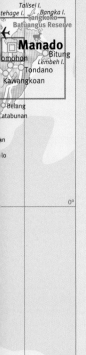

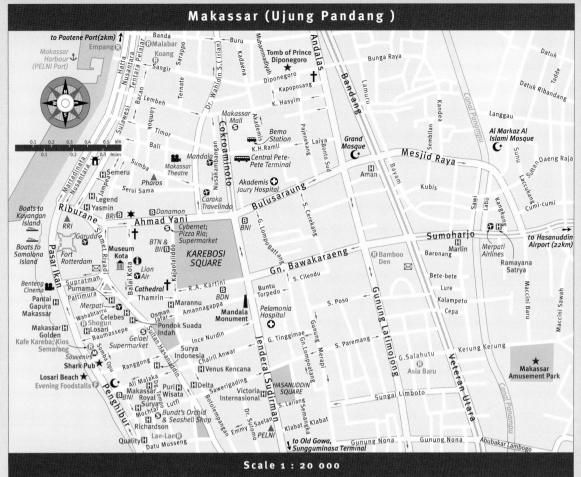

Scale 1 : 20 000

SULAWESI

The peninsulas of Sulawesi — once known as the Celebes — reach out into the Sulawesi, Maluku, Banda, and Flores Seas. Within its odd, contorted outlines—the product of the collision of ancient continents— are extraordinary landscapes. Rugged mist-covered mountains, tropical rainforest, rice terraces, and deep lakes dominate the interior. Along the coast, coral reefs encircle dormant volcanoes, while white sandy beaches fringed with coconut trees and scattered fishing villages are flanked by rugged limestone outcroppings.

The total land area of Sulawesi and its adjacent islands is 227,000 sq km. The distance from the northernmost island, **Miangas** to the southernmost, **Satengar**, is nearly 2,000 km.

VOLCANOES Most of the island lies above 500 m and fully one-fifth lies above the 1,000-metre mark. The highest peaks are found in Central and northern South Sulawesi; the island's highest point is on **Mt. Rantemario**, north of **Enrekang**, at 3,450 m. Sulawesi has 11 active volcanoes and many fumaroles and volcanic springs. The most active are Soputan-Aeseput, Lokon-Empung, and Gunung Api Siau on the island of Siau, between the mainland and Sangihe Island.

NATURAL RESOURCES Sulawesi has considerable mineral deposits. Parts of the north are currently experiencing a gold rush, oil has been found south of the eastern arm of Sulawesi near Luwuk and large reserves of natural gas exist near **Lake Tempe**. **Buton Island** off Southeast Sulawesi holds Asia's largest deposits of natural asphalt. The island's largest mine, at **Soroako** on the shores of Lake Matana, is a huge deposit of low-grade nickel.

LAKES Sulawesi has 13 lakes of more than 5 sq km surface area, including Towuti and Poso, the second and third largest lakes in Indonesia. In the wet season, **Lake Tempe** rivals **Lake Poso** in size. Some are extremely deep, such as **Lake Matana**; the bottom of which, 540 m from the surface, lies 160 m below sea level.

REEFS The reefs around **Bunaken** and neighbouring islands off **Manado** in the north are easily accessible. Less well-known are the unique coral reefs of the **Togian Islands** in Tomini Bay and the spectacular, remote, and little-disturbed reefs and shoals of the **Tukang Besi** Islands in Southeast Sulawesi.

WILDLIFE Sulawesi is home to an imcomparable range of wildlife which can be seen in any of the national parks, including the **Lore Lindu National Park** in Central Sulawesi and the **Tangkoko-Batuangus-Dua Saudara Reserve** and the **Dumoga Bone National Park** in North Sulawesi. 62 percent of Sulawesi's native mammal species and 88 species of birds are found only on Sulawesi.

Makassar

Makassar is the largest city and communications centre east of Surabaya. It is the focal point not only for the populous province of South Sulawesi, but for the thousands of islands and hundreds of ethnic groups which make up the social fabric of eastern Indonesia.

The massive walls of the waterfront Dutch fortress formerly known as **Fort Rotterdam** guard fine buildings of the 17th to 18th centuries. Now a museum and cultural centre, the "Benteng" houses offices of the Indonesian Archaeological Service. The **Makassarese**, the **Bugis**, and the **Mandar** are the great seafaring peoples of Indonesia. Their ships are remarkable for their sturdiness and grace, the result of the exceptional skill of the builders who fashion these heavy ships purely from wood. Many styles of fishing and sailing boats ply the seafront in the harbour of **Makassar**, giving the town a unique charm and ambience.

TANA TORAJA

After some 130 km of hugging the coastline of South Sulawesi, the long highway heading north from Ujung Pandang begins its winding ascent to the mountains. Out of **Parepare**, the road to **Rantepao** turns inland and begins to wind steeply upwards into the rolling hills. Past the "gateway" arch of **Tana Toraja**, the road opens onto a hilly plateau, then begins its gradual 200-m descent into the **Makale** and **Rantepao** valleys and a majestic landscape of rugged grey granite outcrops and distant blue mountains.

Karampuang Island
Rangas Point
Tapandulu
Ujung Lumpatang
Ngalo Point
Pasabu · Tapalang

Lombang
Tasio
Tanete Rantekalua 986m
Balakalumpang
Saluena Salusokan
Taludu
914m
Buttu Ulutaang 945m
Buttu Ulutaang 1313m
1012m
2531m
1965m

Tanete Patawe 1130m
Tanete Pelatang 2986m
3037m
2176m
Mt. Gandadiwata 3074m
+2117m
2438m
2335m
Rindingallo
Buttu Kapusaang +1519m

Pattung
Limbong
Lasa
Tanete Siraun 2462m
Buntu Barada 2580m
Buntu Mabi 1740m
2328m
Taba
Sangkaropi
Rantepang

Buntu Tabang +1369m Buntu Raketabuan 1335m
Sabbang
Tandung
Dangang
Bundu Bajai 1324m
Seponbuntu Lamasi
Walenrang
Tulungasari
586m
Sukamaju
Bonebone
Lata
Mangale
Bondesawa
Amassangan
Munte
Pangko
Pasorongan to Teluk Ussu Estuary

Mamuju
X
Mamasa
Tandialo
Mambi
Deking
Buttu Panda 1336m

Quarles Mountains
Rantepao
Tana Toraja Culture ★
Bittuang
Sipatte
Rea
Karoan
Tangratte
Paurrungan

Rantepang
TANA TORAJA
Batan
★ Typical Torajan Villages
Ampadang
Sanggala
Getengan
Makale
1468m
Buakayu

Batusitanduk
Tokaili
Batu Putih
Palopo
Beringinjaya
Padangkalua
Bua
Lamikomiko Estuary

Bone Bay

Malunda
935m
Udung Point
Bondebonde
Salutambung
Kolendang
1517m
Buttu Tamanipi 1181m
Buttu Tamedingin 1296m

Balambang
Sumarorong
Buttu Parinding 2619m
+2020m
1743m
Buttu Jolenata 1743m
Buttu Waylimbong 1743m

Mangngi
Tangratte
1468m
Buakayu
Buttu Ambeso 194m
Lumbaja

Buntu Tampatena 912m
Buttu Tabang 832m
Beuma
Padangsappa
Ponrang Estuary
Ponrang
Bauma
Patedong
Olang Pt.
Banejambong Pt.
Buntu Miraring 893m
Babana
Cilallang
Belopa
Cimpu

Puppuuring 1209m
Somba
Apoleang
Galunggalung
Majene
Kalitarung
Pandengpareng
Andau
Capego
Bumbung
Paleloan
Campalagian
Tinambung

Wonomulyo
Polewali
Kayuanging
Lampuko/ Mampie Reserve
Panampeang Island

Salu Mappak
Belajen
Patongan
Buntu Rantemario 3478m
Dadeko
Baraka
Dantemalua
+2674m
Tibusan
Latimojong Mts. Reserve
Buntu Malici 1513m
Bajo
Lempokasi
Larompong

Rampusa
Karawa
Buttu Talubenua 2165m
Cakke
780m
Panassang
Buttu Pasapai 1534m
907m

1207m

Enrekang

Mandar Strait
Sadang Estuary

Buttu Kassa
Buttu Tirasa 985m
Lampa
Cempapasar
Pinrang
Langnga

Harapankarya
Ujunglero
Lappakaka

SOUTH SULAWESI
1348m
Tambolang
Botto Tallu 3086m
Botto Lebu +1322m
680m

Siwa
Lokoloko Point
to Susua

Malimpung
Teppo
Baranti
Rappang
Lapalopo
Uluale
Maiwa
Larumpu
Tanrutedong
Anabanua
Posselloreng

to Kolaka
Pusung Marasanga
Pusung Tellang

to Kolaka

Makassar Strait

to Balikpapan, Pantoloan, Samarinda

to Batulicin

Sidenreng
Amparita
Parepare
Bilokka
Bulu Botu
Torong Batu 827m
Bulu Palicu
Palanro 984m
Wawagulung
Mangkoso
Donridonri

Paria
Jalang

Lake Shadereng
Tamparang Lapompaka

Sengkang
★ Silk Weaving
Maroanging
Tamparang Palisu
Kotabaru
Lakamporo
Tawaru
Pampanua

Lake Tempe

Watansoppeng
Panikiang Island
Coppo Mabolae +1253m
Galung
1465m
Kessi
Nampo
Cabbenge
Cangadi
Tokaseng
Uloe ★ Mampu Caves
Pallime

Pekkae
Ralla
1030m
Jembulu
Takalala
Taccipi
Macope
Kampung Tenga
Bajoe
Watampone

Tamarupa Barat
Segeri
Bontobonto
Bulu Marukuruku 1335m
Lalebata
Benrongeng
Lawelu
573m
Ponreng
Apala
Matango
Pattiro Bajo
Ujung Patitiro

Binangatoa
Labakkang
Lejang
Tumampua
Toceppa
812m
Tanabatue
802m
Buludua

Pangkajene
607m
Padangtanga
Camba
Kalibong
640m
1687m
Camming
Bulubulu
Kadai
Ujung Salangketo

Barrang Caddi Island
Talawe
Kasuarang
Bantimurung Reserve
Camba
Palattae

Maros
Mandai
Bantimurung
★ Waterfall, Caves
Bulu Bualo 1504m
824m
Kahu
Balange
Bojo
Sinjai
Samataring
Batanglempe Island
Sembilan Islands
Kambuno Island
Burungloe Island

to Banjarmasin, Batulicin

Makassar (Ujungpandang)
Fort Rotterdam & Museum ★
Sungguminasa
Ballalompoa Museum
Bontolebang
Limbung
Galesong
Pattallasang
Satanga Island
Bauluang Island
Takalar
Cilalang
Mangadu

Biringkanaya
Bontobotoa
Parang
558m
Patuku
618m

1110m
1140m
Bulu Balang
Bili Resort
Malino
Mt. Lompobattang 2871m
Mt. Lompobattang Reserve
Malakaji
905m
Bulupodo
Lappadata
Amesangeng
Tanete
Bikeru
Batusantung
Kassi
Tanuntung
Hilahila
Tanahberu

Jakarta, Semarang, Surabaya

Tanekeke Island
Ujung Pepe
Laikang Bay
Ujung Mangasa
Malasoro Bay

Mangkoso
Malakaji
Pukangan
Panaikang
Bontowa
Togotogo
Teneta
Jenep@sh to Badas, Baubau, Bonerate, Labuanbajo, Maumere
Jeneponto

Pullaweng
Gantarangkeke
Bissapu Waterfall ★
Bantaeng
Ujungkatingting
Ponre
Bontosunggu

Balantieng River
Bulukumba
Bira
Ujung Bira
Liukanglu Island

N
W · E
S

10 20 30 40 50 km
10   20   30 miles

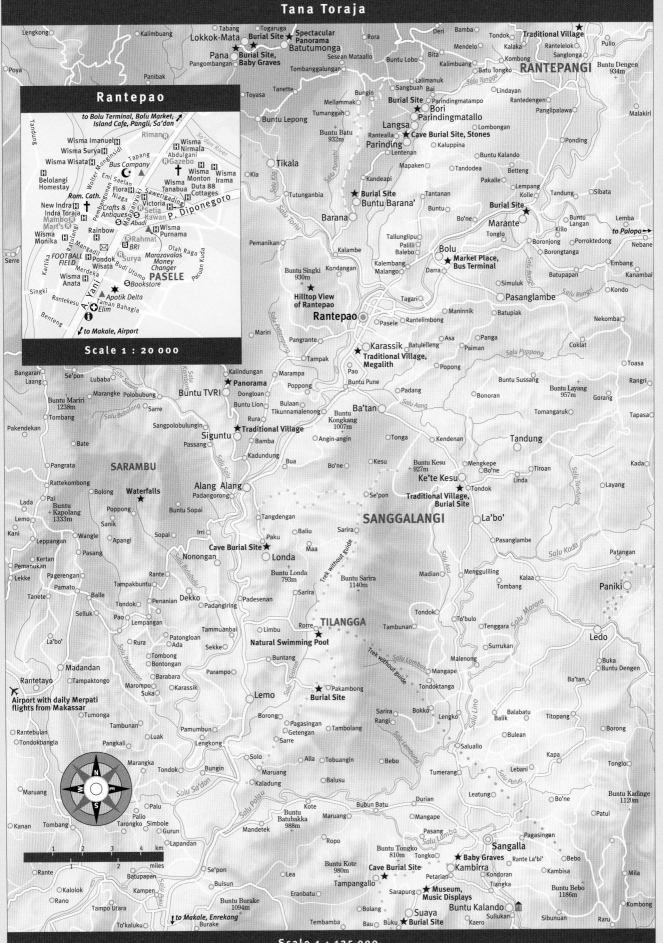

Sulawesi

74

Celebes Sea

Likupang Strait

Bangka Island

Nain I.

Lehaga I.

Gangga I.

Sahaong Pt.

Tarabitan Pt.

Tarabitan

Serei

Korakora Bay

Bokol Pt.

Sonsilo

Mobune

Montehage I.

Montehage

Tinabunan I.

Munte

Tamperong I.

Likupang

Mokotamba Pt.

Pulisan Pt.

Planned Site for NDC

Paputungan

Lantung

Werot

Maen

Likupang Paradise

**Bunaken-Manado Tua
Marine Park**

Bulo

Darunu

Budo

Talawan Bajo

Kokoleh

Rondor

Pinenek

Mogogimbun I.

*Manadotua
Island*

Manadotua

Bunaken I.

Siladeng I.

Wori

Patokoan

Wanguran

Batuputih

Bunaken

Pisok Pt.

Mt. Tumpa
637m

Sam Ratulangi
Airport

Waterfall

Dimembe

Pinasungkulan

**Tangkoko-Batuangus-
Duasaudara Reserve**

Mt. Batuangus
+1109m

to Paleleh

Barracuda Diving

Molas

Nusantara Dive Center (NDC)

Mapanget

Talawaan

Mt. Tandei
743m

Manado Bay

Manado

Klabat

Duasudara

Mt. Duasudara
+1351m

Makawidei

Malalayang

Mt. Klabat
1995m

Danowudu

Madidir

Kunkungan
Bay Resort

Tanduk Rusa

Bitung

Kalesei Pt.

Murex Dive Centre

Tateli

Girian

Tanjung
Merah

Aer Tembaga

Papusungan

Lembeh Island

Manado Beach

Tanawangko

Pineleng

Tuanku
Imam Bonjol
Grave

Airmadidi

Kauditan

Dua I.

Tinoor

Liang

Sawangan

Lembean

to Kwandang, Lirung, Tahuna, Tolitoli

Mt. Lokon
1595m

Tembona

Mt. Mahawu
1311m

Waterfall

Waruga

Ranotongkor

Kakaskasen

Rurukan

Woloan

Tomohon

Temboan

Kema

Taratara

Kasuang

Japanese Cave

Makalisung

to Ternate

Tondano

Mt. Kaluta
1179m

Rerer

*Lake
Linau*

Lahendong

Mt. Tompusu
1202m

Leilem

Tounsaru

Tandengan

Sonder

Kombi

Rumoong

Remboken

Karumenga

Eris

Japanese Cave

Pulutan

Tulap

*Lake
Tondano*

Kawangkoan

Toraget

Kakas

Watulaney

Molucca Sea

Watu Pinabetengan

Tompaso

Kotamenara

Langowan

Mt. Kaweng
1179m

Teep

Mt. Soputan
1830m

Wailang

Pinarut

Rarumis

Mt. Manimporok
1661m

Pangu

Mt. Kawatak
1179m

Mahembang

Tombatu

Wongkat

Bukit Tinggi

Mundung

to Banggai, Gorontalo

2.5 5 7.5 10 12.5 km

2.5 5 7.5 miles

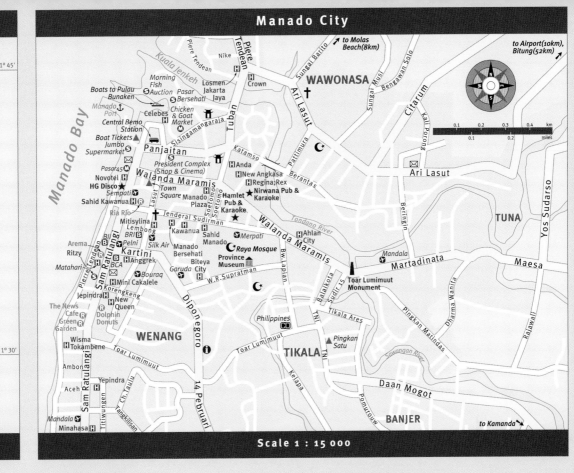

Scale 1 : 15 000

MANADO

North Sulawesi is one of the most prosperous and scenic areas in Indonesia. Made up of two large districts (Minahasa and Bolaang Mongondow) and one smaller one (the Sangihe-Talaud Islands), the province of North Sulawesi occupies the long (350 km) and narrow (average width is only 50 km) northern arm of the island.

Much of the beauty and fertility of the region derives from its towering volcanoes. Many are extinct or dormant, but **Mt. Lokon** near Tomohon erupted in 1986 and 1991, and **Mt. Soputan** in central Minahasa in 1989. Earth tremors are not at all uncommon. The volcanoes are responsible for the exceptionally fertile soils that are the province's major economic asset. Agriculture in the form of coconut, clove and nutmeg tree cultivation, forms the basis for great wealth in many parts of the province.

Minahasa, the hinterland of Manado, is the most heavily populated and highly developed district. Only 20 percent of its land remains under forest cover and the population density has soared to over 300 persons per sq km—less than half that of Java, but still high. The Minahasa area is extremely mountainous, but has a narrow coastal fringe where coconuts thrive, and an interior plateau around **Lake Tondano** (altitude 600 m; surface area 46 sq km), where irrigated rice fields provide abundant harvests.

The fame of the reefs of the **Bunaken** group has spread among lovers of the underwater world. And rightly so: the 75,000 ha **Bunaken-Manado Tua Marine Park**, one hour by boat from Manado, offers excellent snorkelling and scuba diving. The clear waters harbour a tremendous amount of marine life —reef fishes in great variety, healthy, diverse coral growth and just about every invertebrate on the evolutionary scale, from sponges to squids.

The hilltop town of **Tomohon**, known locally as the "City of Flowers" sits in a saddle between two volcanoes, **Lokon** and **Mahawu**. The climate is temperate and suited for the fruits and a wide range of flowers that are grown commercially to supply markets in Manado.

Just beyond **Airmadidi**, east of Manado, a road to the right leads south to **Tondano**. The village of **Sawangan**, just further on, is the site of the largest collection of ancient sarcophagi, or waruga, in the province.

Tondano town, the administrative centre of the Minahasa region, lies on the northern shores of Lake Tondano. Smaller roads from Tondano skirt both shores of the lake and a trip all the way around it provides ever-changing vistas of the nearby mountains, rice fields and the lake itself.

The road south of Tomohon to **Sonder** passes first through **Lahendong**, where seething energy just below the earth's surface is dramatically apparent. With ominously hissing fissures and gurgling pools of mud, there is a primeval feel about the site; the sulfuric odours are powerful.

South of Sonder and Kawangkoan toward Langowan lies **Watu Pinabetengan**— a stone believed to be the most spiritually powerful site in Minahasa. Through the ages, this site has been a politically potent gathering spot for Minahasan leaders. Pictographic carvings on the stone have never been deciphered and most had unfortunately already been encased in concrete along with much of the stone before the government declared it a public monument. Ceremonies involving chicken and pig sacrifices are still held during the full moon, and people come here to consult with the spirits of their deceased ancestors.

Mt. Klabat, located directly to the east of Manado, a dormant volcano, is the highest peak in Minahasa. At 1,995 m it offers fine views from the summit across the entire northern end of the peninsula.

The entire tip of the peninsula to the north and east of Mt. Klabat is covered in lush, tropical rainforests which have been declared a nature reserve. The **Tangkoko-Batuangus-Dua Saudara Reserve**, as it is known (the name refers to three peaks in the reserve) encompasses 9,000 ha ranging from sea level up to 1,100 m. This is a spectacular area which offers one the possibility to see not only some of Sulawesi's unique animals and plants, but also a wealth of corals and fishes.

Bitung is the other main point of interest in this area. Neatly laid out with wide boulevards, it boasts two bizarre replicas of the Eiffel Tower and a striking church. Bitung is the main port of North Sulawesi and has a fine natural harbour protected by the island of Lembeh. It is also the centre for commercial fishing in the region.

MANADO CITY

Manado, bustling capital of North Sulawesi province, sprawls inland across low, palm-clad hills around a wide bay fringed with luxuriant tropical vegetation. In the distance, a backdrop of three volcanoes completes the city's spectacular setting. As a service and administrative centre for the entire province, it is also the site of numerous educational institutions, banks, and government offices. The **North Sulawesi Provincial Museum** on Jl. WR. Supratman has interesting displays of historical and cultural relics from all around the province.

Maluku (The Moluccas)

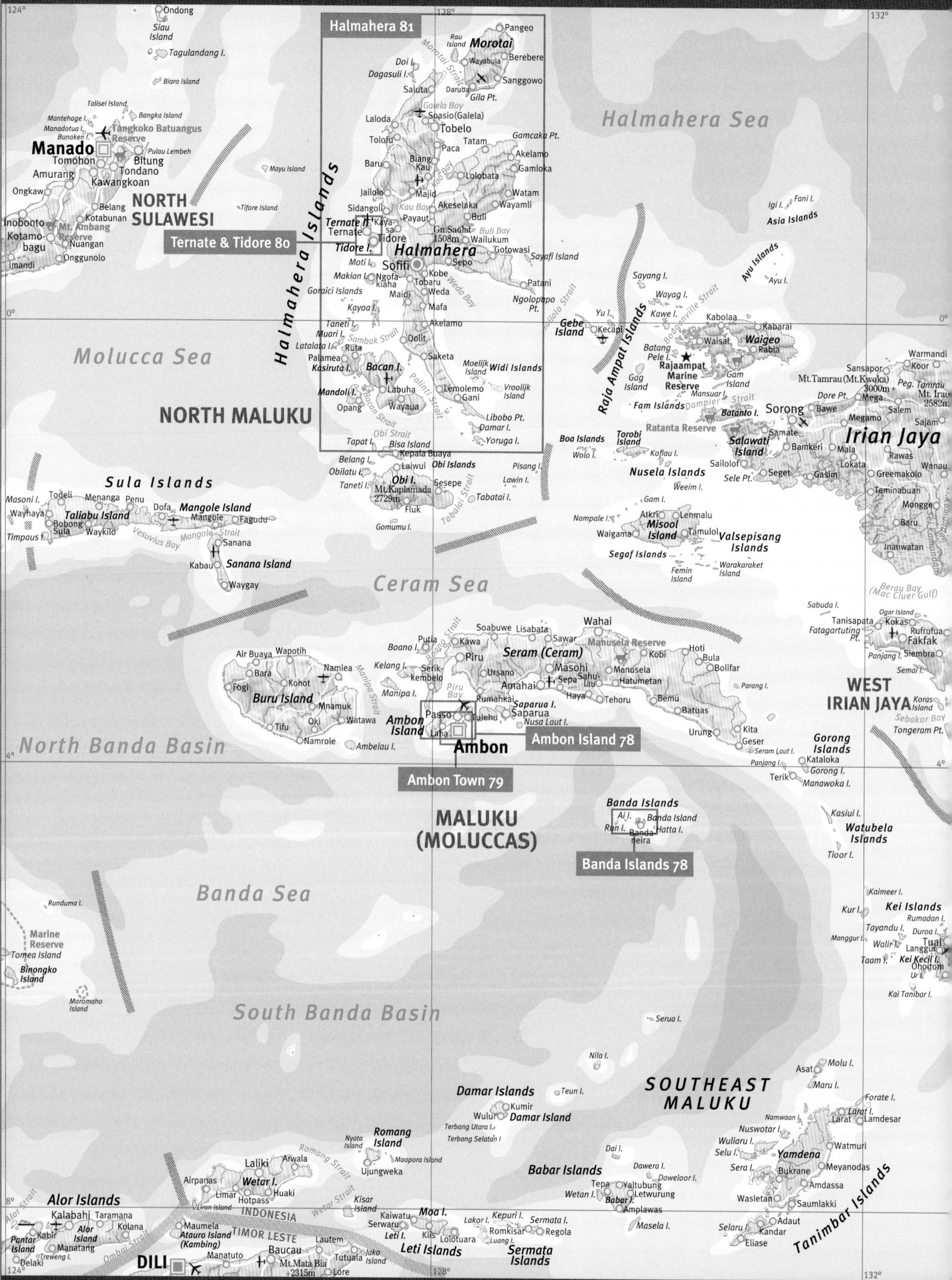
Halmahera 81
Ternate & Tidore 80
Ambon Island 78
Ambon Town 79
Banda Islands 78
Halmahera Sea
Molucca Sea
Ceram Sea
North Banda Basin
Banda Sea
South Banda Basin
NORTH SULAWESI
NORTH MALUKU
MALUKU (MOLUCCAS)
SOUTHEAST MALUKU
WEST IRIAN JAYA
Irian Jaya
INDONESIA
TIMOR LESTE
Ondong
Siau Island
Tagulandang I.
Biaro Island
Talisei Island
Bangka Island
Mantehage I.
Manadotua I.
Bunaken I.
Tangkoko Batuangus Reserve
Manado
Tomohon
Bitung
Pulau Lembeh
Amurang
Tondano
Kawangkoan
Mayu Island
Ongkaw
Belang
Kotabunan
Tifore Island
Inobonto
Mt. Ambang Reserve
Kotamobagu
Nuangan
Onggunolo
Imandi
Halmahera Islands
Pangeo
Rau Island
Morotai
Morotai Strait
Wayabula
Berebere
Doi I.
Dagasuli I.
Sanggowo
Saluta
Daruba
Gila Pt.
Galela Bay
Soasio (Galela)
Loloda
Tobelo
Tolofu
Tatam
Gamcaka Pt.
Paca
Akelamo
Baru
Biang
Kau
Gamlaka
Lolobata
Jailolo
Majid
Watam
Sidangoli
Kau Bay
Akeselaka
Wayamli
Ternate I.
Kayasa
Payaut
Buli
Ternate
Gn.Saolat 1508m
Buli Bay
Wailukum
Tidore I.
Tidore
Halmahera
Gotowasi
Sayafi Island
Moti I.
Sofifi
Sepo
Makian I.
Ngofakiaha
Kobe
Tobaru
Weda Bay
Patani
Goraici Islands
Maidi
Weda
Ngolopopo Pt.
Kayoa I.
Mafa
Jailolo Strait
Taneti I.
Akelamo
Muari I.
Sambak Strait
Latalata I.
Ruta
Dolit
Palamea
Saketa
Kasiruta I.
Bacan I.
Moelijk Island
Widi Islands
Mandoli I.
Labuha
Lemolemo
Vroolijk Island
Opang
Wayaua
Gani
Bacan Strait
Patinti Strait
Libobo Pt.
Damar I.
Obi Strait
Tapat I.
Bisa Island
Yoruga I.
Kepala Buaya
Belang I.
Laiwui
Obi Islands
Obilatu I.
Obi I.
Sesepe
Pisang I.
Taneti I.
Mt.Kaplamada 2729m
Lawin I.
Tabatai I.
Fluk
Tobalai Strait
Gomumu I.
Sula Islands
Masoni I.
Todeli
Menanga
Penu
Dofa
Mangole Island
Wayhaya
Taliabu Island
Mangole
Fagudu
Bobong
Sula
Waykilo
Timpaus I.
Vesuvius Bay
Mangole Strait
Sanana
Kabau
Sanana Island
Waygay
Yu I.
Gebe Island
Kecapi
Raja Ampat Islands
Sayang I.
Wayag I.
Kawe I.
Bougainville Strait
Ayu Islands
Ayu I.
Igi I.
Fani I.
Asia Islands
Kabolaa
Kabarai
Waisai
Waigeo
Rabia
Batang Pele I.
Rajaampat Marine Reserve
Gag Island
Gam Island
Mansuar I.
Dampier Strait
Fam Islands
Batanto I.
Sorong
Ratanta Reserve
Boa Islands
Torobi Island
Salawati Island
Samate
Wolo I.
Kofiau I.
Bamkeri
Nusela Islands
Sailolof
Seget
Sele Pt.
Weeim I.
Gam I.
Nampale I.
Atkri
Lenmalu
Misool Island
Tamulol
Waigama
Valsepisang Islands
Segaf Islands
Femin Island
Warakaraket Island
Sansapor
Koor
Warmandi
Mt.Tamrau (Mt.Kwoka) 3000m
Peg. Tamrau
Mt. Irau 2582m
Dore Pt.
Mega
Salem
Bawe
Megamo
Sajam
Mala
Rawas
Lokata
Wanau
Gasim
Greemakolo
Teminabuan
Mongge
Baru
Inanwatan
Berau Bay (Mac Cluer Gulf)
Sabuda I.
Ogar Island
Tanisapata
Kokas
Fatagartuting Pt.
Rufrufua
Fakfak
Panjang I.
Siembra
Semai I.
Koras Island
Sebakor Bay
Tongeram Pt.
Wahai
Soabuwe
Lisabata
Sawai
Manusela Reserve
Putia
Kawa
Boano I.
Boano Strait
Seram (Ceram)
Hoti
Kobi
Bula
Piru
Kelang I.
Serik-kembelo
Ursano
Masohi
Manusela
Bolifar
Amahai
Sepa
Sahulau
Hatumetan
Manipa I.
Piru Bay
Rumahkai
Haya
Tehoru
Bemu
Parang I.
Saparua I.
Saparua
Batuas
Passo
Tulehu
Nusa Laut I.
Ambon Island
Laha
Ambon
Urung
Kita
Geser
Seram Laut I.
Air Buaya
Wapotih
Bara
Namlea
Manipa Strait
Fogi
Kohot
Buru Island
Mnamuk
Tifu
Oki
Watawa
Namrole
Ambelau I.
Gorong Islands
Kataloka
Panjang I.
Gorong I.
Terik
Manawoka I.
Banda Islands
Ai I.
Banda Island
Run I.
Hatta I.
Bandaneira
Kasiui I.
Watubela Islands
Tioor I.
Runduma I.
Marine Reserve
Tomea Island
Binongko Island
Moromaho Island
Kaimeer I.
Kur I.
Kei Islands
Rumadan I.
Tayandu I.
Duroa I.
Manggur I.
Walir I.
Tual
Langgur
Taam I.
Kei Kecil I.
Ohoitom
Ur I.
Kai Tanibar I.
Serua I.
Nila I.
Asat
Molu I.
Maru I.
Forate I.
Larat I.
Larat
Lamdesar
Namwaan I.
Nuswotar I.
Teun I.
Damar Islands
Kumir
Wulur
Damar Island
Terbang Utara I.
Terbang Selatan I.
Wuliaru I.
Selu I.
Yamdena
Watmuri
Sera I.
Meyanodas
Bukrane
Amdassa
Wasletan
Saumlakki
Tanimbar Islands
Adaut
Kandar
Selaru I.
Eliase
Dai I.
Dawera I.
Daweloor I.
Babar Islands
Tepa
Yaltubung
Wetan I.
Babar I.
Letwurung
Amplawas
Masela I.
Romang Island
Nyata Island
Maopora Island
Romang Strait
Laliki
Arwala
Ujungweka
Airpanas
Wetar I.
Limar
Huaki
Hotpass
Liran Island
Wetar Strait
Kisar Island
Alor Islands
Alor Strait
Kalabahi
Taramana
Pantar Island
Kabir
Alor Island
Kolana
Manatang
Treweng I.
Delaki
Maumela
Atauro Island (Kambing)
Ombai Strait
Manatuto
DILI
Baucau
Lautem
Tutuala
Jaco Island
Mt.Mata Bia 2315m
Lore
Kaiwatu
Moa I.
Serwaru
Leti I.
Kisar
Lakor I.
Kepuri I.
Sermata I.
Lolotuara
Romkisar
Regola
Luang I.
Leti Islands
Sermata Islands
124°
128°
132°
0°
4°
8°

Scale 1 : 5 300 000

MALUKU

Maluku's thousand-odd islands (one count claims 999; another 1,029) extend across an area of some 851,000 square km, only 10 percent of which is land. Geologically, biologically and culturally, these islands form a fascinating zone of transition between the Sunda Islands to the west and the Sahul zone to the east. Some of the islands are volcanic and dressed in luxuriant vegetation. Others are coral atolls, lined with swaying palms. But they are all beautiful and blessed with some of the finest beaches in the world: oases of soft sand and impossibly blue water. About two million people live here in scattered, usually small, villages. **Ambon**, the provincial capital of Maluku, is of a sufficient size to be called a city.

In geological terms, the Malukan island chain is an infant, no more than a few million years old. However, it is amazingly complex. Three of the earth's great tectonic plates meet under Maluku. The plates collide directly, scrape past each other, force another plate up or down, or fragment, producing a variety of geological effects.

This island arc splits through the length of Maluku. In the south, the outer arc is formed of contorted, mostly calcareous mudstones, limestones and a rare intrusive rock. This outer arc marks the northern boundary of the shallow **Arafura Sea**. It begins in the west with the barren, uplifted coral reefs of the **Leti** and **Babar islands,** and continuing counterclockwise, includes the forested, slightly larger **Tanimbars,** the **Kei, Watubela,** and **Gorong** groups, and finally hooks sharply back to include large, almost inaccessibly mountainous, **Seram** and **Buru.** Somewhat east of this outer arc is the Aru group, built of raised coral reefs cut through with narrow, mangrove-lined channels.

The inner arc is geologically quite different. A continuation of a chain that includes Sumatra, Java and Bali, here are the volcanic islands, beginning with large **Wetar** in the west, and extending northeast through the **Damar** group to include tiny **Gunung Api** in Banda. These islands mark a plate boundary, where molten rock has worked up through fissures in the earth's crust.

North of Seram, the double line of islands becomes less distinct. The island of **Halmahera** (like Sulawesi which was formed by the slow collision of two narrow islands) is marked on its western side by a line of young, active volcanoes, including Ternate. The rest of Halmahera is made up of older volcanic rock, calcareous sediments, and ultrabasic materials forced up from beneath the ocean.

VOLCANOES Of the nine or more still-smoking volcanoes here, two are easy to reach. **Gunung Api** ("Fire Mountain") in the middle of the tiny **Banda** archipelago, is a perfect cone reaching 656 m above the surface of the Banda Sea. This volcano erupted in 1988, devastating crops and forcing the thousands of people who lived on Gunung Api's lower slopes to evacuate. **Gamalama** volcano, crowning tiny Ternate, tops 1,700 m.

RESOURCES The staples today are mostly root crops such as manioc (also called cassava, the source of tapioca), taro, and sweet potatoes, supplemented by beans and other vegetables. The sago palm also provides prodigious quantities of staple starch. Fishing provides the bulk of the protein in the local diet, although wild pigs and other game are hunted in some areas.

The biggest cash crop is copra, dried coconut meat. Cloves, cacao (for chocolate), nutmeg, and coffee are also exported from the region. Commercial fishermen export a variety of fish, especially tuna, as well as shrimp. Smaller operations yield trepang (sea cucumbers), mother-of-pearl, seaweed for medicines and cosmetics, squid, and sharks' fins.

Many of the larger islands hold large timber resources. In a few areas, rattan is harvested for furniture and on a few islands, damar or gum copal, used in varnishes, is harvested. Other valuable tree products include massoi bark, which produces an aromatic oil used in folk medicine to cure rheumatism and other ills. On Buru island, the cineole rich leaves of a type of tropical myrtle are harvested, yielding the renowned kayu putih medicinal oil used for a wide variety of remedies ranging from muscle aches to nausea.

FLORA AND FAUNA From the biologist's point of view, Maluku — except for Aru — falls into a large area called **Wallacea,** named after Sir Alfred Russel Wallace, who spent eight years here during the 1850s. Wallacea is the island region between the **Sunda** and **Sahul** continental shelves. The transitional zone bridges two very different types of plant and animal species — those characteristic of Asia (e.g. placental mammals), and those characteristic of Australia (e.g. marsupials). As a result of selective migrations of species and their ensuing isolation on these islands, many unique hybrids and evolutionary holdovers found nowhere else in the world flourish in Maluku.

Found here are exotic clove and nutmeg trees, coconut palms, bananas, and trees sprouting strange and fragrant tropical fruits. A great variety of birds — pigeons, sunbirds, lories, cockatoos and kingfishers — fly and screech overhead. Just offshore, the coral-filled seas teem with bright fish, anemones, and sponges.

Most Malukans live a stone's throw from the water, and these clear tropical seas are teeming with life. Maluku is near the centre of species diversity for the entire Indo-Pacific region, and has more species of fish and invertebrates than just about anywhere in the world. Most of the reefs are pristine and ideal for snorkelling, scuba diving or fishing.

SPICES Maluku is most famous for two trees: the nutmeg and the clove. At one time, the **Banda Islands** were the nutmeg garden of the world. Few cultivated plants are more beautiful than nutmeg trees (Myristica frangrans), which thrive on Banda's moist air and light volcanic soils. The hard, aromatic "nut" or seed of this tree is ground into the familiar spice. Even more valuable, however, is mace, a spice prepared from the bright red, waxy aril that covers this nut. Cloves were the most valuable of Maluku's spices. Until the Dutch intruded, all of the world's cloves came from five small islands off the west coast of Halmahera: Ternate, Tidore, Moti, Makian, and Bacan. In 1583, the Dutch shifted the centre of clove production to **Ambon,** an island more firmly in their grasp. Subsequently, clove trees on Ternate and the nearby islands were almost entirely exterminated.

Europe's search for the source of these spices, the 15th century's great mystery, fueled the Age of Exploration, radically changing the course of world history. The spices, used in flavorings, medicines and as preserving agents, were almost priceless. The search realigned Europe as, in turn, the Portuguese, the Spanish, the Dutch, and the English became wealthy from the spice trade. Only the Dutch, through brutal suppression of indigenous sovereignty, were finally able to establish a monopoly.

Today, clove and nutmeg groves recall the days of European exploration. Currently, all the clove production is used within Indonesia, as the chopped spice is rolled up with tobacco in fragrant kretek cigarettes. Centuries-old Portuguese and Dutch forts, sometimes crumbling and overrun with vegetation, stand as reminders that the European trade monopolies were established here by force.

Today, **Ambon** is the capital of Maluku province and serves as the area's communications hub. Jets fly to and from Jakarta, Bali, Ujung Pandang, and Irian Jaya and smaller planes fan out from Ambon to the many tiny, out-of-the-way islands in the Malukan group. Mixed passenger and freighter ships make their slow way along convoluted loops that reach the far corners of the archipelago.

In the interiors of some of the larger islands, like **Buru, Halmahera, Seram,** and the **Sula,** people live in a way more or less uninfluenced by the outside world. On several of the islands, including Ambon, traces of ancient and poorly understood megalithic civilizations remain in stone altars and thrones, and in ancient costumes, dances, and rituals.

The chain of tiny islands, stretching from **Wetar,** near East Timor, to the **Aru group** next to New Guinea, is probably the most remote part of all of Indonesia. The beaches of the **Kei archipelago** are unsurpassed and the exquisite birds of paradise inhabit Aru's thick forests.

Maluku

Maluku

78

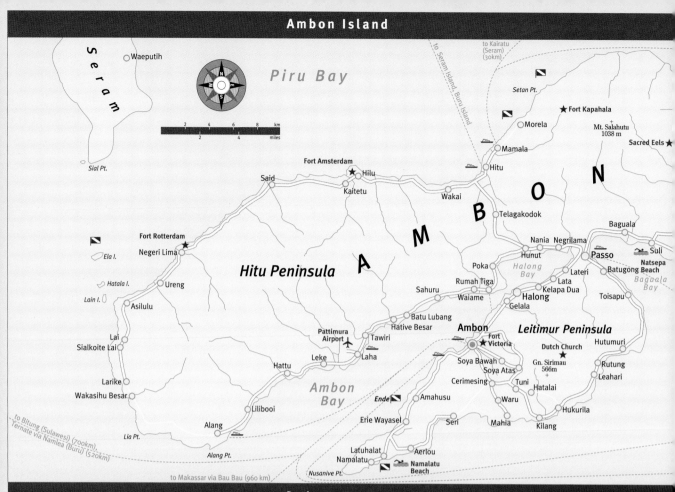

Seram

Waeputih

Piru Bay

to Kairatu (Seram) (30km)

to Seram Island, Buru Island

Setan Pt.

★ Fort Kapahala

Morela

Mt. Salahutu 1038 m

★ Sacred Eels

Sial Pt.

Mamala

Hitu

Fort Amsterdam ★ Hilu

Said

Kaitetu

Wakai

Telagakodok

Baguala

Nania Negrilama

Fort Rotterdam ★

Ela I.

Negeri Lima

Hitu Peninsula

A M B O N

Hunut

Poka

Lateri

Passo

Suli

Natsepa

Batugong Beach

Bagaala Bay

Hatala I.

Ureng

Lain I.

Asilulu

Sahuru

Rumah Tiga

Waiame

Halong Bay

Lata

Kelapa Dua

Halong

Gelala

Toisapu

Lai

Sialkoite Lai

Batu Lubang

Hative Besar

Ambon

★ Fort Victoria

Leitimur Peninsula

Hutumuri

Pattimura Airport ✈

Tawiri

Dutch Church

Gn. Sirimau 566m +

Larike

Wakasihu Besar

Hattu

Leke

Laha

Soya Bawah

Soya Atas

Cerimesing

Tuni

Hatalai

Rutung

Leahari

to Bitung (Sulawesi) (700km)

Ternate via Namlea (Buru) (520km)

Lilibooi

Ambon Bay

Ende

Amahusu

Waru

Mahia

Kilang

Hukurila

Alang

Lia Pt.

Erie Wayasel

Seri

Alang Pt.

Latuhalat

Namalatu

Aerlou

Namalatu Beach

Nusanive Pt.

to Makassar via Bau Bau (960 km)

Scale 1 : 300 000

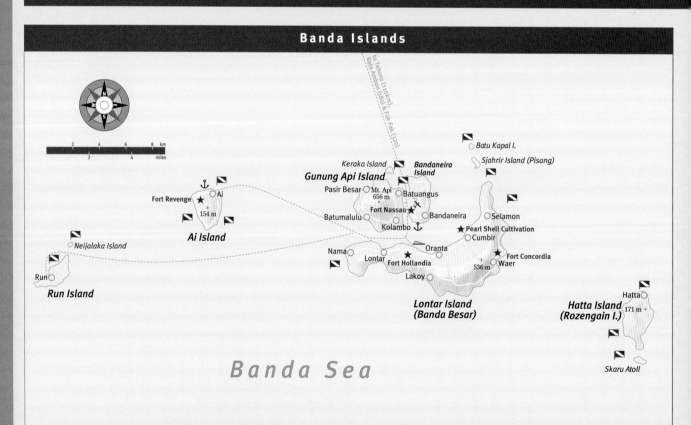

to Tehoru (110km), Kota Ambon (160) & Fak-Fak (320)

Batu Kapal I.

Sjahrir Island (Pisang)

Keraka Island

Bandaneira Island

Gunung Api Island

Pasir Besar

Mt. Api 656 m +

Batuangus

Fort Revenge ★ Ai

154 m +

Neijalaka Island

Ai Island

Batumalulu

Fort Nassau ★

Kolambo

Bandaneira

Selamon

★ Pearl Shell Cultivation

Cumbir

Run

Run Island

Nama

Lontar

Oranta

★ Fort Hollandia

Lakoy

★ Fort Concordia

536 m + Waer

Hatta

171 m +

Lontar Island (Banda Besar)

Hatta Island (Rozengain I.)

Skaru Atoll

Banda Sea

Scale 1 : 275 000

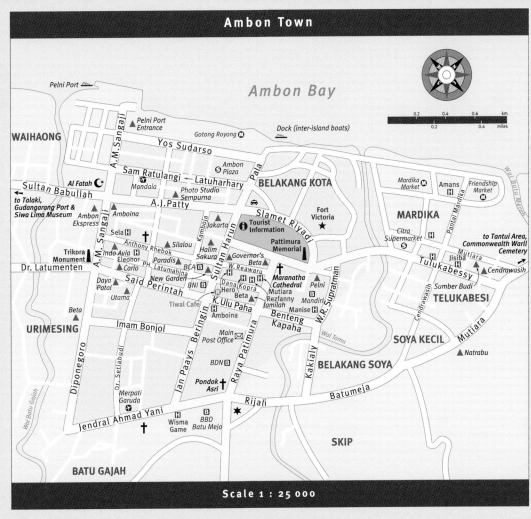

Scale 1 : 25 000

AMBON ISLAND

An excellent harbour and strategic location have made Ambon the Moluccas' best known island. Paved roads reach most of the important villages along the coast, and their paths unfold beautiful panoramas: steep mountains, curved bays and deep blue seas.

The mountainous, volcanic island takes roughly the shape of a mitten, with the Hitu Peninsula defining the bulk of the territory and the much smaller Leitimur Peninsula sticking out like a thumb from its south coast.

The island has many beaches of clean sand, lapped by warm, transparent tropical waters. One of the most popular beaches is **Natsepa**, at **Baguala**, 17 km from Ambon Town, just past **Paso** on Hitu's southeast coast. This is a favorite family picnic spot with a gently-sloping sea bottom and calm seas.

Further along the coast the paved road to **Tengah-Tengah** makes a beautiful trip, revealing ocean panoramas of brilliant color. Past Tengah-Tehgah, is **Tulehu**, the ferry landing for Saparua, Haruku, Seram and the other Lease Islands to the east. Five kilometres from Tulehu is the village of **Waai**, where sacred eels, the embodiment of ancestral spirits, are pampered and fed fresh chicken eggs.

Pombo Island (best reached by speedboat from **Honimua**), a few kilometres off the northeast tip of Hitu, offers excellent snorkelling on beautiful shallow reefs. On the northeast coast, **Satan's Cape** is the best spot for scuba diving, with drop-off reefs, spectacular overhangs, caves and deep clefts.

On the Leitimur Peninsula, south of Ambon, the sandy beach at **Amahusu**, 7 kilometres from Ambon town, is the closest place for a quick dip. **Namalatu** beach 16 kilometres away on Leitimur's southern tip, attracts a large weekend crowd. The view from the cliff tops above nearby **Latuhalat** overlooks the white sandy beach with its fringing coral reefs.

The most pleasant trip out of Ambon is to the village of **Soya Atas**, perched 400 metres up the flank of **Gunung Sirimau**, with its pretty, little church faced by a raja's house filled with momentos from the days of past splendor. From a sacred site at the top of the hill, a stone throne faces a splendid panorama—Hitu's Mount Salahutu, the Lease Islands, Leitimur's southern coast and, sometimes in the far distance, Banda's **Gunung Api** volcano.

AMBON TOWN

Born as a tiny Portuguese trading outpost more than 400 years ago, Ambon soon grew to become the centre of the clove trade under the Dutch. At the height of the Dutch East Indies Company's wealth and power Ambon town was referred to as "The Queen of the Eastern Islands."

Ambon's urban landscape is full of churches and there is a famous statue of the energetic Saint Francis Xavier in front of the Catholic Church on Jl. Raya Pattimura. Two mosques stand right next to each other on Jl. Sultan Babullah. This is a unique arrangement. According to Islamic traditions, when the stylish new **Al Fatah Mosque** was completed, the old one should have been destroyed, but the elderly servants of Allah loved the ambience of the old Jame Mosque and put up such a fuss that it still stands.

Ambon's main street is Jl. Raya Pattimura, named for the 19th-century Malukan patriot Thomas Matulessy, a.k.a. Pattimura. On the shopping strip on Jl. A.Y. Patty, the shops offer unique Moluccan souvenirs: mother-of-pearl montages, model ships crafted of cloves, handwoven ikat and embroidered traditional shirts.

The **Siwalima Museum**, on the slope of Gunung Nona above the city, displays fine ancestral woodcarvings, mock-ups of traditional Moluccan lifestyles, displays of natural history, fine porcelain and weapons.

BANDA

Situated some 140 km southeast of Ambon, the Bandas cover barely 50 square kilometres of dry land, of which half is taken up by crescent-shaped **Lontar Island** (also called Banda Besar, "Great Banda"). Lontar's coastline traces the crown of a huge sunken caldera, which also forms tiny Sjahrir, formerly Pisang ("Banana") Island. Rising out of the sea in the centre of the crater are **Banda Neira** and the perfect cone of **Gunung Api** ("Fire Mountain"), the still smoking snout of a once-huge volcano.

Banda is one of the world's finest spots for scuba and snorkelling. The reefs surrounding the islands are healthy and lush with fish and colourful invertebrates. For the serious diver, the reefs surrounding the outer islands often border on spectacular drop-offs at this transition between shallow reef and deep water.

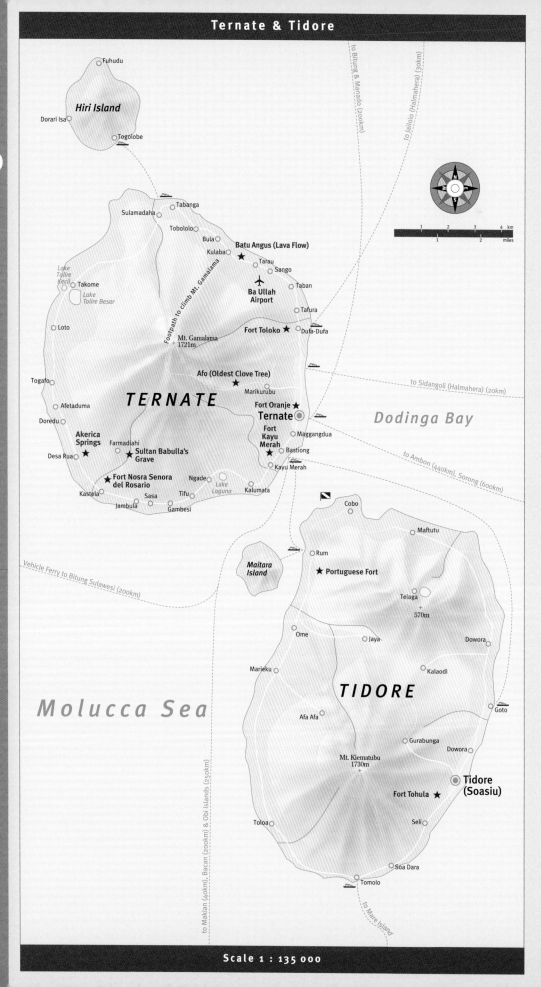

Map labels (Halmahera Island):

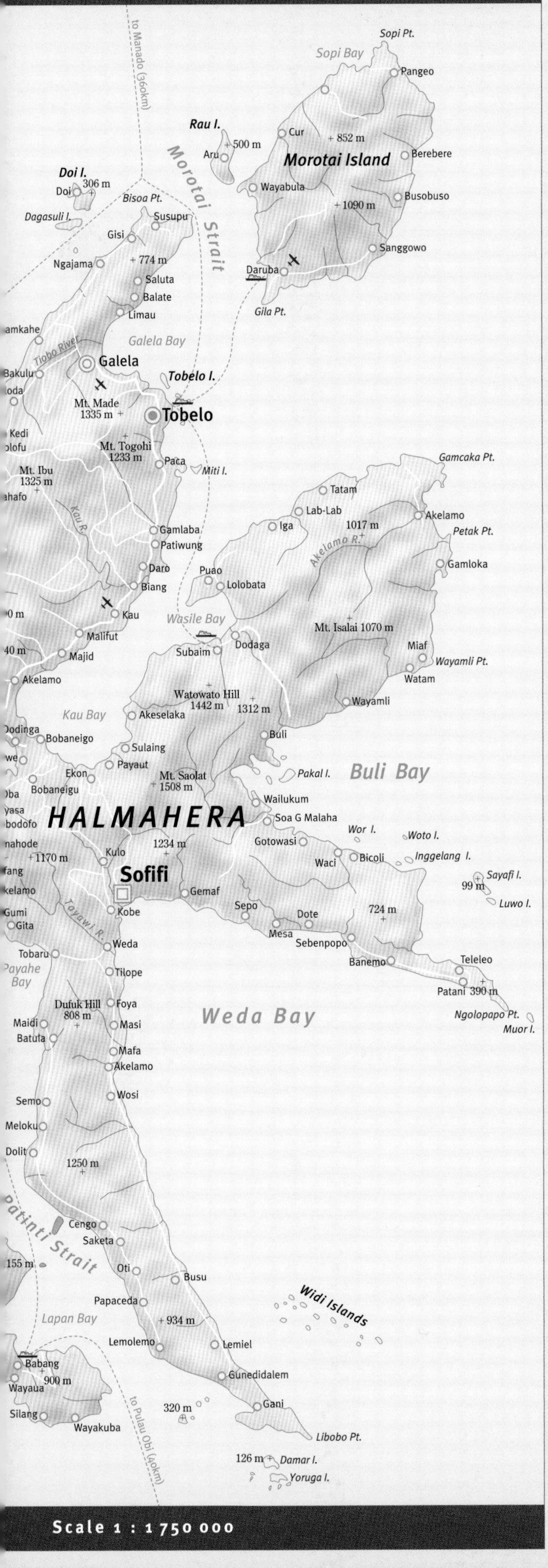

to Manado (356km) · Sopi Pt. · Sopi Bay · Pangeo · Rau I. · Cur · +852 m · Aru · +500 m · Berebere · Morotai Island · Doi I. · Doi · 306 m · Bisoa Pt. · Wayabula · Busubuso · Dagasuli I. · Susupu · +1090 m · Gisi · Saluta · Morotai Strait · Balate · Sanggowo · Ngajama · +774 m · Limau · Daruba · amkahe · Gila Pt. · Bakulu · Tiobo River · Galela · Galela Bay · Tobelo I. · oda · Mt. Made 1335 m · Tobelo · Kedi · olofu · Mt. Togohi 1233 m · Paca · Miti I. · Gamcaka Pt. · Mt. Ibu 1325 m · Tatam · Lab-Lab · 1017 m · Akelamo · ahafo · Iga · Petak Pt. · Kau R. · Gamlaba · Akelamo R. · Gamloka · 40 m · Patiwung · Puao · Daro · Lolobata · 0 m · Biang · Wasile Bay · Mt. Isalai 1070 m · Miaf · Kau · Wayamli Pt. · Malifut · Subaim · Dodaga · Watam · Majid · Watowato Hill 1442 m · 1312 m · Wayamli · Akelamo · Kau Bay · Akeselaka · Buli · Dodinga · Bobaneigo · Sulaing · Pakal I. · Buli Bay · we · Ekon · Payau · Mt. Saolat 1508 m · Bobaneigu · Wailukum · yasa · **HALMAHERA** · Soa G Malaha · Wor I. · Woto I. · bodofo · Gotowasi · Inggelang I. · nahode · 1234 m · Kulo · Waci · Bicoli · Sayafi I. · +1170 m · **Sofifi** · 99 m · Luwo I. · fang · Gemaf · Sepo · Dote · 724 m · kelamo · Kobe · Mesa · Gumi · Weda · Sebenpopo · Gita · Banemo · Teleleo · Tobaru · Tilope · Patani 390 m · Payahe Bay · Foya · Ngolopapo Pt. · Maidi · Dufuk Hill 808 m · Masi · Muor I. · Batula · Mafa · **Weda Bay** · Akelamo · Semo · Wosi · Meloku · Dolit · 1250 m · Patinti Strait · Cengo · Saketa · 155 m · Oti · Widi Islands · Busu · Papaceda · Lapan Bay · +934 m · Lemolemo · Lemiel · Babang · 900 m · Wayaua · Gunedidalem · Silang · Gani · 320 m · Wayakuba · to Pulau Oti (60km) · Libobo Pt. · 126 m · Damar I. · Yoruga I.

TERNATE & TIDORE

Just west of sprawling, four-armed Halmahera Island, two volcanoes rise from the Maluku Sea: Ternate and Tidore, the famous clove islands. Three centuries ago, the great kingdoms of Europe fought bitterly for control of these tiny isles and their precious harvest of cloves. Today, Ternate and Tidore have faded from the world's attention, but these lush, breezy islands are just as beautiful as they were when the first Portuguese sailors landed.

TERNATE is one of the cities in North Maluku. Daily flights connect Ternate with Manado in north Sulawesi and Ambon and on a weekly basis planes head for the towns of Galela and Kao in north Halmahera.

Ternate is a tiny island, less than 10 km in diameter, dominated by **Gunung Gamalama**. This still active volcano, whose 1,721-m top has erupted with lava and ash at least 70 times in the last half millenium, keeps all development to a tight circle along the coast.

The commercial centre of the island is **Ternate** town, which spreads out along the southeast coast facing an excellent deep-water harbour. Ternate town has grown around **Fort Oranje**, built by the Dutch in 1607 when they set about enforcing a monopoly on the sultan's cloves. Just south of town, past the main docks, a run down, graffiti-covered fort crumbles by the seaside. Begun by the Portuguese in 1510, the fort is now called Kayu Merah ("Red Wood"). The view from here across the narrow strait to Tidore and Maitara Islands is beautiful.

Ternate was once the site of a splendid sultanate. Today, the sultan's crown is on display in the palace, its magic powers undiminished from the days of Sultan Awal, the first of the line. The town mosque, an old, multi-tiered wooden structure, stands next to the main road to the airport in the northern part of town. Its foundations date back to the first sultan's conversion in the 15th century. Several of Ternate's long line of sultans are buried behind the mosque. Just north of the mosque is the sultan's residence, perched on a small hill next to the road.

A few km north of town, a path leads to the beachside village of **Dufa-Dufa**, which sits under the dominating presence of **Fort Toloko**. This well-preserved fort is perched on upraised coral. Its entrance still bears its 16th century Portuguese seal. Continuing in the same direction on the main road, the forest is replaced by a desolate moonscape of bare, jagged black rocks, running all the way to the sea. This is **Batu Angus** ("Burned Rock"), a lava flow remaining from a disastrous eruption in the 18th century.

Rounding the northern tip to the western side of the island, a short side road leads inland to lovely **Danau Tolire Besar** (Big Tolire Lake). Emerald waters fill this steep-sided, vegetation-encircled crater lake. **Danau Tolire Kecil** (Little Tolire Lake), a smaller lake, lies between the main road and the nearby beach. Its smooth surface is a perfect mirror reflecting the Gamalama volcano.

South from Ternate, the main road climbs to **Ngade** village. Just past the little settlement, is **Danau Laguna**, a lake which is the home of sacred crocodiles. About 1.5 km from the gate, a short side path to the right leads to a magnificent view of spring-fed Laguna Lake and Tidore Island.

TIDORE, slightly larger than Ternate, lies just one kilometre south of her better known twin's closest shore. Like Ternate, Tidore is also dominated by a volcano, 1,730-m **Gunung Kiematubu**, which rears up in a perfect cone to form the southern part of the island. **Gurabunga** village, at the foot of Kiematubu, is the centre of adat traditions for Tidore, perhaps because of its protected, inland position. A partially-paved, 130-km network of roads opens Halmahua's wonderful beaches, reefs and World War II relics to the traveller.

Tidore town, (Soasiu)is the capital of the **Central Halmahera District**, which includes Tidore and central Halmahera. Seaside villages ring the island, however, most of the Tidorese are concentrated on the southern coast. A paved road follows most of Tidore's 45-km circumference, but gets progressively worse the further one gets from Soasiu. The scenery from the road is superb. Just north of Tidore and off Maitara Island's north and northeast coasts the clear seas are fine for snorkelling.

HALMAHERA

North to south, Halmahera measures 330 km and at its widest point, 160 km across, for a total land area of just under 18,000 sq km. The whole of the island is mountainous, rough, and densely forested. Although Seram is slightly larger, Halmahera spreads over a much greater area and is a more imposing presence.

The four fingers of Halmahera cut a striking figure. Separated by three great bays, these long peninsulas are reminders that the island was once two separate islands that, over the eons, slowly crashed together. The separate mountain chains now come together in a jumble of peaks in the centre of the island. Only the northern finger is volcanic; three cones still occasionally smoke and rumble. Its eastern coast is dotted with off-shore islands, with wide beaches, profusions of coconut trees, and clear, coral-filled waters.

IRIAN JAYA

The island of **New Guinea** is enormous, spanning 2,400 km end to end, and 740 km at the shoulder. Covering 792,540 sq km, it is the world's second-largest island, behind Greenland, and just ahead of Borneo.

The island is neatly bisected at longitude 141°E (except for a slight westward blip at the Fly River), with the western half being the Indonesian province of **Irian Jaya**, and the eastern half being part of **Papua New Guinea**, an independent country. This boundary was settled by the Dutch with the British in 1895 and with the Germans in 1910, the latter two maintained a presence in the eastern part of the island. Irian's 421,981 sq km constitute 22 percent of Indonesia's total land area.

The shape of New Guinea has been likened to that of the cassowary bird, and the westernmost peninsula, nearly cut off from the "body" by Bintuni Bay, is "called the Bird's Head—Kepala Burung" in Indonesian and "Vogelkop" in Dutch.

A 2,000-km long cordillera of craggy mountains running the length of the island is New Guinea's most distinctive topological feature. The crests of the main divide top 3,000 m in many places and a handful of rocky peaks soar above 4,500 m. Small permanent snowfields and relict glaciers still grace the highest elevations. Volcanic rock is not common in the mountains, but in one of the few places an igneous intrusion has appeared the outcrop has proved to be incredibly rich in copper, gold and silver. Irian's highest peak is the pride of the **Sudirman Range: Puncak Jaya**. Reaching 4,884 m, this is the highest point between the Himalayas and the Andes.

East of **Puncak Jaya**, the southern coastal forest broadens, and the swamplands around the Casuarina Coast are vast, reaching 300 km inland. Several rivers here are navigable almost to the mountains, and the land is so flat that tides affect river height far inland. At the far southeastern corner of Irian Jaya, near **Merauke**, there is a large, anomalous stretch of dry, grassy savannah.

The northern slopes of the mountains descend gradually, yielding to foothills and then the vast **Mamberamo** basin. This is the Lake Plains region, flat and swampy, full of mipa palms and lowland forest, and little explored. The Mamberamo and its two main tributaries — the **Taritatu** flowing from the east, and the **Tariku** from the west — are slow, silty, meandering rivers.

Bintuni Bay cuts deep into Irian and its inner reaches form one of the most extensive mangrove swamps in the world. North of Bintuni is the Bird's Head peninsula, which is made up of lowland forest in the south, and more mountainous regions in the north, marked by the **Tamrau Mountains**, and the **Arfak Mountains** near **Manokwari**.

WILDLIFE Irian has the richest concentration of plant life in all of Indonesia, and perhaps in all the world. Scientists estimate there are 16,000 species of plants growing in New Guinea, including hundreds of species that are of medicinal importance. At least 124 genera of New Guinea's flowering plants are unique to the island.

New Guinea is well on the Australian side of **Wallacea**. Since the Arafura Sea is quite shallow, the rising and falling of the sea brought on by the Ice Ages have caused the two land masses to have periodically connected. Because of this — and because of the existence of marsupials and monotremes in both places — New Guinea is typically considered part of the Australian faunal province.

Biologists have identified 643 species of birds in Irian Jaya, including the Victoria crowned pigeon (the world's largest pigeon), the beautiful birds of paradise, and the large, flightless cassowary.

The swampy south coast of Irian is too silty to allow the growth of coral, but around **Triton Bay** near Kaimana, off the **Raja Ampat Islands**, and around the islands of **Cendrawasih Bay** are some of the finest and least disturbed coral reefs in the world. Since it is so close to the epicentre of species diversity for the vast Indo-Pacific region, these coral reefs harbour well over 3,000 species of fish.

IRIANESE Irian's two million people form a patchwork of ethnicities, speaking, by most estimates, as many as 250 distinct languages. The island's great size, rugged terrain and the practice of perpetual warfare between neighbouring groups have resulted in the independent development and maintenance of distinct languages and lifestyles.

The **Dani** of the central highlands, perhaps the best-known of the Irianese, live in communities of tidy little thatch and wood huts surrounded by neatly kept gardens of sweet potato vines. If the Dani are Irian's most famous group, the **Asmat** of the south coast are the island's most notorious, with a ritual culture that once centred around a cycle of headhunting.

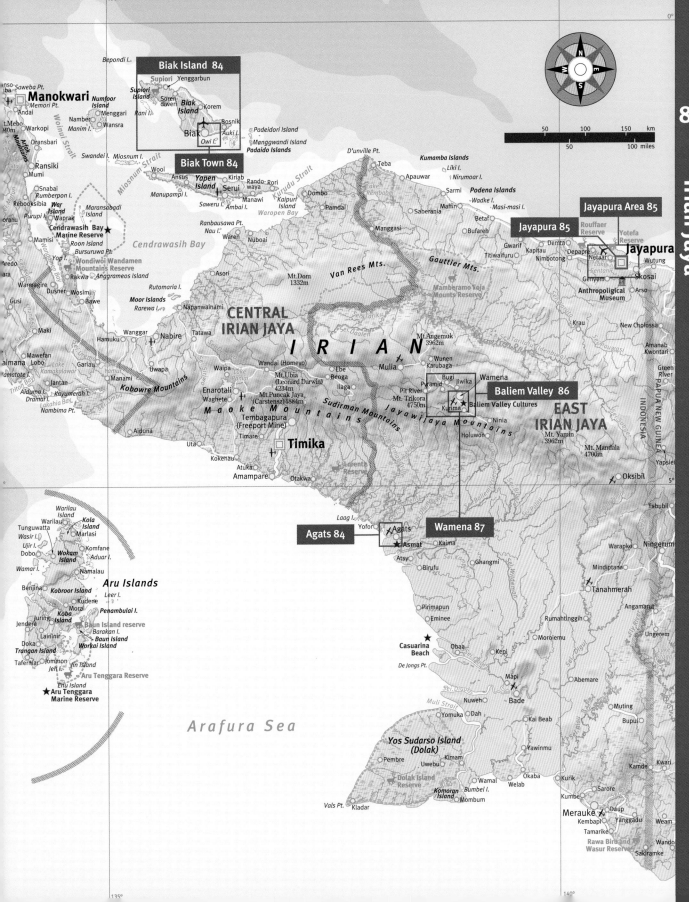

Biak Island 84

Biak Town 84

Jayapura Area 85

Jayapura 85

Baliem Valley 86

Agats 84

Wamena 87

Saweba Pt.
Memori Pt.
Manokwari
Andai
t.Mebo
140m
Warkopi
Oransbari
Ransiki
Mumi
Snabai
Rumberpon I.
Rebooksibia
Purupi I.
oranu
Mamisi
Maki
Mawefan
Gariau
Jantan
Aiduma I.
Dramal I.
Nambira Pt.
Ajduna

Bepondi I.

Supiori
Island
Soren-
diweri
Rani I.

Yenggarbun

Korem

Biak
Island

Bosnik
Auki I.
Owi I.

Biak

Numfoor
Island
Namber
Manim I.
Wansra
Menggari
Swandei I. Miosnum I.

Maransabadi
Island
Cendrawasih Bay
Marine Reserve
Roon Island
Bursuruwa Pt.
Rakwa
Yop I.
Warmagire
Dusner
Wosimi
Bawe

Wanggar

Hamuku

Wondiwoi Wandamen
Mountains Reserve
Anggrameos Island

Wool
Ansus
Manupampi I.
Serui
Manawi
Saweru I.

Yapen
Island
Kiriab

Rando-Rori
waya

Kaipuri
Island
Kurudu Strait
Waropen Bay

D'unville Pt.
Teba

Kumamba Islands
Liki I.
Nirumoar I.

Apauwar

Sarmi
Wadke I.
Podena Islands
Masi-masi I.

Dombo
Pamdai
Maffin
Betaf
Bufareh

Saberania

Gauttier Mts.

Mamberamo Foja
Mounts Reserve

Rouffaer
Reserve

Gwarif
Titiwaifuru
Demta
Kapitau
Nimbotong
Depapre
Netaar

Yotefa
Reserve

Jayapura
Wutung
Skosai

Lake
Sentani
Genyem
Anthropoligical
Museum

Arso

New Cholossa

Krau

Amanab
Kwontari

Green
River

PAPUA NEW GUINEA

INDONESIA

Napanwainami
Tatawa

Nabire

Uwapa

Waren
Nuboai

Asori

Van Rees Mts.

Mt.Dom
1332m

Sei Tariku

I R I A N

Rutomaria I.
Rarewa I.
Moor Islands

CENTRAL
IRIAN JAYA

Wandai (Homeyo)

Waipa

Enarotali
Waghete

Mt.Ubia
(Leonard Darwin)
4234m
Mt.Puncak Jaya
(Carstensz) 4884m

Maoke Mountains

Tembagapura
(Freeport Mine)
Timare

Uta

Timika

Kokenau

Atuka
Amampare
Otakwa

Lorentz
Reserve

Ebe
Beoga
Ilaga

Mulia

Mt.Angemuk
3962m

Wunen
Karubaga

Bugi
Pit River
Mt.Trikora
4750m

Pyramid

Jiwika
Kurima

Wamena

Baliem Valley Cultures

Sudirman Mountains

Jayawijaya Mountains

Ninia

Holuwon

EAST
IRIAN JAYA

Mt.Yamin
3962m

Mt.Mandala
4700m

Yapsiei

Oksibil

Tabubil

Ningerum

Warapko

Mindiptana

Tanahmerah

Angamarut

Ungerem

Warilau
Island
Warilau
Tunguwatta
Wasir I.
Ujir I.
Dobo
Wamar I.
Benjina

Kola
Island
Marlasi
Komfane
Aduar I.
Wokam
Island
Manalau

Kobroor Island

Aru Islands

Leer I.

Kudene
Morai
Penambulai I.

Laag I.
Yofor

Agats

Asmat

Atsy
Birufu
Ghangmi

Kaima

Sei Wildeman

Rumahtingggih

Moroiemu

Abemare

Muting

Bupul

Juring
Koba
Island
Jendera
Laininir
Doka
Trangan I.
Tafermar
Jommon
Jefi I.
Jin Island
Baun Island reserve
Barakan I.
Baun Island
Workai Island

Pirimapun
Eminee

Casuarina
Beach
De Jongs Pt.
Obaa
Kepi
Mapi
Bade

Yawinmu

Enu Island
Aru Tenggara Reserve

Aru Tenggara
Marine Reserve

Arafura Sea

Nuweh
Yomuka
Dah
Kai Beab

Yos Sudarso Island
(Dolak)
Pembre
Uwebu
Kimam

Muli Strait

Dolak Island
Reserve

Komoran
Island

Wamal
Okaba
Welab
Bumbel I.
Mombum

Kurik
Kumbe

Kamde
Kwari

Merauke
Kembapi
Daup
Yanggadu
Weam

Tamarike
Rawa Biru and
Wasur Reserve

Sakiramke

Wando

Vals Pt.
Kladar

km
50   100   150

50   100 miles

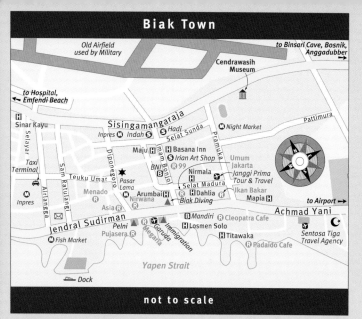

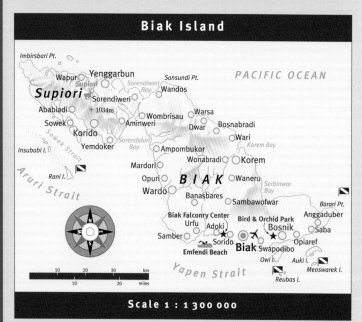

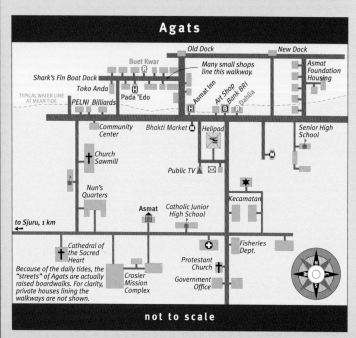

BIAK

Biak is the best-known and most populated of the former **Schouten Islands**. The boot-shaped island covers 1,834 sq km, extends 50 km northwest to southeast, and averages 18 km wide. The northernmost shore reaches within 60 km of the equator and the middle of the island lies 1° south. It is often hot and humid.

Geologically, all these islands consist of uplifted coral limestone, with coastlines often ending in impressive cliffs as much as 60 metres from the waves below. The heavy rainfall has eroded the soft limestone into caves, which on **Biak Island** in particular, played a historic role in World War II as hideouts for Japanese soldiers. Inland, the terrain is generally flat, with occasional low hills, except in the north of **Biak** and in **Supiori**.

Paved roads radiate out from **Biak** town heading toward the north, east and west. To the east, it's 18 km and a half-hour ride to **Bosnik**, where there are sandy beaches and near-shore reefs. This is a good place to hire boats to the **Padaido Islands**, which dot the sea southeast of Biak. These islands are ringed with coral and offer fine snorkelling in some of the richest and most unspoiled reefs in all of Indonesia.

About two kilometres beyond **Bosnik**, a narrow beach and picnic area abuts a sweep of raised coral. In the clear, shallow seas here one can see the rusting remains of American-built World War II piers. The paved road continues to **Opiaref Village**. At the back of the elementary school there is a beautiful and mysterious blue-water pool in the **Goa Serumi** cave.

Heading north from Biak town, just outside the urban area, a turnoff leads to **Goa Binsari**, a complex of caves used by the Japanese as hideouts during World War II. The bay-side market of Wardo lies at the western end of a 50-km paved road from Biak town. Much of the area is uninhabited. A couple of km before reaching the market, a paved strip to the right leads to the Wapsdori waterfall.

BIAK TOWN

Biak town has some lively markets, an interesting harbour, and a small museum full of relics. Further out from the town, there are beautiful waterfalls and reefs. The total population of the Biak district (including Supiori and Numfor) is just over 81,000, with about half living in Biak town and the surrounding areas.

AGATS

Agats is the capital of the **Asmat** region; the communications, commercial, and educational centre, and the centre for the Catholic mission in the area. This small town sits barely propped above the mud on the south bank of the mouth of the **Aswetsj River**, where it empties into Flamingo Bay.

Wooden walkways raised on posts, serve as streets. When the tide is in, the water reaches to within a metre of the boards, and children jump in with glee, using either the boardwalks or half-submerged trees as diving boards. Twice a year, in late December and in June, the tides can exceed five metres. When this happens, great stretches of boardwalk can be submerged, and it is not the best time to visit.

Five metres of rain fall each year in **Agats**, but since the town's drinking water comes exclusively from cisterns fed by rainfall off rooftops, a two or three week long dry spell can mean a lack of drinking water.

Just in and to one side of the old dock is "downtown" Agats, a stretch of a couple dozen small stores and shops selling clothing, tinned or packaged food, tobacco, cheap household items, and basic hardware. The daily green market, **Bhakti Market**, is a small building facing the Asmat Inn. Activities start at 5 am and are over within the hour.

The Roman Catholic church, which pioneered the proselytising of the Asmat, continues to maintain its headquarters in Agats, largely run today by the American Crosiers. The **Asmat Museum of Culture and Progress** has accumulated an excellent collection of Asmat carvings, masks, costumes, and artifacts.

Visiting the Asmat region around Agats requires hiring a dugout canoe and guide, and sleeping at night on the bark floor of a jeu, the long, raised men's huts that serve as the architectural and cultural centres of Asmat villages.

JAYAPURA

Jayapura, Irian's capital and largest city, began it's life as a Dutch port and administrative centre. The city was placed here to mark the border with the German colony just a stone's throw away, and one can see into Papua New Guinea from the hills north of town.

Jayapura began its life as Hollandia in 1910, became Kota Baru after Irian's integration into Indonesia, and then changed briefly to Sukarnopura before assuming its current name. Today, Jayapura is a thriving city with a mixed population of Irianese, Javanese, Makassarese and Bugis Muslims, as well as many Ambonese and Manadonese Christians.

The **Cenderawasih University Museum** in nearby **Abepura** has a fine collection of artifacts from many areas of Irian, and the **Museum Negeri**, also displays objects of material culture from Irian's various ethnic groups.

From Jayapura, a short hop to **Yotefa Bay** offers the spectacle of scattered World War II relics — half-sunken ships, beached tanks, and landing craft. Nearby **Lake Sentani**, dotted with islands offers a stunning panorama of velvet-green hills easing their way into the lake. Just out of Sentani, a paved road winds upward for 6 km and climbs to **Mount Ifar** in the Cyclops Mountains. At Ifar stands a monument to General MacArthur, whose World War II headquarters were here. The site overlooks the humid lowlands and offers a splendid view of the lake. Craftsmen make bark cloth paintings and sculptures in the traditional style on **Apayo Island** in the middle of Lake Sentani.

The beachside suburb of **Hamadi** is located off the main road to Sentani about 4 km out of town. The best beach in the area is 7 km in the opposite direction from Jayapura, at the old Allied "Base G." The sand is clean and the water clear.

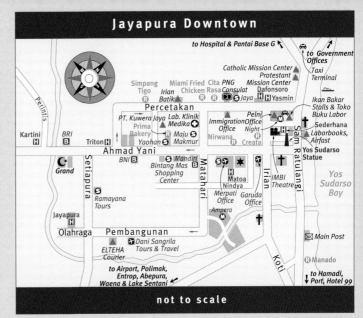

Jayapura Downtown

not to scale

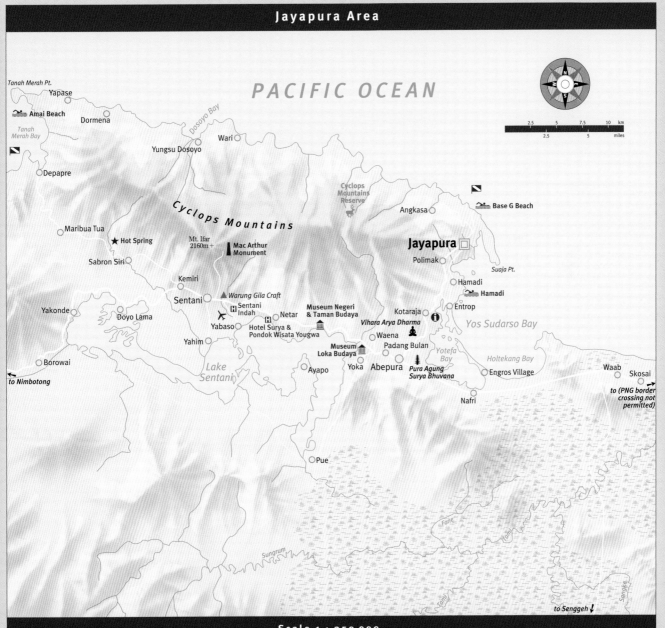

Jayapura Area

PACIFIC OCEAN

Scale 1 : 350 000

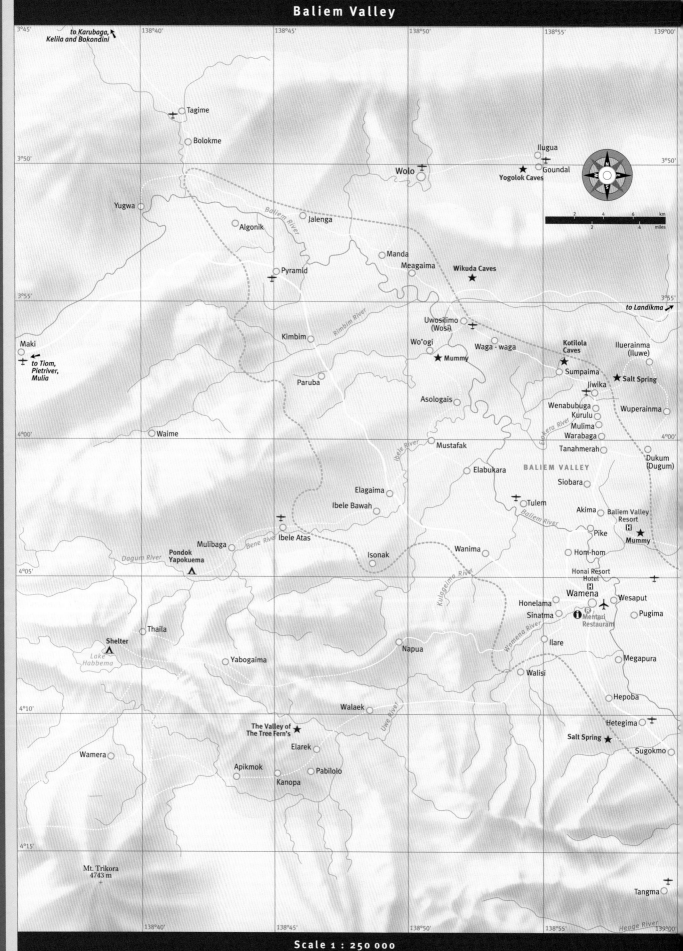

Baliem Valley

to Karubaga,
Kelila and Bokondini

Tagime

Bolokme

Ilugua

Wolo
Goundal
Yogolok Caves

Yugwa

Baliem River
Jalenga

Algonik

Manda
Meagaima

Wikuda Caves

Pyramid

to Landikma

Rimbim River

Kimbim
Uwosilimo
(Wosi)

Maki

Wo'ogi
Waga - waga
Kotilola
Caves
Iluerainma
(Iluwe)

to Tiom,
Pietriver,
Mulia

Mummy
Sumpaima
Salt Spring

Jiwika

Paruba
Asologais
Wenabubuga
Wuperainma

Kurulu
Mulima

Waime
Mustafak
Warabaga

Tanahmerah
Dukum
(Dugum)

Elabukara
BALIEM VALLEY

Elagaima
Siobara

Ibele Bawah
Tulem
Akima
Baliem Valley
Resort

Baliem River
Pike
Mummy

Mulibaga
Ibele Atas
Bene River
Isonak
Wanima
Hom-hom

Pondok
Yapokuema
Dagum River

Honai Resort
Hotel

Wamena
Wesaput

Honelama
Pugima

Thaila
Sinatma
Mentari
Restaurant

Shelter
Napua
Ilare
Megapura

Lake
Habbema
Yabogaima
Walisi

Hepoba

Walaek
Uwe River
Hetegima

The Valley of
The Tree Fern's
Salt Spring
Sugokmo

Elarek

Wamera
Apikmok
Pabilolo
Kanopa

Mt. Trikora
4743 m

Tangma

Heage River

Scale 1 : 250 000

3°45'
3°50'
3°55'
4°00'
4°05'
4°10'
4°15'

138°40'
138°45'
138°50'
138°55'
139°00'

Kulageimo River
Wamena River
Eiekera River
Ibele River

BALIEM VALLEY

The Grand Valley of the **Baliem River**, green and fertile, nestles incongruously in Irian's cordillera of rocky peaks. Coursing down its centre is the silt-rich Baliem River, a branching stripe of cafe au lait against the valley's green floor. The Grand Valley is beautiful; with trees and grass, and everywhere, tidy plots of sweet potatoes. Looming on all sides, shrouded by mist and clouds, is the mountain wall.

The Grand Valley lies at an elevation of 1,600 m is 60 km long and 15 km wide, and is surrounded by 2,500–3,000 m peaks. The **Baliem River** flows into the valley from the north from two sources: the **East Baliem**, which begins near **Gunung Trikora**, and the **West Baliem** which begins in the **Ilaga–Tiom** valley system. These two rivers join, then briefly disappear underground in the **Baliem Swallet**, just southwest of **Tiom**. The waters join the North Baliem and then drop to the floor of the Grand Valley, where they become a slow brown river.

The Grand Valley is home to the **Dani**, the most populous of Irian's highlanders. Most famous for their ritual warfare, the Dani are also first-rate farmers, the key to the valley's high population. The Dani's numbers are increasing even today, rising from 50,000 in the early 1960s to currently more than 100,000 in the valley itself. There are also 130,000 **Western Dani** (or Lani), who speak a slightly different language and live west of the Grand Valley.

The village of **Pugima**, just east of **Wamena**, is actually a loose grouping of house compounds, each of which is home to from two to six related families. A strong wooden fence encircles several thatch-covered huts: the round men's house, the similarly shaped women's houses and a long, rectangular kitchen adjoining the covered pig sty.

The most popular and easiest trek from Wamena is to **Jiwika** (pronounced either Djiwika or Yiwika), some 20 km to the northwest along one of the few roads in the Baliem. Shortly after crossing the bridge, a short side road leads to **Akima Village** and its famous mummy. Men of importance were not given the usual cremation after death. Their bodies were desiccated and kept in the men's house as a conduit to the supernatural to obtain good health, abundant harvests, wives, pigs, and victory in war.

Jiwika, an administrative centre, lies a couple of hundred metres off the main road. The market (Sundays only) is a quiet, if crowded affair. About a hundred metres past La-uk Losmen in Jiwika is a footpath that leads to Kampung Sampaima, with another mummy. Another path starts out from the back of the Jiwika market, up a steep mountain side to a saltwater spring called **Iluerainma** (or just Iluwe). The salt pool is about 300 m above the valley and the steep climb takes about an hour.

At **Waga-Waga**, further north from Jiwika, is a limestone cave called **Kontilola**. A dark passageway leads from a large chamber to a pool of water and a section of the cave filled with bats.

Some of the Grand Valley's most spectacular scenery lies southeast of Wamena, where the mountain wall parts in the Baliem Gorge. **Kurima** is a tiny, spread-out town with schools, military and police posts and the administrative centre of the district. Tuesday is the weekly market day here. Hikes out of Kurima lead to incredible mountain scenery.

A mostly paved road now runs the entire way from Wamena to Pyramid (and beyond, to Tiom) in the northwest corner of the Baliem Valley. On the way to **Pyramid**, a side-trip leads to **Lake Habbema** and **Mt. Trikora**, which, at 4,743 m, is one of Irian's highest peaks. Lake Habbema sits in a broad alpine marsh, a sponge of mosses, tea-brown streams, and strange vegetation. The air is thin and cold, and at night, every star is visible. Pyramid is the site of the main highland base and conference centre of the fundamentalist Protestant Christian and Missionary Alliance (CAMA). Kimbim, just 5 km south of Pyramid, is the district centre. From **Kimbim**, there is a good trail to the village of **Wo'ogi**, where there is another mummy.

WAMENA

Wamena is the administrative and communications hub of the Baliem Valley. Roads lead across the river and north, all the way to **Pass Valley**, northwest to Pyramid and beyond, and south to **Sugokmo**. The town of Wamena is growing dramatically. Much of this increase is due to Indonesians arriving from elsewhere in the archipelago (mainly from East and Central Java, Manado, Ambon, and South Sulawesi) to take advantage of job and business opportunities. The district's only high school and a number of specialized colleges have added hundreds of students to Wamena's population.

The **Pasar Nayak** market is crowded with the colourful produce of Dani gardens and equally colourful crowds. Souvenirs available include bows with multipurpose arrows, stone axes, penis gourds, and belts of cowrie shell money.

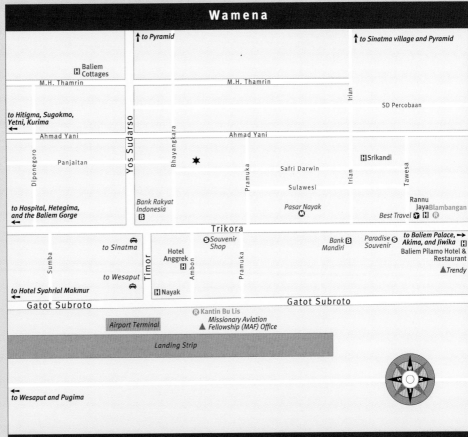

HOW TO USE THIS INDEX

There are three sections. The first lists villages, towns and cities. The second lists significant points of interest, while the last one indexes national parks and reserves. All items give page number and map title. If an entry appears on a large area map and also a more detailed map in the same chapter, only the page with the more detailed map is listed. To conserve space, places in Malaysia, Singapore, Brunei and Timor Leste are omitted.

Cities and Towns

Aan 47 Bali
Ababiadi 84 Biak Island
Abangiwang 62 Timor
Abemare 83 Irian Jaya
Abepura 85 Jayapura Area
AbiankapasKaja 48 S Bali
Abiansemal 47 Bali
Abuan 47 Bali
Ada 73 Tana Toraja
Adaut 76 Maluku
Adiandamar 10 Lake Toba
Adoki 84 Biak Island
Adonara 61 Flores
Adu 59 Sumbawa
Aekgorat 11 Lake Toba
Aekguo 12 W Sumatra
Aekkanopan 08 N Sumatra
Aekmatolu 11 Lake Toba
Aektintin 10 Lake Toba
Aerlou 78 Ambon Island
AerTembaga 74 Manado Region
AfaAfa 80 Ternate & Tidore
Afetaduma 80 Ternate & Tidore
Afia 08 N Sumatra
Afulu 09 Nias Island
Ai 78 Banda Islands
Aiduna 83 Irian Jaya
Aikbuka 57 Lombok
Aikdarek 57 Lombok
Aikembuk 57 Lombok
Aiklomak 57 Lombok
Aikmel 57 Lombok
AikmelUtara 57 Lombok
Aikmual 57 Lombok
Aikperapa 57 Lombok
Aimere 60 Flores
Airangat 12 W Sumatra
Airbangis 12 W Sumatra
AirBari 58 Sumbawa
AirBuaya 76 Maluku
Airdikit 12 W Sumatra
Airhilang 15 Minang Highlands
Airmadidi 74 Manado Region
Aisuning 58 Sumbawa
Ajibarang 20 Java
Ajibata 11 Lake Toba
Akarakar 57 Lombok
Akelamo 81 Halmahera Island
Akeselaka 81 Halmahera Island
Akima 86 Baliem Valley
Alahanke 12 W Sumatra
Alahanpanjang 12 W Sumatra
Alamsari 48 S Bali
Alang 78 Ambon Island
AlangAlang 73 Tana Toraja
Alas 59 Sumbawa
Alasombo 37 Solo Area
Algonik 86 Baliem Valley
Alindau 70 Sulawesi Island
Alla 73 Tana Toraja
Allu 72 SW Sulawesi
Amahai 76 Maluku
Amahusu 78 Ambon Island
Amampare 83 Irian Jaya
Amandaraja 09 Nias Island
Amassangan 72 SW Sulawesi
Ambarawa 21 Java
Ambarita 11 Lake Toba
Ambengan 48 S Bali
Ambon 78 Ambon Island
Ambuaki 82 Irian Jaya
Ambulu 21 Java
Ambunten 21 Java
Amdassa 76 Maluku
Amesangeng 72 SW Sulawesi
Aminweri 84 Biak Island
Amlapura 47 Bali
Ampadang 72 SW Sulawesi
Ampah 66 Kalimantan
Ampang 15 Minang Highlands
Amparita 72 SW Sulawesi
Ampel 36 Yogyakarta Area
Ampelbanjar 45 Mount Bromo
Ampenan 56 Lombok
Ampibabo 70 Sulawesi Island
Amplawas 76 Maluku
Ampoa 70 Sulawesi Island
Ampombukor 84 Biak Island
Amuntai 66 Kalimantan
Amurang 70 Sulawesi Island
Anabanua 72 SW Sulawesi
Anakalang 65 Sumba
Ancak 48 S Bali
Ancol 34 Bandung Area
Anculai 17 Batam & Bintan Island
Andai 83 Irian Jaya
Andau 72 SW Sulawesi
Andelara 64 Sumba
Andir 34 Bandung Area
Andonosari 45 Mount Bromo
Anggaduber 84 Biak Island
Anggana 69 Lower Mahakam River
Angin-angin 73 Tana Toraja
Angkasa 85 Jayapura Area
Anjani 57 Lombok
Anlagak 87 Baliem Valley
Ansus 83 Irian Jaya
Antap 46 Bali
Anyar 48 S Bali
Anyar 57 Lombok
Anyaranyar 48 S Bali
AnyarKelod 48 S Bali
Anyer 20 Java
Apala 72 SW Sulawesi
Apangi 73 Tana Toraja
Apatana 70 Sulawesi Island
Apauwar 83 Irian Jaya
Apiapipanjang 16 Riau Island Group
Apikmok 86 Baliem Valley
Apitaik 57 Lombok
Apoleang 72 SW Sulawesi
Apuan 47 Bali
Arcamanik 35 Bandung Area
Aredo 83 Irian Jaya
Argosari 45 Mount Bromo
Aritonang 11 Lake Toba
Arjasari 34 Bandung Area
Arobaadsyauwa 09 Nias Island
Arso 83 Irian Jaya
Aru 81 Halmahera Island
Arubara 61 Flores
Asa 73 Tana Toraja
Asahan 56 Lombok
Asahduren 46 Bali
Asam 16 Riau Island Group
Asat 76 Maluku
AsemanKangin 48 S Bali
Asembagus 21 Java
Asera 70 Sulawesi Island
Asilulu 78 Ambon Island
Asologais 86 Baliem Valley
Asolu 70 Sulawesi Island
Asori 83 Irian Jaya
Astaraja 34 Bandung Area
Atambua 62 Timor
Atap 67 Kalimantan
Atapupu 62 Timor
Atkri 82 Irian Jaya
Atsy 83 Irian Jaya
Atuka 83 Irian Jaya
Aukakehok 65 Sumba
Aurcina 13 W Sumatra
Awang 57 Lombok
Awoni 09 Nias Island
Ayapo 85 Jayapura Area
Baa 55 E Nusa Tenggara
Baamang 66 Kalimantan
Ba'baBa'ba 73 Tana Toraja
Babadan 37 Solo Area
Babahan 47 Bali
Babakan 35 Bandung Area
Babakan 48 S Bali
Babakan 66 Kalimantan
BabakanAndir 34 Bandung Area
Babakandago 35 Bandung Area
Babakandesa 34 Bandung Area
Babakandesa 35 Bandung Area
BabakanJati 35 Bandung Area
Babakanjeruk 34 Bandung Area
Babakanpangajaran 34 Bandung Area
Babakanpicung 35 Bandung Area
Babakansirna 34 Bandung Area
Babakantanjung 35 Bandung Area
Babana 70 Sulawesi Island
BabanaCilallang 72 SW Sulawesi
Babang 81 Halmahera Island
Babar 58 Sumbawa
Babat 21 Java
BabatToman 04 Sumatra
Babau 62 Timor
Babo 82 Irian Jaya
Badau 05 Sumatra
Bade 83 Irian Jaya
Badran 36 Yogyakarta Area
Bagan 16 Batam & Bintan Island
Bagansiapiapi 04 Sumatra
Bageklawang 57 Lombok
Bagikcendo 57 Lombok
Bagikmanis 57 Lombok
Bagikpapan 57 Lombok
Bagikpolak 56 Lombok
Bagiktemah 57 Lombok
Bagu 57 Lombok
Baguala 78 Ambon Island
Bahalbatu 08 N Sumatra
Baharu 12 W Sumatra
Baho 08 N Sumatra
Bahodopi 70 Sulawesi Island
Bahsawa 11 Lake Toba
Bai 73 Tana Toraja
Baing 65 Sumba
Bajawa 60 Flores
Bajera 46 Bali
Bajo 58 Sumbawa
Bajo 59 Sumbawa
Bajo 72 SW Sulawesi
Bajo 80 Halmahera Island
Bajoe 72 SW Sulawesi
Bajur 56 Lombok
Bakahuni 05 Sumatra
Bakalan 45 Mount Bromo
Bakara 11 Lake Toba
Baki 37 Solo Area
Bakongan 04 Sumatra
Bakulu 81 Halmahera Island
Bakungsari 48 S Bali
Balabatu 73 Tana Toraja
Balaiberkuak 66 Kalimantan
Balaikarangan 66 Kalimantan
Balaipungut 04 Sumatra
Balairiam 66 Kalimantan
BalaiSelasa 12 W Sumatra
Balaitangah 12 W Sumatra
Balakalumpang 72 SW Sulawesi
BalakasapTengah 34 Bandung Area
Balambang 72 SW Sulawesi
Balangan 36 Yogyakarta Area
Balange 72 SW Sulawesi
Balaraja 20 Java
Balate 81 Halmahera Island
Balauring 62 Timor
Baleagung 48 S Bali
Balebo 73 Tana Toraja
Balerbaleagung 46 Bali
Balige 11 Lake Toba
Balik 73 Tana Toraja
Balikpapan 67 Kalimantan
Balimbing 05 Sumatra
Balimbing 15 Minang Highlands
Baliu 73 Tana Toraja
Balle 73 Tana Toraja
Balo 70 Sulawesi Island
Baloa 70 Sulawesi Island
Baloga 09 Nias Island
BaloiLaut 16 Batam & Bintan Island
Balong 21 Java
Balun 48 S Bali
Balusu 73 Tana Toraja
Bama 61 Flores
Bamba 73 Tana Toraja
Bambang 04 Sumatra
Bambang 45 Mount Bromo
Bambapuang 70 Sulawesi Island
Bamkeri 82 Irian Jaya
Ban 47 Bali
Banaran 36 Yogyakarta Area
Banasbares 84 Biak Island
Bancak 37 Solo Area
BandaAceh 04 Sumatra
BandaElat 77 Maluku
Bandaneira 78 Banda Islands
Bandaragung 05 Sumatra
Bandardurian 08 N Sumatra
Bandarpasirmandogai 08 N Sumatra
Bandingagung 04 Sumatra
Bandona 60 Flores
Bandongan 36 Yogyakarta Area
Bandung 34 Bandung Area
Bandung 36 Yogyakarta Area
Bandung 48 S Bali
Bandut 45 Mount Bromo
Banemo 81 Halmahera Island
Bangaran 73 Tana Toraja
Banggo 59 Sumbawa
Bangil 21 Java
Bangin 48 S Bali
Bangkalan 21 Java
Bangkanol 35 Bandung Area
Bangkatmolon 57 Lombok
Bangket 48 S Bali
Bangkinang 12 W Sumatra
Bangklr 70 Sulawesi Island
Bangko 04 Sumatra
Bangko 56 Lombok
Bangli 47 Bali
Bangsal 56 Lombok
Bangsalan 37 Solo Area
Bangun 11 Lake Toba
Bangun 68 Lower Mahakam River
Bangunjawa 11 Lake Toba
Bangunpanci 11 Lake Toba
Bangunpapan 36 Yogyakarta Area
Bangunpurba 08 N Sumatra
Bangunrejo 69 Lower Mahakam River
Bangunseribu 10 Lake Toba
Banjar 20 Java
Banjar 58 Sumbawa
Banjaran 36 Yogyakarta Area
BanjarBaru 66 Kalimantan
Banjarmasin 66 Kalimantan
Banjarnato 12 W Sumatra
Banjarnegara 20 Java
Banjarsiantar 11 Lake Toba
Banjatharjo 20 Java
Bantaeng 72 SW Sulawesi
Bantang 47 Bali
Bantarbolang 20 Java
BantarKalong 35 Pangandaran
Bantas 48 S Bali
Banten 20 Java
Bantimurung 72 SW Sulawesi
Bantul 36 Yogyakarta Area
Banualuhu 11 Lake Toba
Banyak 37 Solo Area
Banyuaeng 36 Yogyakarta Area
Banyuanyar 36 Yogyakarta Area
Banyubiru 46 Bali
Banyudono 37 Solo Area
Banyumas 20 Java
Banyumeneng 36 Yogyakarta Area
Banyumulek 56 Lombok
Banyupoh 46 Bali
Banyuwangi 21 Java
Bara 11 Lake Toba
Bara 59 Sumbawa
Bara 76 Maluku
Barabai 66 Kalimantan
Barabali 57 Lombok
Barabara 73 Tana Toraja
Baraka 72 SW Sulawesi
Barana 73 Tana Toraja
Baranti 72 SW Sulawesi
Barate 62 Timor
Barejulat 57 Lombok
BarekMotor 17 Batam & Bintan Island
Bari 60 Flores
Barossenang 34 Bandung Area
Baru 16 Batam & Bintan Island
Baru 80 Halmahera Island
Baru 82 Irian Jaya
Baruh 12 W Sumatra
Barung 67 Kalimantan
Barus 08 N Sumatra
Barusjahe 08 N Sumatra
Barutunggul 34 Bandung Area
Baserah 13 W Sumatra
Baso 15 Minang Highlands
Basri 45 Mount Bromo
Bastiong 80 Ternate & Tidore
Batahan 12 W Sumatra
Ba'tan 73 Tana Toraja
Batanancak 48 S Bali
Batanbuah 48 S Bali
Batang 20 Java
Batankendal 48 S Bali
Batannyuh 48 S Bali
Batauga 70 Sulawesi Island
Bate 73 Tana Toraja
Batipuh 15 Minang Highlands
Batu 44 Mount Bromo
Batu 48 S Bali
Batuaji 47 Bali
Batuampar 04 Sumatra
Batuangus 78 Banda Islands
Batuas 76 Maluku
Batubatu 72 SW Sulawesi
Batubelin 08 N Sumatra
BatuBesar 17 Batam & Bintan Island
Batubesurat 12 W Sumatra
Batubidak 48 S Bali
Batubolong 56 Lombok
Batubolong 57 Lombok
Batubulan 47 Bali
Batubuwih 56 Lombok
Batuculing 48 S Bali
BatuDulang 58 Sumbawa
Batugajah 34 Bandung Area
Batugalas 15 Minang Highlands
Batugong 78 Ambon Island
Batugosok 64 Komodo & Rinca
Batuhoda 11 Lake Toba
Batui 70 Sulawesi Island
Batuidu 62 Timor
Batujai 57 Lombok
Batujaya 20 Java
Batujimbar 48 S Bali
Batukaang 47 Bali
Batukangkung 13 W Sumatra
Batukarut 34 Bandung Area
Batukumbung 57 Lombok
Batula 81 Halmahera Island
BatuLante 59 Sumbawa
BatuLayar 56 Lombok
Batulelleng 73 Tana Toraja
BatuLian 16 Riau Island Group
Batulicin 67 Kalimantan
Batulolong 62 Timor
BatuLubang 78 Ambon Island
Batumalulu 78 Banda Islands
Batumea 70 Sulawesi Island
Batumelinggang 09 Nias Island
BatuMerah 16 Batam & Bintan Island
Batumonga 12 W Sumatra
Batununggal 47 Bali
Batunyale 57 Lombok
Batupandang 57 Lombok
Batupanjang 04 Sumatra
Batupapan 73 Tana Toraja
Batupiak 73 Tana Toraja
BatuPutih 17 Batam & Bintan Island
Batuputih 21 Java
BatuPutih 72 SW Sulawesi
Batuputih 74 Manado Region
Batur 48 S Bali
Baturaden 20 Java
Baturaja 05 Sumatra
Baturakit 57 Lombok
Batureok 34 Bandung Area
Baturono 45 Mount Bromo
BatuRotok 58 Sumbawa
BaturSelatan 47 Bali
BaturTengah 47 Bali
Baturube 70 Sulawesi Island
Baturumpil 35 Bandung Area
Batusangkar 15 Minang Highlands
Batusantung 72 SW Sulawesi
Batusitanduk 72 SW Sulawesi
Batutabal 15 Minang Highlands
Batutering 58 Sumbawa
BatuTongko 73 Tana Toraja
Batutulis 57 Lombok
Batutumonga 73 Tana Toraja
Batuyang 57 Lombok
Bau 73 Tana Toraja
Baubau 70 Sulawesi Island
Bauberepa 62 Timor
Baula 70 Sulawesi Island
Bauma 72 SW Sulawesi
Baun 62 Timor
Bawahterutu 68 Lower Mahakam River
Bawalia 09 Nias Island
Bawe 82 Irian Jaya
Bawe 83 Irian Jaya
Bawelowalani 09 Nias Island
Bawomataluo 09 Nias Island
Bayah 20 Java
Bayan 57 Lombok
Bayat 37 Solo Area
Bayu 04 Sumatra
Bayunglincir 04 Sumatra
Bayur 14 Minang Highlands
Bebae 55 E Nusa Tenggara
Bebek 16 Riau Island Group
Beber 57 Lombok
Bebile 57 Lombok
Bebo 73 Tana Toraja
Bebuak 57 Lombok
Bebulu 67 Kalimantan
Beburung 57 Lombok
Bedulu 47 Bali
Begaden 37 Solo Area
Begawan 45 Mount Bromo
Beji 37 Solo Area
Beji 44 Mount Bromo
Bekokong 68 Lower Mahakam River
Bekonang 37 Solo Area
Bekul 48 S Bali
Belai 14 Minang Highlands
Belajen 72 SW Sulawesi
BelakangSidi
17 Batam & Bintan Island
Belandingan 47 Bali
Belang 71 Sulawesi Island
Belanga 47 Bali
Belanjong 48 S Bali
Belanting 57 Lombok
Belawan 09 Nias Island
Beleka 57 Lombok
Beleke 56 Lombok
Belet 57 Lombok
Belian 16 Batam & Bintan Island
Belimbing 46 Bali
Belinyu 05 Sumatra
Belong 48 S Bali
Belopa 72 SW Sulawesi
Beloro 69 Lower Mahakam River
Beluk 37 Solo Area
Beluntas 57 Lombok
Beluran 48 S Bali
Bemu 76 Maluku
Benamang 66 Kalimantan
Benangin 66 Kalimantan
Benaya 48 S Bali
Bendan 37 Solo Area
Bendosari 37 Solo Area
Bendung 37 Solo Area
Bendungan 35 Bandung Area
Bendungan 36 Yogyakarta Area
Bendungan 37 Solo Area
Bener 45 Mount Bromo
Benete 58 Sumbawa
Bengkalis 04 Sumatra
Bengkayang 66 Kalimantan
Bengkel 56 Lombok
Bengkoang 56 Lombok
BengkongLaut
16 Batam & Bintan Island
Bengkulu 04 Sumatra
Bengkung 57 Lombok
Benjina 77 Maluku
Benjor 45 Mount Bromo
Benlelang 62 Timor
Benoa 47 Bali
Benrongeng 72 SW Sulawesi
Bentek 57 Lombok
Benteng 70 Sulawesi Island
Benua 70 Sulawesi Island
Benuaapahan
69 Lower Mahakam River
Beoga 83 Irian Jaya
Beraban 47 Bali
Beraban 48 S Bali
Beraim 57 Lombok
Berakit 17 Batam & Bintan Island
Berambang 56 Lombok
Beran 36 Yogyakarta Area
Berastagi 08 N Sumatra
Berbah 36 Yogyakarta Area
Berbankrikilan 36 Yogyakarta Area
Berebere 81 Halmahera Island
Beringin 68 Lower Mahakam River
Beringinjaya 72 SW Sulawesi
Beringintinggi 13 W Sumatra
Beriolou 12 W Sumatra
Berloka 60 Flores
Berora 56 Lombok
Besakih 47 Bali
Beseran 36 Yogyakarta Area
Besikama 62 Timor
Besitang 09 Nias Island
Besuki 21 Java
Besuki 45 Mount Bromo
Betaf 83 Irian Jaya
Betteng 73 Tana Toraja
Betugunggung 08 N Sumatra
Betun 62 Timor
Betung 05 Sumatra
Beuma 72 SW Sulawesi
Biak 84 Biak Island
Biang 81 Halmahera Island
Biangono 62 Timor
Biawak 66 Kalimantan
Bicoli 81 Halmahera Island
Bikeru 72 SW Sulawesi
Bilebente 57 Lombok
Bilo 70 Sulawesi Island
Bilokka 72 SW Sulawesi
Bilungala 70 Sulawesi Island
Bima 59 Sumbawa
Binagaara 10 Lake Toba
Binangatoa 72 SW Sulawesi
Bingintelok 04 Sumatra
Binjai 05 Sumatra
Binjai 08 N Sumatra
BinohKelod 48 S Bali
Binontoan 70 Sulawesi Island
BintanBuaya 17 Batam & Bintan Island
Bintang 11 Lake Toba
Bintuhan 04 Sumatra
Bintuni 82 Irian Jaya
Bira 72 SW Sulawesi
Birak 57 Lombok
Bireuen 04 Sumatra
Biringkanaya 72 SW Sulawesi
Birufu 83 Irian Jaya
Bita 73 Tana Toraja
Bittuang 72 SW Sulawesi
Bitung 74 Manado Region
Blahbatuh 47 Bali
Blahkiuh 47 Bali
Blangkejeren 04 Sumatra
Blau 44 Mount Bromo
Blawu 70 Sulawesi Island
Blega 21 Java
Blimbing 36 Yogyakarta Area
Blimbing 44 Mount Bromo
Blimbing 67 Kalimantan
Blimbingsari 46 Bali
Blitar 21 Java
Blondo 36 Yogyakarta Area
Blongas 56 Lombok
Blora 21 Java
Blubuk 45 Mount Bromo
Bluto 21 Java
Boal 59 Sumbawa
Boalemo 70 Sulawesi Island
Boas 62 Timor
Boawae 60 Flores
Boba 60 Flores
Bobaneigo 81 Halmahera Island
Bobaneigu 81 Halmahera Island

Places of Interest

National Parks & Reserves